Study Guide for the Telecourse
Discovering Psychology

coordinated with

Gerrig and Zimbardo

Psychology and Life

Nineteenth Edition

prepared by

Nancy Franklin
Stony Brook University

"Discovering Psychology: Updated Edition" is a production of WGBH Boston

Funded by Annenberg Media

Allyn & Bacon

Boston Columbus Indianapolis New York San Francisco Upper Saddle River
Amsterdam Cape Town Dubai London Madrid Milan Munich Paris Montreal Toronto
Delhi Mexico City Sao Paulo Sydney Hong Kong Seoul Singapore Taipei Tokyo

Allyn & Bacon
is an imprint of

www.pearsonhighered.com

ISBN-10: 0-205-75708-1
ISBN-13: 978-0-205-75708-4

This study guide was developed for use by students enrolled in the *Discovering Psychology: Updated Edition* telecourse. The telecourse consists of twenty-six half-hour public television programs, the Study Guide, Faculty Guide, and the Gerrig/Zimbardo *Psychology and Life* textbook. *Discovering Psychology: Updated Edition* was produced by WGBH-TV, Boston, Massachusetts. Major funding was provided by Annenberg Media. This series is closed captioned for the hearing impaired.

To order the study guide, contact:

Pearson
Allyn & Bacon
75 Arlington Street, Suite 300
Boston, MA 02116
http://www.pearsonhighered.com

For further information about the course call 1-800-LEARNER or visit Annenberg Media's website at www.learner.org

To purchase *Discovering Psychology: Updated Edition* DVD/videocassettes and/or other video series from Annenberg Media, contact:

Discovering Psychology
Annenberg Media
P.O. Box 2345
South Burlington, Vermont 05407-2345
1-800-LEARNER

For more information about telecourse licenses, contact:

Discovering Psychology
PBS Adult Learning Service
1320 Braddock Place
Alexandria, Virginia 22314-1698
1-800-ALS-ALS-8

ACKNOWLEDGMENTS

The advisory board of nationally recognized experts from diverse areas of psychological knowledge has significantly contributed to creating this important telecourse.

Updated Edition

John Darley, Ph.D.
Professor of Psychology
Princeton University

Jane Halonen, Ph.D.
Director, School of Psychology
James Madison University

James Jones, Ph.D.
Professor of Psychology
University of Delaware
Director of Minority Fellowships, APA

Philip G. Zimbardo, Ph.D.
Professor of Psychology
Stanford University
President of the American Psychological Association 2001–2002

Original Series

Philip G. Zimbardo, Ph.D.
Professor of Psychology
Stanford University

W. Curtis Banks
Professor of Psychology (deceased)
Howard University

Ludy T. Benjamin, Jr.
Professor of Psychology
Texas A & M University

Tom Bond
Williamsburg Sleep Disorder Center
Sleep Disorder Specialist

Freda Rebelsky Camp
Former Professor of Psychology
Boston University

Daniel Goleman
Psychologist, Journalist, Author

James B. Maas
Professor of Psychology
Cornell University

Margaret S. Martin
Associate Professor of Professional Development and Health Services Administration
Medical University of South Carolina

Joe L. Martinez, Jr.
Director, Division of Life Sciences
The University of Texas at San Antonio

Fay-Tyler M. Norton
Retired President
Colleague Consultants in Higher Education

Michael Wertheimer
Retired Professor of Psychology
University of Colorado, Boulder

Special thanks also go to Robert Arkin, Dean of Undergraduate Studies at Ohio State University and the project's chief print advisor, who carefully reviewed the manuscript at several stages in its development and suggested many valuable improvements. The print materials also benefited greatly from the editing and fine-tuning provided by Naomi Angoff. Winifred Dunn deserves considerable credit for developing the faculty test bank, as well as review questions for students. Researchers Frank Yao and Chaz Sylvester spent many hours locating anthology readings, citations for studies, additional resources, and other information necessary to complete the project. Patricia Crotty was the editorial assistant for the project and, with Deborah Paddock, oversaw photo research. Karen Barss was the permissions editor; Janet Crowley copyedited the manuscript.

WGBH Educational Foundation
Boston, Massachusetts

Project Directors

Brigid Sullivan
Manager of Special Telecommunications

Kim Storey
Project Director

Print Development

Ann Strunk
Director of Print Projects

Beth Kirsch
Coordinator of Print Projects

Production Team

Updated Edition

Harlan Reiniger
Producer

Jayne Sportelli
Associate Producer

Kim Swensen
Production Assistant

Christine Herbes-Sommers
Senior Producer/Project Director

Michael Korf
Executive Producer

Original Edition

Thomas Friedman
Executive Editor

William C. Brennan
Executive Producer

Tug Yourgrau
Senior Producer

CONTENTS

COURSE OVERVIEW AND GOALS

The first psychology laboratory was established in Leipzig, Germany more than 100 years ago. Yet despite its relative youth as an empirical science, psychology has made an indelible mark on our culture. We have become a psychology-oriented society, especially in the last half-century. Psychological research has changed many of our views on mental illness, learning, perception, motivation, sex and gender, aging, decision making, and health. Today, researchers and clinicians worldwide continue to investigate the puzzles of human behavior, studying questions of great interest not only to psychologists, but also to all of us as we strive to unravel the mysteries of mind and body—why we think, act, and feel as we do.

Discovering Psychology: Updated Edition, an introductory psychology course consisting of twenty-six half-hour programs and corresponding curriculum materials, will help students understand the variety of approaches to the study of human nature. Each program is designed to stand alone as well as to fit into the overall focus and scope of the course, which begins with psychology's basic conceptual frameworks and progresses to more complex extensions and applications. It is supported by a web site with a page for each video program featuring an "academic footnote" to further update the content of the videos. The site also offers four special interactive features as well as an extensive webography. Visit www.learner.org for more information.

Discovering Psychology: Updated Edition will expose students to leading researchers and the latest developments in the field, from new ways of treating anxiety and depression to the psychological factors involved in space travel. The course explains the scientific method of gathering and evaluating evidence as well as how psychological knowledge can improve the quality of life. Important psychological concepts and principles are brought to life by documentary footage, interviews, demonstrations, classic experiments, simulations, computer graphics, and animation. The course encourages open-minded curiosity and critical thinking.

Goals

Discovering Psychology: Updated Edition

- ∞ Explores the major psychological approaches to the study of behavior, including its history, contributors, methods, research findings, terminology, and current directions.

- ∞ Promotes the development of scientific values and skills, recognition of individual bias in experimentation, and the ability to evaluate generalizations.

- ∞ Encourages personal development through increased understanding and tolerance of the behavior of others and a curiosity about the forces that make us behave as we do.

∞ Integrates new developments with classic research findings.

∞ Challenges some traditional perspectives in light of new knowledge.

∞ Illuminates the decision-making processes used by researchers.

∞ Interweaves the theme of psychology as a scientific enterprise with that of psychology as a course of knowledge and practice that can improve the quality of life.

The Host

Philip Zimbardo is Professor of Psychology at Stanford University. Internationally applauded for his vibrant teaching style, he is the recipient of many distinguished teaching awards from universities and national associations. Zimbardo has also won awards for his research, writing, and media activities. He has published more than twenty books and more than 250 articles on a wide range of topics, including evil, shyness, time perspective, madness, anxiety, and animal behavior. The chief academic advisor for the Discovering Psychology Telecourse, Professor Zimbardo has been teaching introductory psychology for more than forty years. He has also been elected as President of the American Psychological Association.

COURSE COMPONENTS

Discovering Psychology: Updated Edition includes five components:

1. Twenty-six half-hour television programs
2. Gerrig/ Zimbardo *Psychology and Life* textbook
3. Telecourse Faculty Guide
4. Telecourse Study Guide
5. Telecourse Web Site (visit www.learner.org for more information)

The Television Programs

1. Past, Present, and Promise

An introduction to psychology as a science at the crossroads of many fields of knowledge, from philosophy and anthropology to biochemistry and artificial intelligence.

2. Understanding Research

An examination of the scientific method and the ways in which data are collected and analyzed — in the lab and in the field — with an emphasis on sharpening critical thinking regarding research findings.

3. The Behaving Brain

The structure and composition of the brain: how neurons function; how information is collected and transmitted; and how chemical reactions determine every thought, feeling, and action.

4. The Responsive Brain

How the brain controls behavior, and, conversely, how behavior and environment influence the brain's structure and functioning.

5. The Developing Child

The nature versus nurture debate, and how developmental psychologists study the effects of heredity and environment on the development of children.

6. Language Development

The development of language and how psychologists hope to discover truths about the human mind, society, and culture by studying how children use language in social communication.

7. Sensation and Perception

How visual information is gathered and processed, and how our culture, previous experiences, and interests influence our perceptions.

8. Learning

The basic principles of classical and operant conditioning and how renowned researchers—Pavlov, Thorndike, Watson, and Skinner—have influenced today's thinking about the nature of animal and human learning.

9. Remembering and Forgetting

A look at the complex process called memory: how images, ideas, language, and even physical actions, sounds, and smells, are translated into codes, represented in memory, and retrieved when needed.

10. Cognitive Processes

An exploration into higher mental processes—reasoning, planning, and problem solving—and why the "cognitive revolution" is attracting such diverse investigators, from philosophers to computer scientists.

11. Judgment and Decision Making

A look at the process of making judgments and decisions, how and why people make good and bad judgments, and the psychology of risk taking.

12. Motivation and Emotion

A review of what researchers are discovering about why we act and feel as we do, from the exhilaration of love to the agony of failure.

13. The Mind Awake and Asleep

The nature of sleeping, dreaming, and altered states of consciousness and how consciousness empowers us to interpret, analyze, and direct our behavior in adaptive, flexible ways.

14. The Mind Hidden and Divided

A review of the events and experiences that take place below the level of consciousness and how they alter our moods, bias our actions, and affect our health.

15. The Self

How psychologists systematically study the origins of self-identity and self-esteem, social determinants of self-concepts, and the emotional and motivational consequences of beliefs about oneself.

16. Testing and Intelligence

The field of psychological assessment and the efforts of psychologists and other professionals to assign values to different abilities, behaviors, and personalities.

17. Sex and Gender

The ways in which males and females are similar and different, and how sex roles reflect social values and psychological knowledge.

18. Maturing and Aging

What really happens, physically and psychologically, as we age, and how society reacts to the last stages of life.

19. The Power of the Situation

How social psychologists attempt to understand human behavior within its broader social context, and how our beliefs and behavior can be influenced and manipulated by other people and by subtle situational forces.

20. Constructing Social Reality

The factors that contribute to our interpretation of reality and how understanding the psychological processes that govern our behavior can help us to become more empathic and independent members of society.

21. Psychopathology

The major types of mental illness, including schizophrenia, anxiety, affective and manic-depressive disorders, and the major factors that influence them both biologically and psychologically.

22. Psychotherapy

The relationships among theory, research, and practice and how treatment of psychological disorders has been influenced by historical, cultural, and social forces.

23. Health, Mind, and Behavior

How research is forcing a profound rethinking of the relationship between mind and body—a new biopsychosocial model is replacing the traditional biomedical model.

24. Applying Psychology to Life

The innovative ways in which psychology is being applied to practical situations and professions in areas concerning human factors, law, and conflict negotiation.

25. Cognitive Neuroscience

How psychologists, biologists, brain researchers, and others are beginning to understand mental processes at the level of the brain and not merely from information-processing models.

26. Cultural Psychology

How cultures construct selves and other central aspects of individual personality, beliefs, values, emotions, and much of what we are and do.

Textbook

This Study Guide has been developed for use with the textbook *Psychology and Life, 19th Edition* by Richard Gerrig and Philip Zimbardo, Allyn & Bacon, copyright 2010. The textbook is an integral part of this television course. The assigned textbook readings for each unit will expand upon the television programs and present new information. The textbook is supported by a web site located at www.mypsychlab.com.

You may find that the television programs present certain concepts or topics somewhat differently from the way the textbook does. Sometimes the information is presented in a different order, or the textbook may provide different examples and illustrations. The Study Guide will help you link the programs with the textbook.

Study Guide

The twenty-six units of the Study unit correspond directly to the twenty-six television programs. The Study Guide previews, reviews, and applies the concepts and information from the television program. Each unit of the Study Guide includes the following elements:

- Objectives—concepts, facts, and themes from the program and textbook that you should be able to define, identify, explain, or apply.

- Reading Assignment—identifies the page numbers in the textbook, *Psychology and Life*, that correspond to the themes and topics of the television program.

- Key People and Terms—lists important terms, concepts, and people introduced in the textbook readings and programs, and defines new terminology from the programs. Textbook page numbers are given for key people and terms, referring to the assigned reading or to other, related sections of the text.

- Program Summary—a narrative description of the themes and highlights of the corresponding television program.

- Program Review Questions—self-test items that enable you to evaluate your understanding of the program. (Answers are included in the Appendix)

- Questions to Consider—open-ended questions to promote critical thinking (with suggested answers included in the Appendix).

- Optional Activities—a variety of optional projects, writing assignments, or experiences to help you gather evidence, raise issues, apply basic concepts, and review important information.
- Additional Resources—a bibliography of related books, articles, films, and Web sites.

Web Site

A web site augments *Discovering Psychology: Updated Edition* with a page for each video program featuring an "academic footnote" to further update the content of the videos. The site also offers four special interactive features as well as an extensive webography. Visit www.learner.org for more information.

Taking *Discovering Psychology: Updated Edition* as a Telecourse

Find out the following information as soon after registration as possible:

- Which books are required for the course.

- If and when an orientation session has been scheduled.

- When *Discovering Psychology: Updated Edition* will be broadcast in your area.

- When examinations are scheduled for the course. (Mark these on your calendar)

- Whether any additional on-campus meetings have been scheduled. (Plan to attend as many review, sessions, seminars, and other meetings as possible)

To learn the most from each unit:

1. Before viewing the television program, read the corresponding unit in the Study Guide, paying particular attention to the Objectives, Key People and Terms, and Program Summary.

2. View the program, keeping the Objectives in mind. *Be an active watcher.* Some students find that taking notes while viewing the programs is helpful. If your area has more than one public television station, there may be several opportunities for you to watch the program. Many public television stations repeat a program at least once during the week it is first shown. The programs may also be available on videocassettes at your school, or you can tape them at home if you own a VCR. If you don't have a VCR, you can make an audiocassette of the program for review.

3. Read the textbook sections listed in the Study Guide. As you read, pay particular attention to the Key People and Terms identified in the Study Guide. In addition, chapter outlines, headings, summaries, and terms in bold type will help you identify the important information.

4. Do the Review Questions and any other questions, activities, essays, or experiments assigned by your instructor.

5. Remember to use the *Discovering Psychology: Updated Edition* web site as a resource for activities and additional readings. Visit www.learner.org for more information.

6. Keep up with the course on a weekly basis. Each unit of the Study Guide builds on knowledge gained in previous units. Stay current with the programs and readings. Make a daily checklist, and keep weekly and term calendars, noting your scheduled activities such

as meetings or examinations and blocks of time for viewing programs, reading, and doing assignments.

7. Keep in touch with your instructor. If possible, get to know him or her. You should have your instructor's mailing address, phone number, and office hours. Your instructor would like to hear from you and to know how you are doing. He or she will be eager to answer any questions you have about the course.

A NOTE FROM PHILIP ZIMBARDO

Welcome to the start of an exciting and challenging adventure in *Discovering Psychology: Updated Edition.* I am delighted that you are about to join in this unique exploration into the nature of human nature. Through the medium of television, we will leave the confines of the traditional classroom to go where the action is, has been, or soon will be in psychology's scientific study of behavior and mental processes.

Our journey will take us to research laboratories throughout the United States to observe experiments in progress that are unraveling the mysteries of how the brain works, how animals and humans develop and change, how the mind guides us through life's mazes, and how our behavior is shaped by internal and external forces acting on us. We will also visit mental hospitals, clinics, and therapists' offices where the pathologies of human functioning are studied, diagnosed, and treated. And we will venture out into the field where other researchers observe behavior in its natural habitat, whether it is stress among African baboons, shyness among chimpanzees, healing practices of Native Americans, competition in the classroom, or the destructive power of cult leaders over their followers.

This introduction to the state of the art of psychological knowledge is shaped by interviews with many of its most distinguished contributors. We will meet more than seventy researchers, theorists, and practitioners, all offering their individual perspectives on why they have devoted their talents to trying to solve the puzzles that brain, mind, and behavior continually present to the curious explorer. In addition to interviews with Nobel Prize-winners David Hubel and Herbert Simon, we will hear from psychology's most prominent figures, among them B. F. Skinner, Neal Miller, Eleanor Maccoby, Noam Chomsky, Carl Rogers, Erik Erikson, Albert Bandura, Hazel Markus, Judy Rodin, John Gabrieli, Jonathan Schooler, and Claude Steele. To get an inside view of the "cutting edge" in psychological knowledge, we will turn also to the new generation of psychologists who present ideas that are influencing the directions psychology is taking and charting the course it is likely to follow in the future.

We will do more than just talk about psychology. We will show it in action—through documentary footage, laboratory experiments re-created in laboratories, case studies, and live demonstrations of perceptual illusions, hypnosis, memory, biofeedback, lie detection, and many other topics of vital concern to today's and tomorrow's psychologists.

We will travel back in time to see the actual archival footage of some of the most significant experiments and demonstrations in the history of psychology: Ivan Pavlov's monumental discovery of the laws of conditioning, John Watson's research on infant emotional reactions, Kurt Lewin's study of democratic and fascist leaders, and Stanley Milgram's provocative look into the conditions that foster blind obedience to authority, and my Stanford prison experiment.

Throughout our series, we will discover that what we know about the content of psychological inquiry is influenced by HOW we know it. So we will look behind the facts and principles to examine the methodology used to collect the data on which our conclusions are based.
 For the most part, the selection of the programs and the sequence of presentation follow what has become traditional in introductory psychology courses. The flow is from the areas considered to be the "hard core" or foundation disciplines of psychology-such as brain processes,

development, perception, learning, memory, cognition, motivation, and emotion-to those that are somewhat more complex, broader in scope, or more recent, or that involve applications of basic psychological knowledge. The latter topics include consciousness, the self, testing and assessment, sex and gender, social psychology, psychopathology, therapies, and health psychology. Finally, our journey, which started by looking inside a single nerve cell in the brain, ventures up and outward to travel in outer space and toward emerging research on the maintenance of peace and conflict negotiation.

An important goal of this series is an increased understanding and tolerance of the behavior of others, along with a wider appreciation of the complex set of influences that determine our own actions, from genetic, cultural, and environmental to political and economic. Just as we as individuals are always part of a broader array of overlapping contexts, so we will see that psychology, too, is at the crossroads of many other disciplines.

Psychology is a unique field of study, a social science that draws from sociology, anthropology, economics, and political science. But it is ever more akin to the biological sciences, especially to the neurosciences, the study of brain processes. For many, the new core of psychology is what it shares with the cognitive sciences, artificial intelligence, computer science, and applied mathematics. And because one of the distinguishing features of psychology is its concern for improving the quality of individual and collective existence, it is also a health science, brimming with ties to education, law, medicine, and the environment.

While this remarkable breadth and depth of modern psychology is a source of attraction to those who become psychologists, it is also what makes the field a difficult challenge for the first-time explorer. As an undergraduate, I certainly found it tough to integrate all that diverse information in my Psych I course; my only college C grade in that course represents an enduring testimonial to that difficulty. But the excitement of being able to contribute to our understanding of human nature as a researcher and to communicate it to others as a teacher has since been a continual source of joy to me. I have taught introductory psychology for more than forty years now, in small seminars and in lectures with thousands of students. With equal delight, I have also shared psychology with high school students, ghetto kids, elders, and teachers and professionals in other disciplines.

Discovering Psychology presents the best of contemporary psychology in a format that is interesting and intellectually stimulating. In a half-hour's time, an enormous amount of knowledge is conveyed, because television can condense information through fast-moving images, graphics, and tightly packed commentary.

Of course, each video program highlights only a limited number of major points, introduces a few major contributors, touches on some historical background, and presents a brief view of current research or practical applications in a given area. But the hope is that by adding this unique visual component to the wealth of information contained in your introductory psychology textbook, *Psychology and Life*, 19th Edition, that I co-wrote with Richard Gerrig, and the exercises and activities in this guide, psychology will come alive for you as never before.

Enjoy this wonderful learning experience, have fun with it, and ideally, contribute your talents to the next generation of psychology.

UNIT 1

Science is the attempt to make the chaotic diversity of our sense-experience correspond to a logically uniform system of thought.

Albert Einstein

Unit 1 introduces psychology as the scientific study of behavior and mental processes. It looks at how psychologists work from a variety of theoretical models and traditions, record and analyze their observations, and attempt to unravel the mysteries of the mind.

Objectives

After viewing the television program and completing the assigned readings, you should be able to:

1. Define *psychology.*

2. Distinguish between the micro, molecular, and macro levels of analysis.

3. Describe the major goals of psychology.

4. Describe what psychologists do and give some examples of the kinds of questions they may be interested in investigating.

5. Summarize the history of the major theoretical approaches to psychology.

6. Describe seven current psychological perspectives.

7. Describe how the concerns of psychologists have evolved with the larger culture.

Reading Assignment

After viewing Program 1, read pages 1-21 in *Psychology and Life*.

Key People and Terms

As you watch the program and read the assignment, pay particular attention to these people and terms. People and terms defined in the text will be found on the given page numbers.

behavior (2)
behavioral data (3)
behavioral neuroscience (11)
behaviorism (10)
behaviorist perspective (10)
biological perspective (11)
cognitive neuroscience (11)
cognitive perspective (11)
sociocultural perspective (12)
evolutionary perspective (11)
functionalism (7)
humanistic perspective (10)
psychodynamic perspective (9)
psychology (2)
scientific method (2)
structuralism (7)
John Dewey (8)
Hermann Ebbinghaus (5)
Sigmund Freud (9)
William James (7)
Abraham Maslow (10)
Carl Rogers (10)
B. F. Skinner (10)
Edward Titchener (7)
John Watson (10)
Max Wertheimer (7)
Wilhelm Wundt (6)

The following people and terms are used in Program 1 but are not described in the text.

∞ *Mahzarin Banaji*—uses indirect measures of reaction time and brain activity to study prejudice.

∞ *ERP (Event-Related Potentials)*—variations in brain waves as recorded by the electro-encephalograph (EEG) that are triggered by specific internal or external events.

∞ *Heisenberg indeterminacy principle*—principle stating that our impressions of other people are distorted by how we observe and assess them.

∞ *Emanuel Donchin*—discovered that brains measure surprise before we are aware of it.

∞ *G. Stanley Hall*—founded the first American Psychology lab in 1883.

∞ *Liz Phelps*—collaborates with M. Banaji in conducting brain-based studies of prejudice.

∞ *Robert Rosenthal*—showed that body language can reflect what we think and feel.

Program Summary

Psychology is a field that asks questions about the relationships among the mind, brain, and behavior. Why do people laugh and cry? What is intelligence? Are we molded more by heredity or experience? What makes us fall in love? And how can we cure mental illness?

Psychologists are people who ask questions about the puzzles of human nature. Like most of us, they are people watchers who make assumptions about their observations. But as scientists, they test their ideas under special, controlled conditions.

During the next 26 programs, we will see psychology in action and discover that it has a lot in common with many other fields of study. From understanding the smallest chemical reaction in the brain to recognizing the special needs of astronauts in space, psychology constantly seeks to answer this fundamental question: What is the nature of human nature?

Professor Philip Zimbardo, the host for the series, will introduce psychologists who work in many different settings: laboratories, classrooms, clinics, hospitals, and prisons. They study animals and people asleep and awake, healthy and ill, alone and in groups. But no matter what their field of expertise, all psychologists are dedicated to gaining a better understanding of behavior. We'll see how they observe behavior and attempt to describe it objectively, using their knowledge to predict behavior, and sometimes to control it.

Psychologists assume that our behaviors—our brain activity, gestures, eye movements, and word choices—are external signs of an inner reality. Even our slightest reaction can raise a host of questions about our underlying perceptions, expectations, feelings, and ideas.
Whatever type of behavior psychologists choose to study, they try to make sense of it by relating the behavior to certain aspects of the individual and to elements of the situation. They ask what it is about the person—gender, sociocultural background, past experiences—that could account for a particular reaction. By looking at the situation and the environment, they try to identify the elements that could have influenced the response.

But not all psychologists work in the same way. In 1975, a psychologist named Emanuel Donchin discovered that our brains register surprise even before we are aware of it. By recording the brain's electrical activity, he discovered that events trigger specific brain electrical patterns. When psychologists focus on a small unit of behavior, such as a brain activity, they are working at the micro level of analysis.

3

Most psychologists operate on the molecular level. They study larger units of behavior, such as body language. Psychologist Robert Rosenthal has shown that our body language can reflect much of what we're thinking and feeling. Rosenthal describes how we can predict behavior in certain situations but emphasizes that the same gestures can have very different meanings in different situations.

At the molar level of analysis, researchers investigate the whole person in complex situations, focusing even more on cultural background and social experiences. Psychologists working at the molar level might study sexual attraction, worker morale, or the nature of prejudice. Because psychologists are scientists, they must always be aware of the limits to their powers of observation and assessment and to their ability to be truly objective.

Mahzarin Banaji of Yale University approaches prejudice from multiple levels of analysis. Her study of reaction times to associate words like "black" and "white" with other concepts (the IAT test) provides an indirect measure of prejudice. In collaboration with Liz Phelps of New York University, she also uses functional magnetic resonance imaging to study prejudice. Using that technique, they examine the activity of the amygdala, which is associated with emotional learning and memory and the evaluation of social groups, when participants look at photographs of unfamiliar white and black faces. They found that people whose amygdalas reacted to black faces also had shown a white bias in the IAT.

Like all disciplines, psychology can be better understood in its own historical context. Modern psychology began in 1879 when Wilhelm Wundt founded the first experimental psychology laboratory in Germany. There he designed studies to collect data on such behaviors as reaction times to sensory stimuli, attention, judgment, and word associations.

The history of psychology took another step forward when G. Stanley Hall founded the first American psychology lab in 1883. Hall became the first president of the American Psychological Association, and he introduced Sigmund Freud to the United States through his translation of Freud's *General Introduction to Psychoanalysis*.

Then in 1890 Harvard professor William James published *Principles of Psychology,* considered by many to be the most important psychology text of all time. And James found a place in psychology for human consciousness, emotions, the self, personal values, and religion.
But James's methods—observation, introspection, and reasoning—were rejected by the Wundtian psychologists as too soft for science. They insisted on patterning psychology on the physical sciences, focusing on such areas as sensation and perception, and later adding studies on learning, memorization, and conditioning.

Since its inception, the field of psychology has included people with very different ideas about what to study and how to study it. Although the field has changed and expanded dramatically, ideas originating over a century ago form the basis of psychological inquiry today, and the methods of science that have developed over many centuries lay the groundwork for all the different levels at which we study human nature.

Program Review Questions

1. What is the best definition of *psychology?*

    a. the scientific study of how people interact in social groups
    b. the philosophy explaining the relation between brain and mind
    c. the scientific study of the behavior of individuals and of their mental processes
    d. the knowledge used to predict how virtually any organism will behave under specified conditions

2. As scientists, psychologists do which of the following?

    a. develop methods of inquiry that are fundamentally at odds with those of physics and chemistry
    b. test their theories under carefully controlled experimental circumstances
    c. ignore their own observational biases when collecting data
    d. rely completely on introspective techniques

3. What is the main focus of Donchin's research involving the P-300 wave?

    a. the relation between brain and mind
    b. the role of heredity in shaping personality
    c. the development of mental illness
    d. the role of situational factors in perception

4. What is the main goal of psychological research?

    a. to cure mental illness
    b. to find the biological bases of the behavior of organisms
    c. to predict and, in some cases, control behavior
    d. to provide valid legal testimony

5. The reactions of the boys and the girls to the teacher in the *Candid Camera* episode were essentially similar. Professor Zimbardo attributes this reaction to

    a. how easily adolescents become embarrassed.
    b. how an attractive teacher violates expectations.
    c. the way sexual titillation makes people act.
    d. the need people have to hide their real reactions.

6. What do EEGs measure?

   a. heart rate
   b. changes in hormone levels in the body
   c. energy expended in overcoming gravity
   d. brain activity

7. According to Robert Rosenthal's research, you are most likely to detect a liar by

   a. observing eye movements.
   b. listening to tone of voice.
   c. considering sociocultural factors.
   d. looking at body language.

8. Which cluster of topics did William James consider the main concerns of psychology?

   a. reaction times, sensory stimuli, word associations
   b. consciousness, self, emotions
   c. conditioned responses, psychophysics
   d. experimental design, computer models

9. What do we learn from our misreading of the "Paris in the the spring" sign?

   a. We are accustomed to an artist's use of perspective.
   b. Experience disposes us to respond in a particular way.
   c. Unexpected events trigger P-300 waves in the brain.
   d. We laugh at those things that violate our expectations.

10. The amygdala is an area of the brain that processes

    a. sound.
    b. social status.
    c. faces.
    d. emotion.

11. According to Mahzarin Banaji, the IAT could potentially be used for what practical application?

    a. studying latent prejudice in police officers
    b. assessing relationships among family members
    c. evaluating intellectual ability
    d. determining when someone is lying during negotiation

12. Who founded the first psychology laboratory in the United States?

    a. Wilhelm Wundt
    b. William James
    c. G. Stanley Hall
    d. Sigmund Freud

13. How did Wundtian psychologists, such as Hall, react to William James' concept of psychology?

    a. They accepted it with minor reservations.
    b. They expanded it to include consciousness and the self.
    c. They rejected it as unscientific.
    d. They revised it to include the thinking of Sigmund Freud.

14. Which level of analysis concerns a person's behavior within a complex situation?

    a. cosmological level
    b. molar level
    c. molecular level

15. Which of the following, according to Robert Rosenthal, predicts success in getting alcoholics into treatment?

    a. their income
    b. the number of years they'd been drinking
    c. the physical appearance of the doctor recommending treatment
    d. the doctor's tone of voice

16. Which of the following psychologists was the first to study people's sensory processing, judgment, attention, and word associations?

    a. G. Stanley Hall
    b. William James
    c. Wilhelm Wundt
    d. Sigmund Freud

17. Most psychologists study human behavior at which level of analysis?

    a. molecular
    b. macro
    c. micro
    d. molar

18. Who wrote *Principles of Psychology* and thereby became arguably the most influential psychologist of the last century?

    a. G. Stanley Hall
    b. Wilhelm Wundt
    c. William James
    d. Sigmund Freud

19. What assumption underlies the use of reaction times to study prejudice indirectly?

    a. People of different ethnic backgrounds are quicker intellectually than people of other ethnicities.
    b. Concepts that are associated more strongly in memory are verified more quickly.
    c. Prejudice can't be studied in any other way.
    d. People respond to emotional memories more slowly than emotionless memories.

20. Prejudice can be studied at

    a. the micro level.
    b. the molecular level.
    c. the molar level.
    d. all of the above.

Questions to Consider

1. Although psychologists are involved in many different kinds of research and professional activities, there are certain fundamental issues that form the basic foundation of psychology. What are they?

2. Why would the study of normal behavior be more important to the science of psychology than an understanding of abnormal behavior?

3. List as many reasons as you can think of for why people who would benefit from seeing a therapist might not do it.

4. How do your culture, age, gender, education level, and past experience bias your observations about events, your own actions, and the behavior of others?

5. Is thinking a behavior? How can it be studied?

6. Imagine the year 2500. How do you think the boundaries of psychological and biological research might have become redefined by then? Do you think the two fields will have become more integrated or more distinct?

Optional Activities

1. Start a personal journal or a log. Make a daily practice of recording events, thoughts, feelings, observations, and questions that catch your attention each day. Include the ordinary and the unusual. Then speculate on the possible forces causing your behavior. As you progress through the course, review your notes and see how your observations and questions reflect what you have learned.

2. Look ahead to one or two psychological principles described in the book. After describing the experimental situation to your friends, ask them to introspect about what their own data would have shown if they had participated. How closely do their introspections match the actual results of the study? What factors might lead their introspections to be more or less accurate?

3. As you go through your day-to-day life, watching the news, battling traffic, and making decisions about how to spend your time and money, consider all the ways that psychologists might be interested in studying, facilitating, or intervening in human behavior.

Additional Resources

Books and Articles

Adler, A. L., & Rubin, R. W. (Eds). (1994). *Aspects of the history of psychology in America 1892-1992.* New York, New York: Academy of Sciences.

Gravetter, W. (2000). *Research methods in psychology.* New York: Brooks/Cole Publishing Company.

Stanovich, K. E. (2000). *How to think straight about psychology*, 6th ed. New York: Addison Wesley Longman.

Web Sites

∞ *http://www.apa.org*—The American Psychological Association is the most diverse professional organization for psychologists.

∞ *http://www.nimh.nih.gov/*—Operated by the federal government and responsible for a large proportion of the research grants awarded to psychologists, the National Institute for Mental Health shapes the direction of research in the U.S.

∞ *http://www.psychologicalscience.org/*—The Association for Psychological Science represents the scientific community of psychologists.

∞ *http://dir.yahoo.com/Social_Science/Psychology/*—You can use one of the most powerful search engines to browse among sites and subcategories that have been identified as related to the broad field of psychology.

∞ *http://www.learner.org/*—This website supports *Discovering Psychology: Updated Edition* with a page for each video program featuring an "academic footnote" to further update the content of the videos. The site also offers four special interactive features as well as an extensive webography.

UNIT 2

Whatever knowledge is attainable must be attainable by scientific method; and what science can not discover, mankind can not know.

Bertrand Russell

Unit 2 demonstrates the hows and whys of psychological research. By showing how psychologists rely on systematic observation, data collection, and analysis to find out the answers to their questions, this unit reveals why the scientific method is used in all areas of empirical investigation.

Objectives

After viewing the television program and completing the assigned readings, you should be able to:

1. Explain the concept of observer bias and cite some techniques experimenters use to eliminate personal bias.

2. Define *placebo effect* and explain how it might be avoided.

3. Define *reliability* and *validity* and explain the difference between them.

4. Describe various psychological measurement techniques, such as self report, behavioral, and physiological measures.

5. Define *correlational methods* and explain why it does not establish a cause-and-effect relationship.

6. Summarize the American Psychological Association's ethical guidelines for the treatment of humans and animals in psychological experiments, and explain why they are necessary.

7. Discuss some ways to be a wiser consumer of research.

8. Describe how a hypothesis leads to a particular experimental design.

9. Discuss how job burnout develops, how it can be studied, and how psychologists can intervene to prevent or combat it.

Reading Assignment

After viewing Program 2, read pages 22-43 in *Psychology and Life*.

Key People and Terms

As you watch the program and read the assignment, pay particular attention to these people and terms. People and terms defined in the text will be found on the given page numbers.

behavioral measures (33)
between-subjects design (28)
case study (35)
confounding variable (26)
control procedures (27)
correlation coefficient (*r*) (29)
correlational methods (29)
debriefing (37)
dependent variable (25)
determinism (23)
double-blind control (27)
expectancy effects (26)
experimental method (26)
hypothesis (24)
independent variable (25)
median (260)
observer bias (24)

operational definition (25)
placebo control (27)
placebo effect (27)
population (28)
reliability (33)
representative sample (28)
sample (28)
scientific method (23)
self-report measures (33)
standard deviation (SD) (276)
standardization (25)
theory (23)
validity (33)
variable (25)
within-subjects design (28)

The following terms and people are referred to in Program 2 but are not identified in the text.

∞ *burnout*—a work-related condition in which stress, lack of support, and negative self-evaluation disrupt performance and well-being.

∞ *field study*—research carried on outside the laboratory where naturally occurring, ongoing behavior can be observed.

∞ *random sample*—an unbiased population selected at random.

∞ *subjective reality*—the perceptions and beliefs that we accept without question.

∞ *Daryl Bem*—psychologist who illustrated the importance of critical thinking in scientific experiments.

∞ *Jerome Frank*—psychiatrist who studies the common features of miracle cures and healings, political and religious conversions and psychotherapy.

∞ *Christina Maslach*—uses psychometric research to study job burnout.

∞ *Leonard Saxe*—studies the use and misuse of polygraphs to detect lying.

Program Summary

Television and radio talk shows commonly feature people peddling psychic powers, astrology, ESP, or mind reading. Because psychology is so often sensationalized and misrepresented, it is difficult for the average person to distinguish science from pseudoscience, fact from fiction.

Program 2 demonstrates how psychologists separate superstition and irrational beliefs from fact and reason. Understanding how ideas are tested enables us to become skeptical consumers of media information and to develop critical thinking skills to protect us against deception and fraud.

Psychologists are guided by a set of procedures for gathering and interpreting evidence using carefully controlled observations and measurements. This is called the scientific method and requires that research be conducted in an orderly, standardized way. Then the results are published so that others can review and perhaps repeat the process.

Scientists employ a variety of study methods. They conduct experiments in laboratories, administer surveys, and take measurements in the field where they observe people and animals in natural settings. Seeing how scientists try to eliminate error and bias from their work helps us avoid some of the faulty reasoning in our own lives.

One factor that scientists consider is the placebo effect. In medicine, a placebo is a substance that is chemically inert, such as a sugar pill. It may, nevertheless, have a therapeutic effect. The placebo effect complicates the job of a researcher because the mere suggestion of a believable treatment will make many people feel better. Some researchers have found that despite different settings or tactics, the power of any change agent relies on the person's belief in the change agent's power.

Any medical or psychological treatment can only be considered successful if it demonstrates a level of effectiveness beyond the placebo effect. To do this, researchers use the double-blind procedure in which neither the participant nor the experimenter knows who is getting the real drug and who is taking the placebo. That information is held by another researcher who has no contact with the experimenter or participants.

We must resist the temptation to conclude that things that merely occur together necessarily have a cause and effect relationship. There may be a third factor that causes the other two. Consider a report that suggests that when the time spent watching TV goes up, grades go down. Should we conclude that watching TV causes poor grades? In fact, students who watch a lot of TV might spend less time on their homework. But students who get bad grades might watch more television because they don't like homework. They would get bad grades whether they watched TV or not.

When interpreting data, we have to make sure that the participants in an experiment are a representative sampling of the population they are meant to represent. Shere Hite's controversial report on women's attitudes about sex and marriage highlights a sampling problem. Her conclusions were based on only four percent of all the people who had received her questionnaire. She had taken no steps to ensure that her sample would be representative of the age, education level, and race distribution in the general population. Hite's sample method was too flawed to be useful (see figure 1).

Shere Hite Study	*ABC News* and *Washington Post* Study
4% of sample responding	random sampling
98% dissatisfied with some aspect of their relationship	*93% satisfied* with their relationship
75% involved in extramarital affairs	7% involved in extramarital affairs

Figure 1: Comparison of Sex and Marriage Studies
Shere Hite's study of women's attitudes toward sex and marriage did not include a representative sampling since only four percent of the women she contacted responded. A similar study conducted by *ABC News* and the *Washington Post,* which included a random sampling of women, found very different results.

Professionals, as well as the general public, can be taken in by pseudoscientific technology. The polygraph, or lie detector, for example, measures changes in physical arousal, such as heart rate or the galvanic skin response. But these machines are fallible. Research has shown that innocent people who believe they might be mistakenly identified may show anxiety. And guilty people may fool the machine by taking drugs or purposely tensing and relaxing their muscles. This so-called lie detector can play a crucial role in people's lives; sometimes it is used to help make decisions about hiring and firing employees.

Good research methods can provide us with information that can then be applied to everyday issues. Christina Maslach studies job burnout and the relation of stress and lack of support on the job to reductions in performance and deterioration of a worker's well-being. Maslach's research focuses on the connections among the person, the situation, and the compatibility of the employee with the job. She collects her data through interviews, surveys, and standardized scales. This research has practical implications for understanding the dynamics between work environments and employees and can be used to develop more constructive workplaces. In turn, the outcomes of the changes instituted in the workplace provide her with new research questions that she can then test.

Getting at the truth about psychological phenomena is difficult, but there are guidelines that help us avoid common pitfalls: Don't assume that two things that occur together have a cause-and-effect relation. Seeing isn't always believing. Question data that aren't collected using rigorous procedures. Keep in mind the power of placebos. Restrain enthusiasm for scientific breakthroughs. Beware of people claiming absolute truth and of attempts to persuade, rather than educate. And remember that conclusions are always open to revision.

Program Review Questions

1. Which of the following describes a field study?

   a. observing a natural, ongoing situation
   b. randomly assigning participants to treatment groups
   c. randomly assigning participants to a control group
   d. distributing a questionnaire to a large group

2. Which of the following is desirable in research?

   a. having the control and experimental conditions differ on several variables
   b. interpreting correlation as implying causality
   c. systematic manipulation of the variable(s) of interest
   d. using samples of participants who are more capable than the population you want to draw conclusions about

3. What is the main reason that the results of research studies are published?

   a. so researchers can prove they earned their money
   b. so other researchers can try to replicate the work
   c. so the general public can understand the importance of spending money on research
   d. so attempts at fraud and trickery are detected

4. Why does the placebo effect work?

   a. because researchers believe it does
   b. because participants believe in the power of the placebo
   c. because human beings prefer feeling they are in control
   d. because it is part of the scientific method

5. What is the purpose of a double-blind procedure?

   a. to test more than one variable at a time
   b. to repeat the results of previously published work
   c. to define a hypothesis clearly before it is tested
   d. to eliminate experimenter bias

6. If you had been one of the participants in the lie detector study, what information would have helped you earn some money?

   a. The results depend on the skill of the person administering the lie detector test.
   b. Lie detectors only measure arousal level, not lying.
   c. The polygraph is used to make millions of decisions each year.
   d. The placebo effect works with lie detectors.

7. According to Jerome Frank, placebos work through

   a. emotional arousal.
   b. brainwashing.
   c. chemical alteration of neural transmission.
   d. cognitive reassessment of the illness.

8. A report on children's television watching found that children who watch more TV have lower grades. What cause-effect conclusion are we justified in making on the basis of this study?

   a. TV watching causes low grades.
   b. Poor school performance causes children to watch more TV.
   c. Cause-effect conclusions can never be based on one study.
   d. None; cause-effect conclusions cannot be based on correlation.

9. What was the major weakness of the Hite report on women's attitudes toward sex and marriage?

    a. The sample was not representative.
    b. Hypotheses were not clearly stated beforehand.
    c. Experimenter bias arose because the double-blind procedure was not used.
    d. No control group was used.

10. A prediction of how two or more variables are likely to be related is called a

    a. theory.
    b. conclusion.
    c. hypothesis.
    d. correlation.

11. Imagine a friend tells you that she has been doing better in school since she started taking vitamin pills. When you express disbelief, she urges you to take vitamins too. Why might the pills "work" for her but not necessarily for you?

    a. Healthy people don't need vitamins.
    b. A belief in the power of the vitamins is necessary for any effect to occur.
    c. She is lying.
    d. They would work for her and not for you if she was a poor student and you were a straight-A student.

12. In which experiment would a double-blind test be most appropriate?

    a. a lab experiment by a technician who does not understand the theory under scrutiny
    b. a study designed to test the researcher's own controversial theory
    c. a survey asking subjects how many siblings they have
    d. an experiment on the effect of a drug on maze running ability in rats

13. The "card trick" in the program demonstrates what about good science?

    a. Predictions should be made explicitly before data collection.
    b. Chance must be ruled out as an explanation.
    c. The experimenter's effect on the subject must be ruled out as an explanation.
    d. All of the above.

14. When long-term stress and lack of support on the job lead to chronic deficits in a worker's productivity and health, the worker is likely to be suffering from

    a. generalized anxiety disorder.
    b. post-traumatic stress.
    c. job burnout.
    d. insomnia.

15. Christina Maslach uses all of the following to study job burnout *except*

    a. interviews.
    b. hospitalization records.
    c. surveys.
    d. psychometric scales.

16. How could you improve on Shere Hite's survey techniques?

    a. Redo her study using her methods, but send the survey to ten times as many recipients.
    b. Hire one subject, pay her for a full day's work, and spend eight hours interviewing her thoroughly.
    c. Redo her study, using her methods, but send the survey to an equal number of men.
    d. Redo her study, but ensure that the percentage of respondents was much higher and much more representative of the population of interest.

17. Why would other scientists want to replicate an experiment that has already been done?

    a. to have their names associated with a well-known phenomenon
    b. to gain a high-odds, low-risk publication
    c. to ensure that the phenomenon under study is real and reliable
    d. to calibrate their equipment with those of another laboratory

18. Because experiments involve careful manipulation of all factors of interest and careful control of all others, which experiment would not be ethically allowable?

    a. the effect of classical music on the ability to solve crossword puzzles
    b. the effect of room lighting on color preference
    c. the effect of supplementary vitamins on retirement age
    d. the effect of prolonged solitary confinement of toddlers on language development

19. Because of what it actually does measure, under what circumstances would an innocent person likely fail a polygraph test?

    a. if she is extremely worried about the possibility of being found guilty
    b. if she is drunk
    c. if she is acquainted with the actual guilty party
    d. if she is confident in the validity of the polygraph test

Questions to Consider

1. If some people really get healed by faith healers, why condemn the practice of faith healing?

2. If there is value in running studies with within-subjects designs, why would an experimenter ever use a between-subjects design?

3. What are some of the practical objections to studying mental processes?

4. What is your reaction to the guidelines prohibiting research if it would require deception and if distress is a likely result? Are there studies you think would be valuable to perform but that could not be? Could the same research questions be answered in some other way?

5. Are animals adequately protected by the APA's guidelines? Why or why not?

6. How could a study be biased simply because it uses volunteer participants?

7. Can the results of experiments conducted mostly on college students, who are among the more highly educated members of our society, really be extended to the rest of society? Which sorts of psychological phenomena would be more likely or less likely to generalize to people of other age groups, socio-economic status, and education levels?

Optional Activities

1. Write operational definitions of the following:

green	thirst	wealth
warm	anger	learning
cleverness	intelligence	jealousy
suffering	comprehension	

2. Design a study that would test whether children come to learn self-control better if they are physically punished vs. receive time-outs for bad behavior. What features of the problem determine whether you can run an experiment to test this? What confounding variables might be present in a study like this? How would you eliminate them as possible alternative explanations?

3. Design an experiment that would allow you to show whether a two-week-old child knows who her mother is. Be sure that your experimental design can eliminate alternative explanations for your data.

Additional Resources

Books and Articles

Adair, J. G. (2001). Ethics of psychological research: New policies; continuing issues; new concerns. *Canadian Psychology (Special Issue), 42*, 25-37.

Bordens, K.S., & Abbott, B. B. (2004). *Research design and methods: A process approach.* New York, NY: McGraw-Hill.

Maslach, C. (2004). Job burnout: New directions in research and intervention. *Current Directions in Psychological Science.*

Schaufeli, W. B., Maslach, C., & Marek, T. (Eds.) (1993). *Professional burnout: Recent developments in theory and research.* Washington, D. C.: Taylor & Francis.

Slife, B. (1998). *Taking sides: Clashing views on controversial psychological issues.* New York, NY: McGraw-Hill.

Wundt, W. (1897). *Ethics.* London: Sommeschine & Co.

Films

Avoiding Burnout: Stress Control. Educational Video Network, Inc., 2002.

Web Sites

∞ *http://www.apa.org/ethics/code2002.html*—Shows the code of ethical conduct currently in effect for the American Psychological Association. The code applies to both use of humans and use of non-human animals in research. It also includes guidelines for issues involving privacy, clinical treatment, sexual harassment, education.

∞ *http://psychexps.olemiss.edu/*—The University of Mississippi ("Ole Miss") sponsors PsychExperiments, an excellent site where you can run demonstration studies in a wide range of psychological fields.

∞ *http://www.learner.org/*—This website supports *Discovering Psychology: Updated Edition* with a page for each video program featuring an "academic footnote" to further update the content of the videos. The site also offers special workshops and video courses.

UNIT 3

There is no scientific study more vital to man than the study of his own brain. Our entire view of the universe depends on it.

Francis Crick

Psychologists who study the structure and composition of the brain believe that all our thoughts, feelings, and actions have a biological and chemical basis. Unit 3 explains the nervous system and the methods scientists use to explore the link between physiological processes in the brain and psychological experience and behavior.

Objectives

After viewing the television program and completing the assigned reading, you should be able to:

1. Explain the major concepts of evolutionary theory, such as natural selection and variation.

2. Identify several methods used to study the brain and give a significant finding associated with each.

3. Identify the major structures and specialized functions of the brain.

4. Cite examples of how the endocrine system affects mood and emotion.

5. List and describe the major divisions and subdivisions of the nervous system and the functions of each.

6. Describe the structure of a neuron.

7. Explain the mechanism of neural transmission.

8. Describe the process of synaptic transmission and list the six important neurotransmitters.

9. Describe hemispheric separation and individual differences pertaining to it.

10. Explain how amnesic patients can be studied to understand normal memory processes.

Reading Assignment

After viewing Program 3, read pages 52-89 in *Psychology and Life*. This textbook reading covers Units 3 and 4.

Key People and Terms

As you watch the program and read the assignment, pay particular attention to these people and terms. People and terms defined in the text will be found on the given page numbers.

action potential (62)

all-or-none law (64)

amygdala (74)

association cortex (76)

auditory cortex (76)

autonomic nervous system (ANS) (71)

axon (61)

brain stem (72)

Broca's area (68)

central nervous system (CNS) (70)

cerebellum (73)

cerebral cortex (74)

cerebral hemispheres (74)

cerebrum (74)

corpus callosum (74)

dendrites (60)

DNA (deoxyribonucleic acid) (56)

electroencephalogram (EEG) (69)

endocrine system (81)

estrogen (82)

evolutionary psychology (59)

excitatory inputs (62)

frontal lobe (75)

functional MRI (fMRI) (70)

genes (56)

genetics (56)

genome (57)

genotype (55)

glia (61)

heredity (56)

heritability (57)

hippocampus (73)

homeostasis (74)

hormones (81)

human behavior genetics (57)

hypothalamus (74)

inhibitory inputs (62)

interneurons (61)

ion channels (63)

lesions (68)

limbic system (73)

magnetic resonance imaging (MRI) (69)

medulla (72)

motor cortex (75)

motor neurons (61)

natural selection (54)

neurogenesis (83)

neuromodulator (66)

neuron (60)

neuroscience (60)

neurotransmitters (64)

occipital lobe (75)

parasympathetic division (72)

parietal lobe (75)

peripheral nervous system (PNS) (70)

PET scans (69)

phenotype (55)

pituitary gland (82)

plasticity (82)

pons (72)

refractory period (64)

repetitive transcranial magnetic stimulation (rTMS) (68)

resting potential (63)

reticular formation (72)

sensory neurons (61)

sex chromosomes (57)

sociobiology (59)

soma (60)

somatic nervous system (71)

somatosensory cortex (76)

sympathetic division (72)

synapse (64)

synaptic transmission (64)

temporal lobe (75)

terminal buttons (61)

testosterone (82)

thalamus (73)

visual cortex (76)

Paul Broca (68)
Charles Darwin (53)
René Descartes (60)
Michael Gazzaniga (78)

The following terms and people are referred to in Program 3 but are not defined in the text.

∞ *agonist*—a chemical or drug that mimics the action of a neurotransmitter.

∞ *amnesia*—a type of profound and generalized forgetting, generally affecting factual information, and involving the inability to learn new information and/or to retrieve important old information.

∞ *antagonist*—a chemical or drug that blocks the action of a neurotransmitter.

∞ *physostigmine*—enhances the effect of acetylcholine in the brain by inhibiting the enzyme that breaks it down.

∞ *scopolamine*—depletes the availability of acetylcholine in the brain by blocking the receptors for acetylcholine.

∞ *Emanuel Donchin*—studies the manner in which the mind is implemented by the brain using psychophysiological measures.

∞ *John Gabrieli*—studies amnesic patients to determine how different types of memory are physically stored in and retrieved from the brain.

∞ *E. Roy John*—studies neurometrics and uses precise electrophysiological measures to determine neural functioning.

∞ *Joseph Martinez*—studies how brain chemicals affect learning and memory.

∞ *Mieke Verfaellie*—studies the effects of amnesia on memory and cognition.

Program Summary

All information that we receive, process, and transmit depends on the functions of the brain, the most complex structure in the known universe. Program 3 describes the brain's biological and chemical foundation for all our thoughts, feelings, and actions.

There are about ten trillion nerve cells in the brain. These cells, called neurons and glia, use a combination of electrical and chemical messengers to perform their specialized functions. Dendrites, or receptor fibers, gather incoming messages and send them to the cell body, or soma.

Then the messages are sent on as electrical discharges down the axon to the neuron's terminal button, which releases a chemical message to adjacent neurons.

Some chemicals generate a nerve impulse by exciting nearby receptors; others reduce or block nerve impulses and regulate the rate at which neurons fire. These nerve impulses are the basis for every change that takes place in the body, from moving our muscles to learning and remembering our multiplication tables.

Although the brain works as a unified whole, some of its parts specialize in particular jobs. The brain stem, which connects the brain to the spinal cord, controls breathing, heartbeat, waking, and sleeping. The cerebellum coordinates body movement and maintains equilibrium. The amygdala, part of the limbic system, seems to control emotional impulses, such as aggressive urges. For example, a mouse receiving electrical stimulation to the amygdala will attack a cat. And suppressing the amygdala will stop a bull in his tracks. The hypothalamus is the liaison between the body and the rest of the brain, releasing hormones to the pituitary gland. The thalamus acts as a relay station, sending signals from the body to the brain.

The cerebrum translates nerve impulses into higher-level cognitive processes, using images and symbols to form ideas and wishes. Its outer layer, the cerebral cortex, is the center of conscious thought and action. The cerebrum's two halves, or hemispheres, are connected by a bundle of millions of nerve fibers called the corpus callosum, which acts as a conduit of messages between the right and left sides of the brain.

Scientists use a variety of methods to understand better the structure and functions of the brain. In the past, autopsies revealed how impaired abilities might be the result of damaged brain tissue. Later, experimenters purposely destroyed specific parts of animal brain tissue so they could observe what sensory or motor losses occurred. Researchers also stimulated specific regions with electricity or chemicals. Today we can get actual pictures of the brain's inner workings using a technique called imaging. Scientists can also record nerve signals from a single neuron or electrical wave patterns from the entire brain. This brain wave pattern is known as an electroencephalogram, or EEG.

But how do scientists know what constitutes normal electrical activity in the brain? By analyzing and comparing brain wave patterns from people all over the world, they have concluded that all healthy members of the human species have similar brains. Variations in electrical patterns may reveal environmental influences, such as poor nutrition or even living at unusually high elevations. This methodology helps scientists identify structural or chemical causes for thought, mood, and behavioral disorders, thus making it easier to evaluate different therapies.

Other neuroscientists study the brain's biochemical activity. They look at many groups of neurotransmitters and hormones that affect brain functions and behavior. Nerve cells manufacture opiate-like molecules, known as endorphins, part of the complex system of neurotransmitters. Endorphins can affect our moods, emotions, and perception of pain. Some long-distance runners report a feeling of euphoria, or "runner's high," after a strenuous workout. This may be the result of exercise increasing the body's endorphin activity.

Endorphins are only one of many chemical influences on the brain. Some scientists investigate the influence of brain chemicals on learning and memory. By comparing the performance of experimental rats given drugs that block or mimic specific neurotransmitters with that of untreated animals, scientists hope to discover which changes in the brain produce specific actions. So, by learning how the brain works or fails to work, they can begin to prescribe new drug therapies to prevent, minimize, even cure diseases, such as learning deficits or memory losses that accompany Alzheimer's disease.

Other scientists, such as Mieke Verfaellie and John Gabrieli, conduct brain imagining studies to learn about the physical mechanisms by which the brain stores and retrieves memories, and to understand what is disrupted in individuals who are amnesic. Amnesic patients suffering from anterograde amnesia have their sense of identity and their earlier memories preserved, but they are unable to learn new information. For example, one patient suffered medial temporal lobe damage in the hippocampal region of his brain because of a viral infection. He was able to provide details about O. J. Simpson from the distant past, but he has no permanent memory of more recent events involving Simpson.

The hippocampus is necessary for laying down new permanent memories. In patients with anterograde amnesia, the hippocampus is so severely damaged that the patient's storehouse of knowledge cannot contain facts about anything to which the patient was exposed after the damage occurred. As the world continues to change, it becomes less and less matched to what the patient "knows." Studying memory and brain functioning in patients for whom basic memory functioning has been disrupted allows neuroscientists to understand how normal brains achieve feats of memory and cognition.

Program Review Questions

NOTE: Review Questions for Units 3 and 4 are provided in Unit 4.

Questions to Consider

1. What is the advantage of knowing that mental illness is caused by neurochemical problems if we don't know how to correct them?

2. There are millions of people who will try just about anything to control their weight. They buy diet pills and nutritional supplements that claim to alter the chemistry of their appetite. Some are so desperate that they have their mouths wired shut. Why don't doctors treat people with eating disorders by placing electrodes in their brains?

3. Different technologies for measuring brain activity help psychologists view structures and functioning of the brain. What advantages do these advanced techniques offer?

4. Imagine that you were a relative of Phineas Gage. How do you think you would have reacted to the changes in his behavior in the years following his accident at the railroad construction site? Would you have been willing to believe that the changes were permanent, or that they weren't under Gage's control?

Optional Activity

Can you feel the effects of your hormones? Try this: Imagine yourself falling down the stairs, stubbing your toe, or suddenly losing control of your car on a busy highway. Did your heart skip a beat? Did you catch your breath or feel a tingle up your back? Did the hair on your neck stiffen? Your imagination has caused a biochemical reaction in your brain, and you are feeling the effect of the hormones it produces. Can you name the hormones involved?

Additional Resources

Books and Articles

Baars, B. J., Banks, W. P., & Newman, J. B. (2003). *Essential sources in the scientific study of consciousness.* Boston, MA: MIT Press.

Corballis, P. M., Funnell, M. G., & Gazzaniga, M. S. (2000). An evolutionary perspective on hemispheric asymmetries. *Brain & Cognition, 43,* 112-117.

Komatsu, L. (2001). *Mind, brain, & computer: An introduction to cognitive science.* New York: Brooks/Cole Publishing Company.

Ramachandran, V. S., & Blakeslee, S. (1998). *Phantoms in the brain.* New York: William Morrow.

Films

Regarding Henry, 1991. Directed by Mike Nichols.

Web Sites

∞ *http://www.psych.ucsb.edu/research/cep/*—Leda Cosmides and John Tooby of the University of California at Santa Barbara host a web site dedicated to theoretical issues and findings concerning evolutionary psychology. They treat the human mind as the product of competition and natural selection, and they present interesting issues that arise from that perspective

∞ *http://www.nhgri.nih.gov/*—The web site for the National Human Genome Research Institute can inform you about the benefits of mapping the human genome and the scientific progress made thus far in understanding the chemical composition of the human genetic blueprint.

∞ *http://www.learner.org/*—This web site supports *Discovering Psychology: Updated Edition* with a page for each video program featuring an "academic footnote" to further update the content of the videos. The site also offers four special interactive features as well as an extensive webography.

UNIT 4

THE RESPONSIVE BRAIN

The Human Brain is a most unusual instrument of elegant and as yet unknown capacity.

Stuart Lyman Seaton

Unit 4 takes a closer look at the dynamic relationship between the brain and behavior. We'll see how the brain controls behavior and, conversely, how behavior and environment can cause changes in the structure and the functioning of the brain.

Objectives

After viewing the television program and reviewing the assigned reading, you should be able to:

1. Cite examples of the brain's capacity to adapt to environmental change.

2. Explain how early experience can affect brain mechanisms that influence stress tolerance in later life.

3. Cite research studies that contribute to an understanding of the role enriched environments play in brain development.

4. Describe the concept of critical periods of development and cite the evidence that supports or contradicts it.

5. Explain how individual maturation is controlled by social needs and group behavior.

6. Describe the sociobiological approach to the explanation of behavior and compare it to the explanation given by proponents of human behavior genetics.

7. Explain the value of observation studies of animals in their natural habitats and how these studies complement laboratory research.

8. Describe various methods currently in use for studying the brain.

9. Describe the interaction between the brain and the endocrine system.

10. Identify the specialized functions associated with each of the four lobes of the brain.

Reading Assignment

After viewing Program 4, review pages 52-89 in *Psychology and Life.*

Key People and Terms

People and terms defined in the text for this unit are provided in Unit 3.

The following terms and people are used in Program 4 but are not introduced in the text.

∞ *enzymes*—protein molecules that act as catalysts in body chemistry by facilitating chemical reactions.

∞ *glucocorticoid*—substances produced by the adrenal cortex that act on the hippocampus to alter the stress response.

∞ *maternal deprivation*—the lack of adequate affection and stimulation from the mother or mother substitute.

∞ *Tiffany Field*—studies the effect of infant massage on the cognitive and motor development of infants.

∞ *Russell Fernald*—neuroethologist who studies how brain, behavior and the environment interact in animals in their natural habitat.

∞ *Michael Meaney*—developmental psychologist who studies how early experiences can change the brains and behavior of animals, especially under stress.

∞ *Saul Schanberg*—works with infant rats to demonstrate how touch is a brain based requirement for normal growth and development. Argues that a mother's touch has real biological value to offspring and is required to maintain normal growth and development.

∞ *Robert Sapolsky*—neurobiologist who studies the social structure of baboon communities. Argues that dominance affects physiological functioning, with higher ranks being associated with greater control, predictability and better physiological functioning.

Program Summary

The brain is the place where an endless stream of electrical nerve impulses, chemical transmitters, and hormone messengers get transformed into experience, knowledge, feelings, beliefs, and consciousness. Learning how it functions helps us better understand human and animal behavior.

The reciprocal relationship between the brain and behavior is the subject of Program 4. The brain controls behavior, and behavior feeds back information to influence the brain. The brain can even alter its own functioning and structure. This capacity for internal modification makes it one of the most dynamic systems on earth.

Several studies demonstrate the responsiveness of the brain's neurochemical system. In one, we learn that humans and animals thrive when they get adequate contact and suffer when they do not. For some infants, especially those born prematurely, touch can mean the difference between illness and health, even life and death.

Psychologist Tiffany Field explains her study in which some premature infants received gentle massages and others received routine care. Those in the massaged group gained more weight, were able to leave the hospital earlier, and showed long-term developmental advantages over the babies who received routine care. This research clearly demonstrates the therapeutic value of touching and suggests a way to save millions of dollars in hospital costs.

Psychologist Saul Schanberg, who conducted research with touch-deprived rats, demonstrated that maternal deprivation can stunt growth. But he also demonstrated that retarded growth can be reversed. Placing the stunted baby rats with their mothers or stroking them with a wet paintbrush restored normal growth.

Lack of touching also seems to affect the production of human growth hormones. When researchers removed touch-deprived, growth-stunted children from their unloving homes and placed them in more affectionate families, they grew dramatically.

Another study demonstrates that early experiences can cause permanent alterations in the structure of the brain. Rats raised in stimulating, visually enriched environments had a thicker cortex and were superior learners compared with rats raised in ordinary or deprived environments. The stimulated rats had more neurotransmitters, more enzymes in the glial cells, and more and larger spines on the dendrites.

Other research studies on early experience and the brain also show long-term effects of touching. Newborn rats who had regular handling were better able to cope with stress throughout their lives. They also showed signs of slower aging and of reduced learning decrements and memory losses.

Developmental psychologist Michael Meaney investigates how early experiences can change the brain and behavior. He explains that when an individual faces a threat, the adrenal glands release hormones called glucocorticoids, which prepare the body to handle stressful situations. But repeated exposure to stress hormones inhibits the glucocorticoid neurons in the hippocampus, a part of the brain that regulates stress and plays a key role in learning and memory. Handling the baby rats in the first three weeks of life seems to reduce the loss of glucocorticoid cells and improves the hippocampus's ability to turn off the stress response.

Observational research is just as important as controlled experiments performed in the laboratory. Russell Fernald studied the African Cichlid fish as an example of how the brain is altered when behavior changes. He observed that dominant male Cichlids have brightly colored patterns and dark eye bars. When these fish acquired territory, changes in the Cichlids' brains caused the fish to grow rapidly and colorfully. When they lost territory, they lost their coloration and sexual maturity.

Another study, conducted by Stanford biologist Robert Sapolsky, demonstrated that in baboon colonies, social rank is the most important principle of social organization. When baboons attained high social rank, they also became healthier and more physically resistant. With reverses in status, they showed a corresponding loss of health and lowering in tolerance for stress.

All these studies contribute to a better understanding of the interplay of environment, behavior, and biology. In the controlled setting of the laboratory, researchers can look more closely at how the brain changes. In the field, they can observe how animals naturally respond to demands from the environment.

Program Review Questions

1. What section of a nerve cell receives incoming information?

   a. the axon
   b. the terminal button
   c. the synapse
   d. the dendrite

2. In general, neuroscientists are interested in the

   a. brain mechanisms underlying normal and abnormal behavior.
   b. biological consequences of stress on the body.
   c. comparison of neurons with other types of cells.
   d. computer simulation of intelligence.

3. Which section of the brain coordinates body movement and maintains equilibrium?

   a. the brain stem
   b. the cerebellum
   c. the hippocampus
   d. the cerebrum

4. Which brain structure is most closely involved with emotion?

    a. the cortex
    b. the brain stem
    c. the limbic system
    d. the cerebellum

5. Which method of probing the brain produces actual pictures of the brain's inner working?

    a. autopsies
    b. lesioning
    c. brain imaging
    d. electroencephalograms

6. E. Roy John cites the example of the staff member responding to a personal question to show how imaging can detect

    a. abnormal structure in the brain.
    b. abnormal personality.
    c. abnormal but transient states.
    d. pathological states, such as alcoholism.

7. If a scientist was studying the effects of endorphins on the body, the scientist would be likely to look at a participant's

    a. memory.
    b. mood.
    c. ability to learn new material.
    d. motivation to compete in sports.

8. Joseph Martinez taught rats a maze task and then gave them scopolamine. What effect   did the drug have on brain functioning?

    a. It enhanced the rats' memory.
    b. It made the rats forget what they had learned.
    c. It enabled the rats to learn a similar task more quickly.
    d. It had no effect.

9. Research related to acetylcholine may someday help people who

    a. have Alzheimer's disease.
    b. have Parkinson's disease.
    c. suffer spinal cord trauma.
    d. suffer from depression.

10. A scientist who uses the methodologies of brain science to examine animal behavior in natural habitats is a

    a. naturalist.
    b. bioecologist.
    c. neuroethologist.
    d. cerebroetymologist.

11. When we say the relationship between the brain and behavior is reciprocal, we mean that

    a. the brain controls behavior, but behavior can modify the brain.
    b. behavior determines what the brain will think about.
    c. the brain and behavior operate as separate systems with no interconnection.
    d. the brain alters behavior as it learns more about the world.

12. Before an operation, men and women were gently touched by a nurse. What effect did this touch have on the patients' anxiety levels?

    a. It decreased anxiety in both men and women.
    b. It increased anxiety in both men and women.
    c. It decreased anxiety in men, but increased it in women.
    d. It increased anxiety in men, but decreased it in women.

13. A group of people comfortable with touching others is compared with a group uncomfortable with touching others. Those comfortable with touch were generally higher in

    a. self-esteem.
    b. social withdrawal.
    c. conformity.
    d. suspicion of others.

14. What long-term effect did Tiffany Field find massage had on premature infants?

    a. Massaged infants had better social relationships.
    b. Massaged infants were physically and cognitively more developed.
    c. Massaged infants slept and ate better.
    d. There were no long-term effects noted.

15. What is the relationship between the results of Saul Schanberg's research and that of Tiffany Field?

    a. Their results are contradictory.
    b. The results of Schanberg's research led to Field's research.
    c. Their results show similar phenomena in different species.
    d. Their results are essentially unrelated.

16. What area of the brain seems to be affected in psychosocial dwarfism?

    a. the hippocampus
    b. the cerebellum
    c. the brain stem
    d. the hypothalamus

17. What physical change did Mark Rosenzweig's team note when they studied rats raised in an enriched environment?

    a. a thicker cortex
    b. more neurons
    c. fewer neurotransmitters
    d. no physical changes were noted, only functional changes

18. In Michael Meaney's research on aged rats' performance in a swimming maze, the rats that performed best were those that

    a. had received doses of glucocorticoid.
    b. had been subjected to less stress in their lives.
    c. had been handled early in life.
    d. could use spatial clues for orientation.

19. Repeated exposure to stress hormones

    a. increases the number of glucocorticoid neurons.
    b. has its greatest effect on the brain stem.
    c. affect learning and memory.
    d. makes brain cells live longer.

20. In his study of Cichlid fish, Russell Fernald found that there was growth in a specific area of the brain following

    a. improved diet.
    b. social success.
    c. gentle handling.
    d. loss of territory.

21. In Robert Sapolsky's study of stress physiology among baboons, what is the relationship between high status and "good" physiology?

    a. Animals attain high status because they have good physiology.
    b. Attaining high status leads to good physiology.
    c. Lowering one's status leads to improved physiology.
    d. Animals with high status produce high levels of stress hormone, which break down the immune system.

22. Which of the following is true about how neurons communicate with each other?

    a. All neuronal communication is excitatory.
    b. Neurons communicate with each other by sending electrical discharges across the connecting synapse.
    c. Neurons of any given type can communicate only with other neurons of the same type.
    d. The sum of excitatory and inhibitory signals to a neuron determines whether and how strongly it will respond.

23. Which part of the brain controls breathing?

    a. cerebellum
    b. brain stem
    c. hypothalamus
    d. limbic system

24. The cerebrum

    a. consists of two hemispheres connected by the corpus callosum.
    b. relays sensory impulses to the higher perceptual centers.
    c. releases seven different hormones to the pituitary gland.
    d. controls temperature and blood pressure.

25. With respect to the neurochemistry of the brain, all of these are true, *except* that

    a. scopolamine blocks the establishment of long-term memories.
    b. opioid peptides are naturally occurring chemicals in the brain.
    c. physostigmine is responsible for information transmission in the perceptual pathways.
    d. endorphins play a major role in pleasure and pain experiences.

26. What did Robert Sapolsky discover is the optimal style of behavior for dominant baboons?

    a. unpredictable aggression
    b. social style
    c. active curiosity
    d. frequent vocalizing

Questions to Consider

1. Many different factors influence your performance on a test: your study habits, recollection of the material, familiarity with the test format, and confidence. Given the choice, would you take a drug that might improve your performance? Would you take a beta-blocker that interferes with the effects of adrenaline (used by some actors and musicians to reduce stage fright) or a drug that enhances retention and recall of information? Would taking a drug give you an unfair advantage over other test takers? Is there any danger in taking drugs for this purpose?

2. Program 4 suggests that children raised with significantly different patterns of physical contact and touching will develop different behavioral, social, and personality characteristics. What do you imagine might happen as the Internet age progresses and people become used to spending less and less time around other people? Will this significantly affect our experience with physical contact?

3. Considering what is known about the damaging effects of poor nutrition, drugs, cigarettes, and alcohol on the fetus, what can be done to protect a baby from the effects of its mother's activities? Should any legal action be taken?

4. Given the advances being made in the imaging of brain activity, will it ever be possible for scientists to "read someone's mind" or to control someone's thoughts?

5. The socialization process in our culture relies heavily on both rewards (for example, praise in school or promotions at work) and punishments of various kinds. Given what we know about the influence of social standing on health, should we restructure our culture to rely more heavily on rewards and gains in status? Do Robert Sapolsky's findings from his work on baboons extend to human social status and health?

6. Speculate on why music, having no survival benefit or pharmacological properties, would have the strong effect on people's emotions and brains that it seems to have.

7. Imagine that you were designing an animal brain. Why would you want to design neurons to have an all-or-none response rather than a graded potential? Why would you want to create a brain that responded to several different neurotransmitters rather than creating one all-purpose neurotransmitter that affected all cells equally?

Optional Activities

1. Interview a few parents from different generations and from different cultures about the infancy of their children. Did they read books on child development or follow an expert's advice? Did they sleep with their babies? How did they comfort them? Which early experiences do they believe were most influential in their children's future development?

2. As science enters an era of being able to study the brain's activities, our imaginations about what is possible run much faster than the development of neuroimaging and simulation techniques. Watch films like *The Cell, The Matrix*, and *AI,* and identify several ways in which the "science" they portray is impossible given the current state of the field. Think about which aspects will likely remain impossible even hundreds of years from now.

Additional Resources

Books and Articles

Changeux, J.-P. (2004). *The physiology of truth: Neuroscience and human knowledge.* Cambridge, MA: Belknap Press.

Gazzaniga, M. S. (2000). *The mind's past.* Berkeley: University of California Press.

Pinker, S. (1999). *How the mind works.* New York: W. W. Norton.

Ramachandran, V. S., & Blakeslee, S. (1998). *Phantoms in the brain: Probing the mysteries of the human mind.* New York: William Morrow.

Films

The Cell. Directed by Tarsem Singh, 2000.
The Matrix. Directed by Andy Wachowski, 1999.

Web Sites

∞   *http://faculty.washington.edu/chudler/disorders.html* —Dr. Eric H. Chudler, of the Department of Anesthesiology at the University of Washington, hosts a Web site that allows people to learn about and compare different kinds of neurological disorders, including Alzheimer's Disease and Tourette Syndrome.

∞   *http://brainmuseum.org/explore/*—Houses a collection of brains from multiple species that you can visually explore. You can also examine brain evolution, individual brain sections, and brain circuitry.

∞   *http://www.biausa.org/*—Find out more about brain injuries, rehabilitation, outcomes, and opportunities at this site operated by the Brain Injury Association. Some types of loss can occur at any time of life and can occur suddenly, such as those associated with head trauma.

∞   *http://www.learner.org/*—This web site supports *Discovering Psychology: Updated Edition* with a page for each video program featuring an "academic footnote" to further update the content of the videos. The site also offers four special interactive features as well as an extensive webography.

UNIT 5

When we hear the baby laugh, it is the loveliest thing that can happen to us.

Sigmund Freud

Unit 5 looks at how advances in technology and methodology have revealed the abilities of newborn infants, giving researchers a better understanding of the role infants play in shaping their environment. In contrast to the nature versus nurture debates of the past, today's researchers concentrate on how heredity and environment interact to contribute to the developmental process.

Objectives

After viewing the television program and completing the assigned readings, you should be able to:

1. State the primary interest of developmental psychologists.

2. Describe the various ways that development is documented, including longitudinal, cross sectional and sequential.

3. Describe cognitive development across the lifespan.

4. Identify Piaget's stages of cognitive development.

5. Describe some contemporary perspectives on early cognitive development.

6. Describe physical development across the lifespan.

7. Describe how habituation studies can be used on infants to determine what they can understand.

8. Describe several ways that we know infants are not born as blank slates, but instead, come equipped with temperaments, preferences, and biases.

9. Describe several ways that the environment is known to affect skills and behaviors.

35

Reading Assignment

After viewing Program 5, read pages 297-313, 317-326, 330-338 in *Psychology and Life*.

Key People and Terms

As you watch the program and read the assignment, pay particular attention to these people and terms. People and terms defined in the text will be found on the given page numbers.

accommodation (306)
assimilation (306)
centration (307)
chronological age (299)
cognitive development (306)
conservation (307)
cross-sectional design (299)
developmental age (299)
developmental psychology (300)
egocentrism (307)
foundational theories (310)
internalization (310)
longitudinal design (299)
maturation (303)
menarche (303)
normative investigations (298)
object permanence (307)

physical development (300)
puberty (303)
schemes (306)
selective optimization with compensation (332)
wisdom (312)
zygote (300)

Renée Baillargeon (309)
Margaret Baltes (332)
Paul Baltes (332)
Eleanor Gibson (302)
John Locke (306)
Jean Piaget (306)
Jean-Jacques Rousseau (306)
Lev Vygotsky (310)
Richard Walk (302)

The following terms and people are used in Program 5 but are not introduced in the text.

∞ *stage theory*—a theory that describes development as a fixed sequence of distinct periods of life.

∞ *Judy DeLoache*—studies cognitive development in older children and how they come to understand symbols.

∞ *Jerome Kagan*—studies inherited behavioral differences between bold and timid children.

∞ *Warner Schaie*---studies the long-term effects of aging

∞ *Steven Suomi*—studies the behavior of genetically shy monkeys. Argues that at least some shyness is an inherited tendency.

Program Summary

Historically, the debate about the true essence of human nature was defined as "nature versus nurture." Empiricists, like John Locke, gave all credit for human development to experience and believed that we arrived in this world as blank tablets devoid of knowledge or skills. Nativists sided with Jean-Jacques Rousseau, arguing that what we bring into the world at birth affects our development the most. This debate was sharpened by the discovery of "The Wild Boy of Aveyron" in 1800 and the attempts by Dr. Itard to educate him. Today, developmental psychologists focus on how heredity and experience interact from the beginning of life throughout the life span.

In the field of child development, the subject of Program 5, there have been many important changes in attitudes about the capacities of newborns. Advances in technology and methodology have rapidly expanded our ability to read the silent language of infants. The growing ability to test for and map their psychological states has led scientists to conclude that infants are born ready to perform many feats and are able to participate in shaping their environment.

Psychologist William James depicted the infant as totally helpless in confronting the world. But today, researchers have powerful evidence that a newborn's behavior is meaningful. Newborns come ready to eat, turn away from bad odors, make friends, and mimic our expressions. We know that newborns can follow a moving face and express preferences for sights, sounds, tastes, and textures.

Researchers infer what newborns are thinking, seeing, and feeling by using techniques that measure how long they look at something or how intensely they suck when presented with stimuli. Researchers can also record and measure electrical responses in the brain, the degree of pupil dilation, and changes in heart rate. Using such indicators, it is possible to determine a baby's preferences and abilities, such as whether a baby is more interested in stripes or spots and whether it recognizes its mother.

One of the first researchers to use a baby's ability to express distinct preferences was Robert Fantz. He was able to show that babies preferred complexity and whole faces over jumbled parts of faces, thus demonstrating their cognitive capacities.

But it is the Swiss psychologist Jean Piaget who has contributed most to understanding the cognitive development of children. Piaget posed a variety of problems for children to solve, and after comparing their responses he demonstrated that understanding of the world varies with age. Piaget theorized that each child passes through four distinct levels of understanding in a fixed sequence, or series of stages—some children more slowly than others.

Despite his major contribution to psychology, Piaget vastly underestimated what children could do and overestimated the ages at which abilities emerged. Today, researchers are careful to design tasks that distinguish a child's ability to perform a task from the ability to explain or understand a concept. The results convince us that infants and children know more than we think they know— and they know it much earlier.

Researcher Renée Baillargeon of the University of Illinois has demonstrated that even six-month-old infants understand the concept of object permanence. Her colleague, Judy DeLoache, has shown that changes in children's ability to use symbols occur between ages two-and-a-half and three. Another well-known experiment that uses the visual cliff has clearly shown that infants develop a fear of heights at about eight and a half months, around the time they learn to crawl.

Researchers have identified activity level and shyness as personality traits that show genetic influence. Harvard psychologist Jerome Kagan, who specializes in the study of inherited behavioral differences between timid and bold children, has found that being born shy does not necessarily mean a lifetime of shyness. Even inherited tendencies can be modified by learning, training, and experience. Researcher Steven Suomi explains how shyness decreased when he placed shy baby monkeys with extremely nurturant foster mothers, demonstrating that both nature and nurture play a significant role in many complex behaviors.

Program Review Questions

1. Imagine that someone familiar with the last twenty years of research on babies was able to converse with William James. What would this time traveler probably say to James?

    a. "You were ahead of your time in understanding babies."
    b. "Babies are more competent than you thought."
    c. "Babies' senses are less sophisticated than you said."
    d. "Babies' perceptions actually depend on their cultures."

2. Which smell do newborns like?

    a. the smell of a banana
    b. the smell of shrimp
    c. newborns can't smell anything.
    d. newborns can smell, but we have no way of knowing what smells they prefer.

3. What task of infancy is aided by a baby's ability to recognize its mother's voice?

    a. avoiding danger
    b. seeking sustenance
    c. forming social relationships
    d. learning to speak

4. A toy company wants to use Robert Fantz's research to design a new mobile for babies to look at in their cribs. The research suggests that the mobile should

    a. be as simple as possible.
    b. use soft colors such as pink.
    c. be made of a shiny material.
    d. have a complex design.

5. Which of a baby's senses is least developed at birth?

    a. hearing
    b. taste
    c. sight
    d. touch

6. Jean Piaget has studied how children think. According to Piaget, at what age does a child typically master the idea that the amount of a liquid remains the same when it is poured from one container to another container with a different shape?

    a. two years old
    b. four years old
    c. six years old
    d. eight years old

7. A baby is shown an orange ball a dozen times in a row. How would you predict the baby would respond?

   a. The baby will make the same interested response each time.
   b. The baby will respond with less and less interest each time.
   c. The baby will respond with more and more interest each time.
   d. The baby will not be interested at any time.

8. Renée Baillargeon and other researchers have investigated object permanence in babies. How do their results compare with Piaget's views?

   a. They show Piaget's age estimates for achieving object permanence were too high.
   b. They contradict Piaget's concept of what object permanence consists of.
   c. They support Piaget's timetable.
   d. They indicate that babies show more variation than Piaget found.

9. When Judy DeLoache hid the small and large toy dogs, what was she investigating?

   a. stranger anxiety
   b. activity level
   c. conservation of volume
   d. symbolic representation

10. In a discussion of the nature-nurture controversy, who would be most likely to cite Steven Suomi's research on shyness in monkeys to support his or her point of view?

    a. someone arguing that nature is the only factor determining shyness or boldness
    b. someone arguing that nurture is the only factor determining shyness or boldness
    c. someone arguing that nature can be modified by nurture
    d. the research does not support any of these viewpoints.

11. At what stage in their development do babies refuse to cross the visual cliff?

    a. as soon as their eyes can focus on it
    b. when they develop conditioned fears
    c. just before they are ready to walk
    d. about a month after they learn to crawl

12. What conclusion has Jerome Kagan come to about shyness in young children?

    a. It is inherent but can be modified by experience.
    b. It is created by parents who misunderstand their child's temperament.
    c. It is an inherited trait that cannot be changed.
    d. It is normal for all children to be shy at certain stages.

13. How does Steven Suomi modify shyness reactions in young monkeys?

    a. by putting them in an enriched environment
    b. by providing highly supportive foster mothers
    c. by placing a shy monkey with other shy monkeys
    d. by administering drugs that reduce the level of social anxiety

14. Which of the following do newborns appear not to already be equipped with?

    a. a temperament
    b. a preference for novelty
    c. a preference for complexity
    d. the ability to understand reversibility in conservation

15. The Wild Boy of Aveyron represents which important issue in developmental psychology?

    a. ethics in experimentation
    b. the relation of physical development to social development
    c. nature vs. nurture
    d. interpretation of experimental data

16. At one month of age, babies

    a. are best described as "a blooming, buzzing confusion."
    b. prefer stimuli that are constant and don't vary.
    c. have not yet opened their eyes.
    d. prefer human faces over other visual stimuli.

17. Which of the following is *not* a method that measures what a two-month-old is interested in?

    a. asking questions in very short, simple sentences
    b. measuring looking time
    c. examining dishabituation
    d. recording heart rate

18. Which of the following developmental psychologists made the mistake of confusing children's physical ability with their cognitive ability and thus believed children were cognitively less capable than they actually are?

    a. Robert Fantz
    b. Jean Piaget
    c. Renée Baillargeon
    d. Eleanor Gibson

19. Which of the following is last to emerge in children?

    a. fear of heights
    b. preference for mother's voice over other people's voices
    c. temperament
    d. ability to see analogies between a real situation and a scale model of it

20. Which of the following psychological characteristics appear(s) to have a genetic component?

    a. activity level
    b. tendency to be outgoing
    c. risk for some psychopathologies
    d. all of the above

Questions to Consider

1. Consider different theories of infant abilities, and contrast the influence of both Gesell and Watson on developmental psychology and child-rearing practices.

2. How might the knowledge of developmental norms affect a parent's response to a child? How might advanced techniques to detect prenatal perception and cognition inform parents? Speculate on what would happen if parents raised their children following inaccurate or out-of-date theories of child development.

3. Is it easier or harder to tell what a child is thinking than to tell what an adult is thinking? How can some of the measures used to detect an infant's interest or learning be used to measure adult cognitive functioning?

4. Can some of the measures used to determine the cognitive capabilities of pre-verbal infants be applied to non-human animals? What would we be able to conclude from patterns of results that are similar to or different from those found in human infants?

5. Besides a predisposition to be interested in humans and to be interested in novelty, what other interests might an infant benefit from being predisposed toward?

6. As people age and restructure their lives based on gains and losses in what they are capable of doing, do you think their values change to fit their capabilities? For example, do you think they come to value physical activity less as they become physically more restricted?

Optional Activities

1. Recall your earliest memory. Speculate as to why you recall it, what you might have distorted in your memory, and what effects the event has had on your development.

2. Can you remember ever having thought in a qualitatively different way from the way you think now? How well do you think you can really take the perspective of a four-year-old who is forming a conceptualization of the world? Do you think there are any barriers to your ability to do that, and how do you think they might affect your ability to interact with the child?

3. Compare yourself to your siblings. What traits, abilities, and interests do you share? Speculate on the roles of genetics and environment in the development of your similarities and differences.

4. Go to a grocery store or mall and observe the children there. At approximately what age does it appear that children engage in cooperative play? Can cooperative play be taught?

5. Interview an elderly person to find out what their experiences have been of the costs and benefits, both cognitively and socially, of aging in this country. Do they ever find that they are discriminated against? Do they find that people are more generous with them than with other people?

Additional Resources

Books and Articles

Asher, J. (1987). Born to be shy. *Psychology Today,* April, 56-64.

Bennett, M. (Ed.) (1993). *The development of social cognition: The child as psychologist.* New York: Guilford Press.

Carey, S., & Markman, E. M. (1999). Cognitive development. In B. M. Bly and D. E. Rumelhart (Eds.), *Cognitive science.* San Diego: Academic Press. pp. 201-254.

Flavell, J. (1999). Cognitive development: Children's knowledge about the mind. *Annual Review of Psychology, 50,* 21-45..

Gibson, E. J., & Walk, R. (1960). The visual cliff. *Scientific American,* 202, 64–71. Classic study of the development of depth perception and the emotion of fear in children.

Goswami, U. (1998). *Cognition in children.* Hove, East Sussex, UK: Psychology Press.

Haith, M. M. (1999). Some thoughts about claims for innate knowledge and infant physical reasoning. *Developmental Science, 2,* 153-156.

Itard, J. (1962). *The wild boy of Aveyron. Translated by G. Humphrey and M. Humphrey.* New York: Appleton-Century-Crofts. Itard's early nineteenth-century memoir tells of his attempts to educate and socialize a child reared in the wild.

Kohlberg, L., & Puka, B. (1994). *Kohlberg's original study of moral development.* New York: Garland Publishing.

Mills, R. S. L. (2000). *The developmental psychology of personal relationships.* New York: John Wiley.

Rogoff, B. (2003). *The cultural nature of human development.* New York: Oxford University Press.

Films

Alzheimer's Disease: What caregivers need to know. Produced by University of South Florida, Suncoast Gerontology Center, 2000. This video was produced to assist caregivers in understanding what they can expect as the disease progresses, from the time the diagnosis is made. It gives suggestions on how to deal with difficult behaviors and where the caregiver can go for community resources.

Child's Play: Prodigies and Possibilities. NOVA #1209, Time-Life Video, 1985. This film introduces us to prodigies who excel in several fields and to current research hoping to uncover more about the nature of giftedness.

The Wild Child. Directed by François Truffaut,1969. Dr. Jean Itard, a nineteenth-century scientist, adopted and attempted to socialize a 12-year-old boy found in the wild. This film, based on Itard's memoirs, explores how children learn language and bond with others. It also shows how the values and expectations of scientists direct their research and may bias their conclusions.

The following popular films capture various aspects of children's perceptions of themselves, adults, and the world around them.

Big. Directed by Penny Marshall, 1988.

E.T. the Extra-Terrestrial. Directed by Steven Spielberg, 1982.

Fanny and Alexander. Directed by Ingmar Bergman, 1983.

My Life as a Dog. Directed by Lasse Hallström, 1985.

The following popular films capture some of the limitations that people begin to face as they age.

Driving Miss Daisy. Directed by Bruce Beresford, 1981.

On Golden Pond. Directed by Mark Rydell, 1981.

A Trip to Bountiful. Directed by Peter Masterson, 1986.

Web Sites

∞ *http://www.acf.hhs.gov/programs/ohs/*—Does early exposure give children a leg-up on development? Visit the Web site of Head Start, a program within the U.S. Department of Health and Human Services. Take a look at their programs and the statistics on their effectiveness.

∞ *http://www.pdf.org/*—Alzheimer's isn't the only disorder associated with the elderly that has widespread effects on the brain and on general functioning. The Parkinson's Disease Foundation provides detailed information about how the disease leads to physical and cognitive deterioration.

∞ *http://www.learner.org/*—This web site supports *Discovering Psychology: Updated Edition* with a page for each video program featuring an "academic footnote" to further update the content of the videos. The site also offers four special interactive features as well as an extensive webography.

UNIT 6

*The birth of language is the dawn of humanity. The line
between man and beast—between the highest ape and the
lowest savage—is the language line.*

Suzanne K. Langer

Unit 6 examines how children acquire language and demonstrates the methods psychologists use to study the
role of biology and social interaction in language acquisition. It also looks at the contribution of language to
children's cognitive and social development.

Objectives

After viewing the television program and completing the assigned reading, you should be able to:

1. Describe the structure of language, including syntax, grammar, and semantics.

2. Define a child's "language making capacity."

3. Provide evidence of the universality of language acquisition and the way it progresses.

4. Explain Chomsky's hypothesis that humans are born with an innate biological capacity for
    language acquisition.

5. Explain how "motherese" (or "parentese") helps babies learn to communicate.

6. Describe the use of intonation by both young children and adults in their communication with
    each other.

Reading Assignment

After viewing Program 6, read pages 312-317 in *Psychology and Life*.

Key Terms and People

As you watch the program and read the assignment, pay particular attention to these people and
terms. People and terms defined in the text will be found on the given page numbers.

44

child directed speech (314)
language making capacity (316)
overregularization (316)
phonemes (314)
Noam Chomsky (315)
Dan Slobin (316)

The following term and person are referred to in Program 6 but are not introduced in the text.

∞ *psycholinguists*—researchers who study the structure of language and communication.

∞ *Jean Berko Gleason*—developmental psychologist who studies the central impact of social interaction on language acquisition.

Program Summary

Learning language, the subject of Program 6, is one of the most amazing of all human accomplishments. How a baby learns to talk so quickly with so little help stimulates intense scientific interest and debate. Until the late 1950s, linguists assumed that children learned to speak by imitating their parents. But observations of young children reveal that early language patterns are unique, and parents rarely try to teach their children to talk.

In 1957, Noam Chomsky revolutionized the study of language when he suggested that babies were born with a built-in language acquisition device. He claimed that babies have the innate capacity for extracting meaning from the words and sentences they hear.

Ideas about the biological capacity for language gave rise to a new field: developmental psycholinguistics. Some psycholinguists, like Jean Berko Gleason, concentrate on the role of social interaction in language development. Gleason explains that environmental and hereditary factors contribute to the process of language acquisition. Communication depends on the ability of both speakers to decode and express their intentions, and includes the use of words and formats with shared meanings.

Research has shown that biology does play a role in language acquisition. Children all over the world follow the same steps as they learn the sounds, words, and rules of their own language. All babies have a built-in preference for voices and can pick out their mother's speech within the first few days of life. The fact that every child goes through the same sequences suggests that learning depends on some form of biological maturation. Scientists believe that a developmental timetable regulates both the maturation of the brain and the muscles in the mouth and tongue that are needed for communication.

Although true language develops later, communication begins at birth. All normal babies cry, coo, and can imitate facial expressions. After a couple of months, they begin babbling and making many varied sounds. By the end of their first year, they tend to specialize in those sounds that have meaning in their own language.

Using words as symbols represents an advance in thinking skills and a new kind of relationship with objects and people. Children increasingly use words as tools for achieving their goals as they move from one- to two-word utterances and simple sentences. Later, they use language for abstract purposes, such as discussing past events (see figure 2).

Age	Language Skills
first few days of life	cry, coo, recognize mother's voice
two months	babbling, varied sounds
one year	specialized sounds in own language
eighteen months	babbles, knows some words
two years	two-word phrases, knows more than fifty words
three years	knows more than 1,000 words
by age six	understands grammar and syntax

Note: The ages in this chart are approximations. Not all children acquire language at the same rate.

Figure 2: Language development occurs in a regular pattern, leading some researchers to think that language is biologically
innate.

Just as the first steps in language development are universal, so is the tendency for parents everywhere to use simplified, high-pitched, melodic baby talk. Anne Fernald explains that people everywhere speak to babies in this adapted style that linguists call motherese, parentese, or child-directed speech (CDS).

Parentese is typically slow, with longer pauses and shorter utterances than the speech used with older children and other adults. It seems to help babies understand units of speech and conveys an emotional content. Researchers observe that caregivers typically adapt to the child's level of language as language skills grow more complex.

The biggest task before age six is discovering the underlying regularities of language—the rules of grammar and syntax. Dan Slobin explains that regularities in children's words and word combinations show that they use a system of grammatical rules that is not based on imitation. For example, children say "foots" and "mouses," although adults do not use those words or reinforce them. The children are using the right rules but in the wrong places.

The complicated social and linguistic strategies of children are part of the language development process. Children need to learn multiple uses of language, how to ask a question, and how to begin and end a conversation. Parents and caregivers teach children the rules of dialogue by asking questions, then teaching them the proper response, like "Thank you" and "Yes, please." These lessons not only help children learn how to use language but also prepare them for more advanced social interactions.

Program Review Questions

1. Lori's parents are thrilled that their daughter has just said her first word. Based on this information, how old would you estimate Lori is?
   a. three months
   b. six months
   c. twelve months
   d. eighteen months

2. Before Chomsky's work, what assumption was generally made about language acquisition?

   a. Babies have an innate capacity for extracting meaning.
   b. There is a built-in language acquisition device.
   c. Language development varies widely, depending on culture.
   d. Language is a skill learned by imitating parents.

3. What sounds do very young babies prefer?

   a. ocean sounds
   b. human voices
   c. other babies
   d. soft music

4. How does an infant react when its mother's voice is paired with the face of a stranger?

   a. by becoming upset
   b. by laughing
   c. by paying closer attention
   d. an infant is not capable of noting any discrepancy

5. What kind of sentences does a mother use in talking to her baby?

   a. one-word commands
   b. short, simple sentences
   c. telegraphic sentences that lack function words
   d. sentences that violate standard English word order

6. How does the development of language competence compare from culture to culture?

    a. It varies greatly.
    b. It is remarkably similar.
    c. Western cultures are similar to each other, while Eastern cultures are very different.
    d. This topic is just beginning to be explored by researchers.

7. Jean Berko Gleason has studied mothers and their babies. Her major focus is on the role of

    a. neurological maturation in language development.
    b. melodic patterns used by mothers in different cultures.
    c. social interaction in language development.
    d. parental patterning of conversational conventions.

8. One difference between cooing and babbling is that babbling allows a baby to

    a. say real words.
    b. express discomfort.
    c. develop its vocal cords.
    d. vary intonations.

9. A seven-month-old American child with American parents is babbling. The sounds that the child produces include

    a. sounds from many different languages.
    b. only sounds used in English.
    c. only sounds found in Western languages.
    d. sounds unlike those of any language.

10. When Anne Fernald says "the melody is the message," she means that

    a. babies take meaning from pitch contours.
    b. mothers need to sing to their babies.
    c. babies need to learn the intonation patterns of their native language.
    d. mothers speak slowly and clearly to their babies.

11. If you heard a mother using a rise–fall pattern with a high pitch and a sharp peak, what would the mother most likely be saying?

    a. "Don't do that."
    b. "That's a good baby."
    c. "See the dog."
    d. "Are you hungry?"

12. What mental ability must a child have developed in order to use words as symbols?

    a. storing and retrieving memory codes
    b. recognizing the letters of the alphabet
    c. composing questions
    d. recognizing the spatial relationships between objects

13. If you hear a child saying "Go store," what is a good estimate of the child's age?

    a. four years old
    b. three years old
    c. two years old
    d. one year old

14. The earliest form of communication that children engage in is

    a. telegraphic speech.
    b. cooing.
    c. babbling.
    d. crying.

15. What does a sentence such as "I bringed the toy" show about how children acquire language?

    a. They imitate their parents, including the parents' errors.
    b. They have no interest in grammar and need training.
    c. They acquire grammatical rules on their own.
    d. They make errors based on watching television and listening to their peers.

16. Which of the following stages of communication consists of simple sentences that lack plurals, articles, and tenses, but tend to have the constituent words in the order appropriate to the child's native language?

    a. telegraphic speech
    b. babbling
    c. question-asking
    d. ritualistic speech

17. Children in the third stage of language development can be characterized by which of the following?

    a. They are about two and a half years old.
    b. They are speaking in full adult-like sentences.
    c. They are speaking in one-word utterances.
    d. They have just begun to make the vowel sounds of their native language.

18. According to Chomsky, what might be necessary to activate the innate language acquisition device in the brain?

    a. sex hormones
    b. social interaction
    c. exposure to multiple languages
    d. the child's own vocalizations

19. According to Dan Slobin, a two-year-old who is not speaking in full sentences yet

    a. cannot know the complex social rules of conversation, like turn-taking.
    b. is more able than ten-month-olds to pronounce speech sounds that aren't native to her language.
    c. is considered to be speech-delayed.
    d. will nonetheless still use the correct word order when speaking telegraphic sentences.

20. What is the correct progression in the development of communication?

    a. babbling, cooing, crying, two-word phase
    b. crying, babbling, cooing, two-word phase
    c. crying, cooing, babbling, two-word phase
    d. cooing, crying, babbling, two-word phase

Questions to Consider

1. Is language unique to humans? Although chimps and gorillas lack the vocal apparatus for spoken language, they can use symbols and signs for communication. Consider your textbook's definition of language. Why is there so much resistance to the idea that animals use language?

2. How closely tied are language and thought? Is language ability necessary for thought?

3. What role does nonverbal communication play in language development? How is it learned?

4. What role might imaginary friends, or human-like relationships with dolls, toys, and pets, play in helping children to master language?

5. If a parent does not use "parentese," what implications might that have for an infant?

6. If most children acquire language before age six, why is grammar instruction such an important part of the school curriculum?

7. When they are introduced to a new word, how do children determine what aspect of the current situation it refers to?

Optional Activities

1. In what ways do television programs designed for adults vs. children differ? Is children's programming superior in any way for helping viewers to learn new words or learn other aspects of grammar? Watch a children's program such as Sesame Street and identify features that may be designed to help specifically with language development.

2. Arrange to observe in a home or day care center. Observe a one-year-old and a two-year-old conversing, one at a time, with an adult, preferably their own mother. For at least fifteen minutes, write down everything each child and the adult say to each other. After you have observed both adult-child pairs, analyze your transcripts. Describe and compare each child's word choices and language skills. Describe the adult's word choices, intonations, and voice and speech patterns. How well did they fit the child's level of language?

3. Watch a pre-verbal child to try to determine what he or she uses to communicate. Do you see the child pointing and grabbing? Do you hear grunts or nonsense syllables accompanied with intonations that carry meaning? Does the child practice sophisticated conversational skills, such as turn-taking, even if no meaningful words are used?

Additional Resources

Books and Articles

Erneling, C. (1993). *Understanding language acquisition: The framework of learning.* Albany: SUNY Press.

Pines, M. (1981). The civilizing of Genie. *Psychology Today,* 28-34.

Schiefelbusch, R. L., & Pickar, J. (Eds.) (1984). *The acquisition of communicative competence.* Baltimore: University Park Press.

Films

The Miracle Worker. 1962. Directed by Arthur Penn.

Web Sites

∞ *http://pinker.wjh.harvard.edu/*—Harvard professor Steven Pinker has written a number of popular books recently with the aim of making cognitive science and Pinker's own specialty, language acquisition, more accessible to the larger population. His excellent and controversial book, *The language instinct,* provided compelling scientific argument for granting the rare distinction of "instinct" to children's language learning capacity. His personal Web page contains a number of outstanding resources.

∞ *http://www.learner.org/*—This web site supports *Discovering Psychology: Updated Edition* with a page for each video program featuring an "academic footnote" to further update the content of the videos. The site also offers four special interactive features as well as an extensive webography.

UNIT 7

We are told about the world before we see it. We imagine most things before we experience them. And those preconceptions, unless education has made us acutely aware, govern deeply the whole process of perception.
Walter Lippmann

Unit 7 explores how we make contact with the world outside our brain and body. We'll see how biological, cognitive, social, and environmental influences shape our personal sense of reality, and we'll gain an understanding of how psychologists use our perceptual errors to study how the constructive process of perception works.

Objectives

After viewing the television program and completing the assigned reading, you should be able to:

1. Define and compare *sensation* and *perception*.

2. Describe how a visual stimulus gets translated into "sight" in the brain.

3. Describe the field of psychophysics.

4. Be able to distinguish distal and proximal stimuli.

5. Explain why illusions provide clues to perceptual mechanisms.

6. Describe Gestalt psychology.

7. Describe the phenomenon of perceptual constancy.

8. Describe the psychological dimensions of sound and the physiology of hearing.

9. Describe the difference between top-down and bottom-up processing.

10. Discuss the senses of smell, taste and touch.

11. Describe attentional processes.

12. Describe identification and recognition processes, including complex visual analysis.

13. Explain how perceptual constancy affects our experience of the world.

Reading Assignment

After viewing Program 7, read pages 90-134 in *Psychology and Life*.

Key People and Terms

As you watch the program and read the assignment, pay particular attention to these people and terms. People and terms defined in the text will be found on the given page numbers.

absolute threshold (93)
accommodation (97)
amacrine cells (99)
ambiguity (127)
attention (114)
auditory cortex (107)
auditory nerve (108)
basilar membrane (108)
bipolar cells (99)
bottom-up processing (125)
brightness (102)
cochlea (108)
complementary colors (102)
cones (98)
convergence (119)
cutaneous senses (111)
dark adaptation (98)
difference threshold (95)
distal stimulus (92)
figure (116)
fovea (99)
frequency theory (108)
ganglion cell (99)
gate-control theory (113)
Gestalt psychology (116)
goal directed selection (114)
ground (116)
horizontal cell (99)

hue (102)
identification and recognition (91)
illusion (124)
just noticeable difference (JND) (96)
kinesthetic sense (112)
lightness constancy (122)
loudness (106)
motion parallax (120)
olfactory bulb (110)
opponent-process theory (104)
optic nerve (100)
pain (113)
perception (91)
perceptual constancy (122)
perceptual organization (91)
pheromones (111)
phi phenomenon (118)
photoreceptors (98)
pitch (106)
place theory (108)
proximal stimulus (92)
psychometric function (94)
psychophysics (93)
receptive field (101)
response bias (94)
retina (98)
retinal disparity (119)
rods (98)

saturation (102)
sensation (91)
sensory adaptation (94)
sensory receptors (96)
set (128)
shape constancy (122)
signal detection theory (SDT) (95)
size constancy (122)
sound localization (109)
stimulus-driven capture (114)
timbre (106)
top-down processing (125)
transduction (96)
trichromatic theory (104)
vestibular sense (112)
visual cortex (100)
volley principle (109)
Weber's law (96)

Donald Broadbent (137)
Hermann von Helmholtz (104)
Ewald Hering (104)
David Hubel (100)
Leo Hurvich (105)
Dorothea Jameson (105)
Wolfgang Kohler (116)
Kurt Koffka (116)
Ernst Weber (96)
Max Wertheimer (116)
Sir Thomas Young (104)

The following term and person are referred to in Program 7 but are not introduced in the text.

∞ *receptor*—a specialized nerve cell sensitive to particular kinds of stimulus energy.

∞ *Misha Pavel*—studies the successive stages of information processing that take place as we continually perceive the world.

Program Summary

Can we believe our eyes? For centuries, magicians and artists have entertained, deceived, and delighted us because we tend to believe what we see. Most of the time our perceptions are remarkably error-free. They have to be; survival in our ever-changing, complex environment depends on accurate perception.

Although psychologists study all sensory processes, including hearing, smell, touch, and taste, Program 7 focuses on visual perception and the processes we rely on to create meaning out of the world's myriad objects and events.

To sense, perceive, and understand the world, we use two different processes. When our eyes, ears, and other sensory apparatus detect stimulation and send the data to the brain, it is called "bottom-up" processing. "Top-down" processing interacts with bottom-up processing, adding in what we already know and remember.

First, the raw sensory data are relayed to the thalamus, which analyzes and directs them to specialized areas in the cortex, the outermost part of the brain. The cortex processes this information and, scientists believe, combines it with old data stored in memory.

Visual perception takes place in three different areas: the retina, the pathways through the brain, and the visual cortex. It is in the visual cortex that flashes of light are broken down and decoded, enabling us to distinguish one object from another.

In addition to identifying objects, the brain has to compute size, distance, and boundaries. It must make these decisions almost instantaneously so we can go about our daily routines safely and smoothly.

Memories, expectations, culture, and language also influence how we derive meaning from sensory information. Unlike a camera, which merely copies an image, our perceptual process is actively processing the world by selecting, classifying, and judging. Consider that a simple curve and a line in the right place on a sheet of paper may took like a nose and a mouth. But when we put these same lines in a different arrangement, they may look like random, meaningless marks, or even like some different object.

The brain also must work to eliminate confusing signals and fill in the blanks. We know that a railroad track doesn't converge and disappear in the distance when we look toward the horizon. And if a shadow falls on our newspaper, we know that the paper isn't really turning black. Perception goes beyond sensory information to impose stability on a constantly changing flow of information.

Psychologists have learned a great deal about how perception works from studying illusions—the perceptual traps we fall into because we use perceptual principles as shortcuts to deal with a flood of sensory input. Fortunately, these shortcuts work most of the time. For example, even when a stop sign is partially obscured by leaves, we still "see" the sign. Although only about seventy percent of the words we hear are given complete sensory processing, we can make sense out of a spoken message because our minds fill in the rest from context.

Have you ever failed to recognize people you knew when you encountered them in a place where you didn't expect to see them? The reason is that our expectations and personal biases have a powerful effect on perception. We may fail to see something because we don't expect or want to see it, which is one reason why people are often unreliable eyewitnesses to an accident or crime.

All of our senses put us in touch with the world around us. But it is our brain that organizes our perceptions, letting us know what's out there and how we should react. Because the perceptual process is the basis for everything we learn, think, and do, scientists and laypersons alike are interested in finding out more about how this extremely sophisticated system works.

Program Review Questions

1. Imagine that a teaspoon of sugar is dissolved in two gallons of water. Rita can detect this level of sweetness at least half the time. This level is called the

   a. distal stimulus.
   b. perceptual constant.
   c. response bias.
   d. absolute threshold.

2. What is the job of a receptor?

   a. to transmit a neural impulse
   b. to connect new information with old information
   c. to detect a type of physical energy
   d. to receive an impulse from the brain

3. In what area of the brain is the visual cortex located?

   a. in the front
   b. in the middle
   c. in the back
   d. under the brain stem

4. What is the function of the thalamus in visual processing?

   a. It relays information to the cortex.
   b. It rotates the retinal image.
   c. It converts light energy to a neural impulse.
   d. It makes sense of the proximal stimulus.

5. David Hubel discusses the visual pathway and the response to a line. The program shows an experiment in which the response to a moving line changed dramatically with changes in the line's

   a. thickness.
   b. color.
   c. speed.
   d. orientation.

6. Misha Pavel used computer graphics to study how

    a. we process visual information.
    b. rods differ from cones in function.
    c. we combine information from different senses.
    d. physical energy is transduced in the visual system.

7. Imagine that a baseball player puts on special glasses that shift his visual field up ten degrees. When he wears these glasses, the player sees everything higher than it actually is. After some practice, the player can hit with the glasses on. What will happen when the player first tries to hit with the glasses off?

    a. He will think that the ball is lower than it is.
    b. He will think that the ball is higher than it is.
    c. He will accurately perceive the ball's position.
    d. It is impossible to predict an individual's reaction in this situation.

8. Imagine that a dog is walking toward you. As the dog gets closer, the image it casts on your retina

    a. gets larger.
    b. gets darker.
    c. gets smaller.
    d. stays exactly the same size.

9. You want to paint your room yellow, so you get some samples at the paint store. When you hold the sample against your white wall, it looks different from the way it looks against the green curtain. A psychologist would attribute this to

    a. perceptual constancy.
    b. visual paradoxes.
    c. contrast effects.
    d. threshold differences.

10. Which of the following phenomena best illustrates that perception is an active process?

    a. bottom-up processing
    b. motion parallax
    c. top-down processing
    d. parietal senses

11. The program shows a drawing that can be seen as a rat or as a man. People were more likely to identify the drawing as a man if they

    a. were men themselves.
    b. had just seen pictures of people.
    c. were afraid of rats.
    d. looked at the picture holistically rather than analytically.

12. Where is the proximal stimulus to be found?

    a. in the outside world
    b. on the retina
    c. in the occipital lobe
    d. in the thalamus

13. How is visual information processed by the brain?

    a. It's processed by the parietal lobe, which relays the information to the temporal lobe.
    b. It's processed entirely within the frontal lobe.
    c. It's processed by the occipital lobe, which projects to the thalamus, which projects to a succession of areas in the cortex.
    d. If the information is abstract, it's processed by the cortex; if it's concrete, it's processed by the thalamus.

14. Which of the following is true about the proximal stimulus in visual perception?

    a. It's identical to the distal stimulus because the retina produces a faithful reproduction of the perceptual world.
    b. It's upside-down, flat, distorted, and obscured by blood vessels.
    c. It's black-and-white and consists of very sparse information about horizontal and vertical edges.
    d. It contains information about the degree of convergence of the two eyes.

15. Which of the following is an example of pure top-down processing?
    a. hallucinating
    b. understanding someone else's speech when honking horns are obscuring individual sounds
    c. perceiving a circular color patch that has been painted onto a canvas
    d. enjoying a melody

16. Which sensory information is *not* paired with the cortical lobe that is primarily responsible for processing it?

    a. visual information, occipital lobe
    b. speech, frontal lobe
    c. body senses, parietal lobe
    d. hearing, central sulcus lobe

17. When your eyes are shut, you cannot

    a. hallucinate.
    b. use contextual information from other senses to make inferences about what's there.
    c. transform a distal visual stimulus into a proximal stimulus.
    d. experience perceptual constancy.

18. The researcher David Hubel is best known for

    a. mapping visual receptor cells.
    b. discovering subjective contours.
    c. identifying the neural pathways by which body sensations occur.
    d. realizing that hearing and smell originate from the same brain area.

19. The primary reason why psychologists study illusions is because

    a. they help to identify areas of the cortex that have been damaged.
    b. they serve as good "public relations" material for curious novices.
    c. they help us to categorize people into good and bad perceivers.
    d. they help us to understand how perception normally works.

20. The shrinking-square illusion demonstrated by Misha Pavel relies on processing of which kinds of feature?

    a. edges and corners
    b. color and texture
    c. torque and angular momentum
    d. density gradients and motion

Questions to Consider

1. Why do psychologists identify sensation and perception as two different fields of study? Does this reflect the relative youth of psychology as a science, or does it represent a scientific distinction that will still be favored in fifty years?

2. As the population ages, adapting the environment for people with a range of sensory abilities and deficits will become increasingly important. Architects will need to improve access to and safety of buildings, taking into account that older people need about three times as much light as young people in order to distinguish objects. They also need higher visual contrasts to detect potential hazards, such as curbs or steps. How might you identify some changes you could make in and around your home to create a safer, more comfortable environment for a disabled or visually- or hearing-impaired person?

3. Investigations of people who claim to have extrasensory perception reveal that the better controlled the study, the less likely it is to support claims of ESP. Does it do any harm to believe in ESP? Why do most psychologists suggest that we should be skeptical of people who claim to have extrasensory perception?

4. Choose a familiar context, like a grocery store, and describe how the Gestalt principles of perceptual organization are used to help people perceive objects and group them.

5. Describe how film and television directors use sight and sound techniques to create meaning and feeling. As you watch a television commercial, program, or film, notice the way the camera frames the image and how angle and motion create a mood or point of view. Notice the use of sound. Consider how these elements shape viewers' desires, expectations, and feelings.

6. Although the neural pathways serving perception are similar in all of us, our internal perceptual experience could theoretically differ. What sorts of differences in our experiences can you imagine as being possible? What sorts of differences would you think would be unlikely?

7. Absolute thresholds seem to differ across species. For example, you are much better at detecting degraded visual stimuli than animals of some other species would be, but at the same time you may be much worse than them at smelling faint odors. Why do you think that humans evolved to favor the visual sense?

Optional Activities

1. Closure and continuity of line are organizing principles that we use to make sense out of stimuli. Make line drawings of familiar objects by tracing pictures from comics, children's coloring books, or magazines. Leave out sections of the drawing, and ask family members or friends to identify the objects. See how incomplete the line drawing can be and still be identified.

2. Blindfold yourself. (Have someone standing by to prevent injury or damage.) Contrast the experience of moving about in a familiar room, such as your bedroom or kitchen, with the experience of moving about a room in which you spend little time. Note the expectations and significant sensory cues you depend on to avoid tripping and bumping into things. How relaxed or tense were you in each room?

3. Listen to a conversation, trying hard to (a) notice all of the other noise going on around you and (b) notice all the instances of imperfect transmission of speech sounds. For example, the speaker might mispronounce something or say it with their mouth full, or an outside noise may obscure the sound coming from the speaker. Is it hard for you to snap out of top-down mode to do this exercise?

4. If you have access to a virtual reality game, try playing it while also monitoring what is going on in the room around you. While interacting with the virtual objects in the game, think about how you must look to passersby, and think about the layout of the objects in the space that physically surrounds you. How good are you at immersing yourself in two worlds at once? Do you find that you have to switch back and forth, or are you able to consider yourself as being in two very different realities simultaneously?

Additional Resources

Books and Articles

Ackerman, D. (1990). *A natural history of the senses.* New York: Random House.

Cobb, V. (1981). *How to really fool yourself: Illusions for all your senses.* New York: Lippincott.

Davis, S. (Ed.) (2000). *Color perception: Philosophical, psychological, artistic, and computational perspectives.* New York: Oxford University Press.

Goldstein, E. B. (Ed.) (2001). *Blackwell handbook of perception.* Oxford: Blackwell.

Narins, P. (2001). In a fly's ear. *Nature* Special Issue, 410, 644-645.

Roeckelein, J. E. (2000). *The concept of time in psychology: A resource book and annotated bibliography.* Westport, CT: Greenwood Press.

Films

Children of a Lesser God. Directed by Randa Haines, 1987. A story of the relationship between a special education teacher and his deaf students. The film gives some sense of the struggles sometimes encountered by the deaf and the ways in which they interact with the world.

Houdini. Directed by George Marshall, 1953. A fictional screen biography of the master magician and escape artist Harry Houdini. Includes faithful recreations of dozens of Houdini's tricks and illusions and his efforts to expose mediums and spiritualists as frauds.

Rashomon (In the Woods). Directed by Akira Kurosawa, 1950. A murder is recounted by four people, including the victim. Each point of view and each story is different, illustrating how people can experience and interpret the same event in different ways. The audience must determine what is real.

The Thin Blue Line. Directed by Errol Morris, 1988. A remarkable and true detective story showing the limits and distortions of perception. Errol Morris calls it "a movie about how truth is difficult to know—not a movie about how truth is impossible to know."

Web Sites

∞ *http://www.psychologie.unizh.ch/sowi/Ulf/Lab/WebExpPsyLab.html*—The University of Zurich's Experimental Psychology on-line laboratory offers a section on perception.

∞ *http://www.learner.org/*—This web site supports *Discovering Psychology: Updated Edition* with a page for each video program featuring an "academic footnote" to further update the content of the videos. The site also offers four special interactive features as well as an extensive webography.

UNIT 8

> *Effective learning means a living at new power, and the consciousness of new power is one of the most stimulating things in life.*
>
> Janet Erskine Stuart

Learning is the process that enables humans and other animals to profit from experience, anticipate events, and adapt to changing conditions. Unit 8 explains the basic learning principles and the methods psychologists use to study and modify behavior. It also demonstrates how cognitive processes, such as insight and observation, influence learning.

Objectives

After viewing the television program and completing the assigned reading, you should be able to:

1. Define *learning*.

2. Describe the process of classical conditioning and show how it demonstrates learning by association.

3. Cite examples of extinction, spontaneous recovery, generalization, and discrimination.

4. Describe the process of operant conditioning.

5. Know the distinction between positive and negative punishment and between positive and negative reinforcement.

6. Describe how observational learning occurs.

7. Discuss the varieties of reinforcement schedules, including fixed ratio, variable ratio, fixed interval and variable interval.

8. Describe cognitive influences on learning.

9. Describe biological constraints on learning and some possible effects that learning can have on the functioning of the body.

Reading Assignment

After viewing Program 8, read pages 163-194 in *Psychology and Life*.

Key People and Terms

As you watch the program and read the assignment, pay particular attention to these people and terms. People and terms defined in the text will be found on the given page numbers.

acquisition (168)
animal cognition (187)
behavior analysis (165)
biological constraints of learning (184)
classical conditioning (166)
cognitive map (187)
conditioned reinforcers (180)
conditioned response (CR) (168)
conditioned stimulus (CS) (168)
discriminative stimuli (178)
extinction (169)
fixed-interval schedule (183)
fixed-ratio schedule (181)
instinctual drift (185)
law of effect (174)
learning (164)
learning performance distinction (164)
negative punishment (178)
negative reinforcement (177)
observational learning (188)
operant (176)
operant conditioning (176)
operant extinction (177)
partial reinforcement effect (181)
positive punishment (178)
positive reinforcement (177)
primary reinforcers (180)
punisher (178)

reflex (168)
reinforcer (177)
reinforcement contingency (176)
schedules of reinforcement (181)
shaping by successive approximations (183)
spontaneous recovery (169)
stimulus discrimination (170)
stimulus generalization (170)
taste aversion learning (185)
three-term contingency (178)
unconditioned response (UCR) (168)
unconditioned stimulus (UCS) (168)
variable-interval schedule (183)
variable-ratio schedule (182)

Albert Bandura (189)
Keller Breland (184)
Marion Breland (184)
John Garcia (185)
Ivan Pavlov (166)
Gerald Patterson (179)
David Premack (181)
Robert Rescorla (171)
B.F. Skinner (165)
Edward Thorndike (174)
Edward Tolman (187)
John B. Watson (165)

The following person appears in Program 8 but is not mentioned in the text.

∞ *Howard Rachlin*—studies how operant principles can be used to train self-control.

Program Summary

Learning is the process by which people and all other animals profit from experience. During the process of learning, behavior is modified. Individuals acquire new skills that ultimately help them survive because they find new ways to anticipate the future and fine-tune their ability to control their environment. In Program 8, we will learn the basic principles of learning along with two methods, developed more than 50 years ago, that psychologists still use today to study behavior, help people to overcome old patterns of behavior, and learn new ones.

One method is called classical conditioning or signal learning. It takes advantage of our ability to anticipate what will happen. The second method is called instrumental conditioning, which takes into account the influence of consequences on future behavior.

Research on learning dominated American psychology for most of the twentieth century. It began around the turn of the century when the Russian scientist Ivan Pavlov noticed that the dogs in his digestion experiments began salivating even before they were given their food. In fact, anything they associated with food caused them to drool—the sight of the food dish, even the sound of Pavlov's footsteps. Pavlov decided to find out why and thereby discovered the basic principles of classical conditioning. He demonstrated that by presenting any stimulus, such as a light or a bell, before the food, the dogs would drool when the stimulus was presented without the food.

Pavlov and others also studied the extinction of such conditioned responses. They found that it was possible for an organism to learn over time that the stimulus no longer elicited the desired event (food, in the dogs' case), so the light or bell no longer elicited drooling. These simple experiments led to an important conclusion: any stimulus an animal can perceive can elicit any response the animal is capable of making.

While the Russians were working on classical conditioning, the American psychologist Edward Thorndike was studying how humans and animals learned new habits and skills. He observed and measured trial and error behavior and discovered that actions that brought a reward became learned—that, in fact, learning is controlled by its consequences. This became known as instrumental conditioning.

John B. Watson, another American psychologist influenced by Pavlov, studied observable behavior. He believed that he could use conditioning and environmental control to train any infant to grow up with any skills he trained them in, regardless of talents or preferences.

Watson's famous test case involved eight-month-old Little Albert. In an experiment that today's ethical guidelines would prohibit, Watson conditioned the boy to fear a white rat by pairing the rat with the sound of a loud gong. Albert learned to fear not only the rat but anything that resembled it -- even a fur coat. Years later, Watson's associate, Mary Cover Jones, developed a way to remove conditioned fears.

Another important figure in the study of instrumental learning was Harvard psychologist B.F. Skinner. By focusing only on observable events that precede and follow behavior, Skinner built upon the ideas of Thorndike and Watson and demonstrated how behavior is influenced by external events in our lives. His basic experimental device, the Skinner box, has become the symbol of behaviorism. In Skinner's simplest experiments, a pigeon learned to control the rate at which it received a reward (food) by pecking a disk. Because the rate of response varied directly with the reinforcing consequences, the behavior could be changed by changing the consequences. Skinner's version of instrumental conditioning is called operant conditioning.

Howard Rachlin of the State University of New York at Stony Brook investigates how establishing a pattern of behavior can reinforce the choices that humans and non-humans make that can lead to self-control. According to Rachlin, self-control is determined partly through environmental contingencies and partly through genetic inheritance. Some animals, like pigeons, tend to be impulsive and not exercise self-control. But with the right set of environmental contingencies, even pigeons can learn self-control. And even human behaviors over which people seem to have little control, such as addiction, can be subject to contingencies that lead to self-control. The approach that allows Rachlin to make headway in this difficult field is to examine the reinforcements not only for the behavior that is ultimately exhibited, but also the reinforcement contingencies for the other available choices.

The behaviorist approach has many other practical applications. Dogs and monkeys have been trained to help disabled people lead more independent lives. Behavioral principles serve as the basis for token systems used to reward healthy behaviors in disturbed patients and criminal offenders. Behavior therapy is also used to help people lose weight and overcome phobias.

Behavioral principles are very powerful—so powerful that they can actually affect our body's immune system. Current research studies that have grown out of these basic learning theories may even shed light on how to enhance our ability to fight off disease.

Program Review Questions

1. Which of the following is an example of a fixed-action pattern?

    a. a fish leaping at bait that looks like a fly
    b. a flock of birds migrating in winter
    c. a person blinking when something gets in her eye
    d. a chimpanzee solving a problem using insight

2. What is the basic purpose of learning?

    a. to improve one's genes
    b. to understand the world one lives in
    c. to find food more successfully
    d. to adapt to changing circumstances

3. How have psychologists traditionally studied learning?

    a. in classrooms with children as participants
    b. in classrooms with college students as participants
    c. in laboratories with humans as participants
    d. in laboratories with nonhuman animals as participants

4. In his work, Pavlov found that a metronome could produce salivation in dogs because

    a. it signaled that food would arrive.
    b. it was the dogs' normal reaction to a metronome.
    c. it was on while the dogs ate.
    d. it extinguished the dogs' original response.

5. What is learned in classical conditioning?

    a. a relationship between an action and its consequence
    b. a relationship between two stimulus events
    c. a relationship between two response events
    d. classical conditioning does not involve learning

6. What point is Professor Zimbardo making when he says, "Relax," while firing a pistol?

    a. There are fixed reactions to verbal stimuli.
    b. The acquisition process is reversed during extinction.
    c. Any stimulus can come to elicit any reaction.
    d. Unconditioned stimuli are frequently negative.

7. What point does Ader and Cohen's research on taste aversion in rats make about classical conditioning?

    a. It can be extinguished easily.
    b. It takes many conditioning trials to be effective.
    c. It is powerful enough to suppress the immune system.
    d. It tends to be more effective than instrumental conditioning.

8. What is Thorndike's law of effect?

    a. Learning is controlled by its consequences.
    b. Every action has an equal and opposite reaction.
    c. Effects are more easily changed than causes.
    d. A conditioned stimulus comes to have the same effect as an unconditioned stimulus.

9. According to John B. Watson, any behavior, even strong emotion, could be explained by the power of

    a. instinct.
    b. inherited traits.
    c. innate ideas.
    d. conditioning.

10. In Watson's work with Little Albert, why was Albert afraid of the Santa Claus mask?

    a. He had been classically conditioned with the mask.
    b. The mask was an unconditioned stimulus creating fear.
    c. He generalized his learned fear of the rat.
    d. Instrumental conditioning created a fear of strangers.

11. What was the point of the Skinner box?

    a. It kept animals safe.
    b. It provided a simple, highly controlled environment.
    c. It set up a classical conditioning situation.
    d. It allowed psychologists to use computers for research.

12. Skinner found that the rate at which a pigeon pecked at a target varied directly with

    a. the conditioned stimulus.
    b. the conditioned response.
    c. the operant antecedents.
    d. the reinforcing consequences.

13. Imagine a behavior therapist is treating a person who fears going out into public places. What would the therapist be likely to focus on?

    a. the conditioning experience that created the fear
    b. the deeper problems that the fear is a symptom of
    c. providing positive consequences for going out
    d. reinforcing the patient's desire to overcome the fear

14. When should the conditioned stimulus be presented in order to optimally produce classical conditioning?

    a. just before the unconditioned stimulus
    b. simultaneously with the unconditioned response
    c. just after the unconditioned stimulus
    d. just after the conditioned response

15. Operant conditioning can be used to achieve all of the following, *except*

    a. teaching dogs to assist the handicapped.
    b. teaching infants English grammar.
    c. teaching self-control to someone who is trying to quit smoking.
    d. increasing productivity among factory workers.

16. Which psychologist has argued that in order to understand and control behavior, one has to consider both the reinforcements acting on the selected behavior and the reinforcements on the reinforcements acting an the alternatives?

    a. E. Thorndike
    b. J. Watson
    c. B.F. Skinner
    d. H. Rachlin

17. If given a choice between an immediate small reinforcer and a delayed larger reinforcer, an untrained pigeon will

    a. select the immediate small one.
    b. select the delayed larger one.
    c. experiment and alternate across trials.
    d. not show any signs of perceiving the difference.

18. In order to produce extinction of a classically conditioned behavior, an experimenter would

    a. reward the behavior.
    b. pair the behavior with negative reinforcement.
    c. present the conditioned stimulus in the absence of the unconditioned stimulus.
    d. model the behavior for the organism.

19. In Pavlov's early work, bell is to food as

    a. unconditioned response is to conditioned response.
    b. conditioned stimulus is to unconditioned stimulus.
    c. unconditioned is to conditioned stimulus.
    d. conditioned stimulus is to conditioned response.

20. Howard Rachlin has discovered that animals can be taught self-control through

    a. reinforcement.
    b. operant conditioning.
    c. instrumental conditioning.
    d. all of the above.

Questions to Consider

1. Approximately two percent of Americans are hooked on gambling, which experts claim can be just as addictive as drugs. Is compulsive gambling a disease or a learned behavior? Consider the kind of reinforcement gamblers get. Using the terms you learned in this unit, how would you characterize the nature of the reinforcement and the reinforcement schedule? What techniques do you predict would work best to help compulsive gamblers change their behavior?

2. You are a school principal, and you are trying to get your students to help clean up the school. Given what you now know about the control of behavior, what sorts of techniques would you use in order to get students to comply?

3. What role does intention to learn play in classical and operant conditioning? Would these techniques work on people who do not know they are being used? Would they work on people who oppose their use?

4. Is it possible that children learn their native language through operant conditioning? When parents and young children interact, do the parents reinforce the use of some grammar and punish others? Are some aspects of language, such as the rules of politeness, more likely to be taught through conditioning than other aspects?

Optional Activities

1. Design your own behavior change program based on the learning principles described in Unit 8. First, identify a specific behavior. Instead of setting a broad goal, such as becoming more fit, design a strategy to reinforce a desired behavior—going for jogs, cutting out midnight snacks, or taking the stairs rather than the elevator. Analyze the specific behavior you would like to change in terms of antecedents-behavior-consequences. Then get a baseline measurement of the target behavior, try out your plan for a predetermined amount of time, and evaluate the results.

2. Have someone teach you something new, such as how to juggle, play basic guitar chords, or serve a tennis ball. Analyze the teacher's method. How does it apply principles of theories of learning? How would you change the teacher's method to be more effective?

3. Choose a member of your family and some trivial behavioral detail, such as standing still. See if you can train the person to reliably perform the behavior without having them catch on to what you're doing.

Additional Resources

Books and Articles

Domjan, M. (2003). *Principles of Learning and behavior. 5th edition.* Belmont, CA: Thomson/Wadsworth.

Rachlin, H. (2000). *Science of self-control.* Harvard: Harvard University Press.

Skinner, B. F. (1971). *Beyond freedom and dignity.* New York: Knopf.

Skinner, B. F. (1972). *Walden two.* New York: MacMillan.

Films

A Clockwork Orange. Directed by Stanley Kubrick, 1971. In the film based on the novel, Malcolm McDowell plays a young thug conditioned to become sick when he thinks of sex or violence.

The List of Adrian Messenger. Directed by John Huston, 1963. Based on Philip MacDonald's novel, this detective film includes some fancy murder methods that illustrate themes of the unit.

The Manchurian Candidate. Directed by John Frankenheimer, 1962. The power of hypnosis plays a central role in the plot of this sophisticated political satire and thriller.

Web Sites

∞ *http://www.animalschool.net/* —Circuses and amusement parks often feature trained animals that can perform impressive and unusual feats. To find out more about how these animals are trained, visit the home page of a program designed to teach people the principles of operant conditioning.

∞ *http://www.schickshadel.com/programs/aversion_therapy_treatment.php*—Some medical treatment programs for addiction rely heavily on counter-conditioning, by which people come to associate nausea or other aversive reactions with the substances they once abused. The Schick Shadel Hospital in Seattle, Washington uses aversion therapy in its treatment regimen. You can find out more by visiting this site.

∞ *http://www.learner.org/*—This web site supports *Discovering Psychology: Updated Edition* with a page for each video program featuring an "academic footnote" to further update the content of the videos. The site also offers four special interactive features as well as an extensive webography.

UNIT 9

REMEMBERING AND FORGETTING

> *Memory is not just the imprint of the past upon us; it is the keeper of what is meaningful for our deepest hopes and fears.*
>
> Rollo May

Unit 9 explores memory, the complex mental process that allows us to store and recall our previous experiences. It looks at the ways cognitive psychologists investigate memory as an information-processing task and at the ways neuroscientists study how the structure and functioning of the brain affect how we remember and why we forget.

Objectives

After viewing the television program and completing the assigned reading, you should be able to:

1. Define *memory*.

2. Compare implicit and explicit memory.

3. Compare declarative and procedural memory.

4. Describe the processes of encoding, storage, and retrieval.

5. Describe the characteristics of short-term, long-term, and sensory memory.

6. Define *schema*.

7. Describe the accuracy of memory as a reconstructive process.

8. Define *amnesia*.

9. Describe processes of encoding and retrieval in Long Term Memory (LTM).

10. Describe short term memory (STM), note its limited capacity, and discuss two ways to enhance STM.

11. Compare semantic and episodic memory.

12. Discuss proactive and retroactive interference.

13. Describe chemical and anatomical factors involved in memory.

Reading Assignment

After viewing Program 9, read pages 195-231 in *Psychology and Life.*

Key People and Terms

As you watch the program and read the assignment, pay particular attention to these people and terms. People and terms defined in the text will be found on the given page numbers.

amnesia (223)

basic level (218)

chunking (202)

concepts (216)

contextual distinctiveness (208)

declarative memory (197)

elaborative rehearsal (213)

encoding (198)

encoding specificity (207)

engram (223)

episodic memories (206)

explicit uses of memory (196)

iconic memory (199)

implicit uses of memory (197)

levels-of-processing theory (209)

long-term memory (LTM) (205)

memory (196)

metamemory (214)

mnemonics (213)

primacy effect (208)

priming (210)

proactive interference (212)

procedural memory (197)

prototype (218)

recall (205)

recency effect (208)

recognition (205)

reconstructive memory (219)

retrieval (198)

retrieval cues (205)

retroactive interference (212)

schemas (218)

semantic memories (206)

serial position effect (208)

short-term memory (STM) (201)

storage (198)

transfer-appropriate processing (210)

working memory (203)

Alan Baddeley (203)

Sir Frederick Bartlett (220)

Hermann Ebbinghaus (211)

J. T. Hart (214)

Karl Lashley (223)

Elizabeth Loftus (222)

George Miller (201)

George Sperling (200)

Endel Tulving (206)

The following people appear in Program 9 but are not mentioned in the text.

∞ *Gordon Bower*—studies how mnemonic techniques can enhance learning and retrieval.

∞ *Richard Thompson*—studies the brain mechanisms underlying classical conditioning.

∞ *Diana Woodruff-Pak*—uses eyeblink classical conditioning to detect early-onset dementia.

Program Summary

When we misplace our keys, forget a name, or go blank in the middle of an exam, we become acutely aware of the complexities of memory. Forgetting can be mildly irritating, or it can be a major frustration. Chronic forgetfulness can even be a symptom of disease. Program 9 explores memory, the basis for all learning, and a process that enables us to survive, by linking the past to the present and the present to the future. To psychologists and neuroscientists, memory is an essential tool for studying the functions of the mind and the structures of the brain.

The early experimental study of memory began 100 years ago when German psychologist Hermann Ebbinghaus attempted to memorize random, three-letter combinations in meaningless series. But his memory faded quickly; he had no frame of reference or familiar context for the nonsense syllables. Because they had no meaning, order, or organization, he forgot them.

With the advent of the computer in the 1960s, psychologists were able to create a working model of the memory. Their approach depicted the mind as an information processor that could be divided into its component processes: selecting, encoding, storing, retaining, and retrieving knowledge.

Today we know that there are differences between long-term memory and short-term memory. Long-term memory contains everything we know about the world and ourselves. It has infinite capacity and stores concepts, smells, words, movements, and all our personal experiences in a complex network of associations. It functions as a passive storehouse, not as an active dispatcher.

The short-term memory holds information currently in use, but only for a very brief time. When we talk with friends, read, or take in the sights and sounds of our environment, we are using our short-term, or working, memory. But without active attention and rehearsal, all items in short-term memory are quickly forgotten and lost forever—unless we transfer them into long-term memory where they become permanent.

Sigmund Freud was the first to recognize that what we remember and forget can help us maintain our personal integrity and sense of self-worth. He developed his concept of repression from this. But even when we push unacceptable ideas into the unconscious, some of them escape and show up in our dreams, slips of the tongue, or mental preoccupations.

Memory is not an exact record of our experience. What we select, retain, and retrieve is influenced by many factors. Our attitudes, expectations, interests, and fears affect what we remember and how we remember it. A student assigned to read a book that seems boring will not retain as much as another student who finds the book fascinating. A witness may provide a distorted report of an accident because of personal expectations or preconceptions. Our schemas—that is, our own set of beliefs about people, objects, and situations—often cause us to ignore some details and add or alter others.

Scientists are learning more about how memory actually works. When something is remembered, the brain changes physically. In fact, every bit of information we remember is encoded in our brains. These traces form the biological foundation for everything we know and do. In the early days of the field, Karl Lashley searched for engrams, or localized addresses for various memories.

He was unsuccessful, but more recently researchers, such as Richard Thompson of USC, have found that simple memories, such as classically conditioned eyeblink, may be localized (in this case, in the interpositus nucleus of the cerebellum). Diana Woodruff-Pak of Temple University has found that disruption of this simple eyeblink response can signal early-onset dementia.

Clearly, memory is essential to individuality and personal identity. But sometimes, people do lose their memories. Organic amnesia is typically the result of injury to the brain, disease, or alcohol addiction. As the tissue is lost and the memory fades, so does the personality, and eventually life itself. Sadly, life without memory is life without a past or a future.

Program Review Questions

1. What pattern of remembering emerged in Hermann Ebbinghaus's research?

    a. loss occurred at a steady rate
    b. a small initial loss was followed by no further loss
    c. there was no initial loss, but then there was a gradual decline
    d. a sharp initial loss was followed by a gradual decline

2. The way psychologists thought about and studied memory was changed by the invention of

    a. television.
    b. electroconvulsive shock therapy.
    c. the computer.
    d. the electron microscope.

3. What do we mean when we say that memories must be encoded?

    a. They must be taken from storage to be used.
    b. They must be put in a form the brain can register.
    c. They must be transferred from one network to another.
    d. They must be put in a passive storehouse.

4. About how many items can be held in short-term memory?

    a. three
    b. seven
    c. eleven
    d. an unlimited number

5. Imagine you had a string of twenty one-digit numbers to remember. The best way to accomplish the task, which requires increasing the capacity of short-term memory, is through the technique of

    a. selective attention.
    b. peg words.
    c. rehearsing.
    d. chunking.

6. According to Gordon Bower, what is an important feature of good mnemonic systems?

    a. There is a dovetailing between storage and retrieval.
    b. The acoustic element is more important than the visual.
    c. The learner is strongly motivated to remember.
    d. Short-term memory is bypassed in favor of long-term memory.

7. According to Freud, what is the purpose of repression?

    a. to protect the memory from encoding too much material
    b. to preserve the individual's self-esteem
    c. to activate networks of associations
    d. to fit new information into existing schemas

8. In an experiment, people spent a few minutes in an office. They were then asked to recall what they had seen. They were most likely to recall objects that

    a. fit into their existing schema of an office.
    b. carried little emotional content.
    c. were unusual within that particular context.
    d. related to objects they owned themselves.

9. The paintings Franco Magnani made of an Italian town were distorted mainly by

    a. repression, causing some features to be left out.
    b. a child's perspective.
    c. sensory gating, changing colors.
    d. false memories of items that were not really there.

10. What was Karl Lashley's goal in teaching rats mazes and then removing part of their cortexes?

    a. finding out how much tissue was necessary for learning to occur
    b. determining whether memory was localized in one area of the brain
    c. discovering how much tissue loss led to memory loss
    d. finding out whether conditioned responses could be eradicated

11. What has Richard Thompson found in his work with rabbits conditioned to a tone before an air puff?

    a. Rabbits learn the response more slowly after lesioning.
    b. Eyelid conditioning involves several brain areas.
    c. The memory of the response can be removed by lesioning.
    d. Once the response is learned, the memory is permanent, despite lesioning.

12. What is the chief cause of functional amnesia?

    a. Alzheimer's disease
    b. substance abuse
    c. traumatic injury to the brain
    d. severe anxiety

13. The best way to keep items in short-term memory for an indefinite length of time is to

    a. chunk.
    b. create context dependence.
    c. use the peg-word system.
    d. rehearse.

14. Long-term memory is organized as

    a. a complex network of associations.
    b. a serial list.
    c. a set of visual images.
    d. a jumble of individual memories with no clear organizational scheme.

15. You remember a list of unrelated words by associating them, one at a time, with images of a bun, a shoe, a tree, a door, a hive, sticks, Heaven, a gate, a line, and a hen. What mnemonic technique are you using?

    a. method of loci
    b. peg-word
    c. link
    d. digit conversion

16. What did Karl Lashley conclude about the engram?

    a. It is localized in the brain stem.
    b. It is localized in the right hemisphere only.
    c. It is localized in the left hemisphere only.
    d. Complex memories cannot be pinpointed within the brain.

17. Long-term memories appear to be stored in the

    a. cortex.
    b. occipital lobe.
    c. hippocampus.
    d. parietal lobe.

18. How has Diana Woodruff-Pak utilized Richard Thompson's work on eyeblink conditioning?

    a. as a precursor to early-onset dementia
    b. as a predictor of musical genius
    c. as a mechanism for growing brain cells in intact animals
    d. as a tool for training long-term visual memories

19. Which neurotransmitter(s) is/are disrupted in Alzheimer's patients?

    a. scopolamine
    b. acetylcholine
    c. both of the above
    d. none of the above

20. Alzheimer's Disease is associated with the loss of

    a. memory.
    b. personality.
    c. life itself.
    d. all of the above.

Questions to Consider

1. What memory strategies can you apply to help you better retain the information in this course? Why is rote rehearsal not the optimal strategy?

2. What is your earliest memory? How accurate do you think it is? Can you recall an experience that happened before you could talk? If not, why not? How does language influence what we remember? How do photographs and other mementos aid memory?

3. Most American kids learn their ABCs by singing them. Why does singing the ABCs make it easier to remember them?

4. Many quiz shows and board games, like Trivial Pursuit, are based on recalling items of general knowledge that we do not use every day. Why is it so much fun to recall such trivia?

5. As a member of a jury, you are aware of the tendency to reconstruct memories. How much weight do you give to eyewitness testimony? Is it possible ever to get "the whole truth and nothing but the truth" from an eyewitness? Do you think memory distortions (for details of what was said during a trial) occur in jurors as well?

6. Why might metamemory, one's knowledge of the capabilities of and principles governing one's memory, be an important skill when one is studying for a test?

Optional Activities

1. Do you have an official family historian? In individual interviews, ask family members to recall and describe their memories of a shared past event, such as a wedding or holiday celebration. Perhaps a photograph or memento will trigger a story. Compare how different people construct the event and what kind of details are recalled. What are different people revealing about their personal interests, needs, and values when they describe the experience?

2. Try to recall an experience from your childhood that at least one friend or family member would also have a memory of. Have each person write down details of their memories, and then compare notes. Are there any details you hadn't remembered that you now do, based on other people's mention of them? Are there any details that you have contradictory memories for? How do you resolve the disagreement?

3. Make up a list of ten unrelated words. Have five friends study the list for one minute with only the instruction to "remember as many of them as you can." After one minute, have them write down as many as they can remember. Have another five friends learn the list for one minute after you teach them the peg-word mnemonic. Do they outperform the control group? What sort of strategies, if any, did the control group tend to use?

Additional Resources

Books and Articles

Koriat. A., Levy-Sadot, R., Edry, E., & de Marcas, G. (2004). What do we know about what we cannot remember? Accessing the semantic attributes of words that cannot be recalled. *Journal of Experimental Psychology: Learning, Memory and Cognition, 29,* 1095-1105.

Loftus, E.F. (2003) Make-believe memories. *American Psychologist, 58,* 864-873

Neisser, U. (1982). *Memory observed: Remembering in natural contexts.* San Francisco: Freeman.

Roediger, H. L., III, & Gallo, D. A. (2001). Processes affecting accuracy and distortion in memory: An overview. In M. L. Eisen, J. A. Quas, and G. S. Goodman (Eds.), *Memory and suggestibility in the forensic interview* (pp. 3-28). Mahwah, N. J.: Lawrence Erlbaum.

Schacter, D. & Tulving, E. (Eds.) (1994). *Memory systems.* Cambridge, MA: MIT Press.

Films

Memento. Directed by Christopher Nolan, 2001.

Web Sites

∞ *http://www.psychology.iastate.edu/faculty/gwells/homepage.htm*—Gary Wells at Iowa State University uses principles of memory research to understand eyewitness testimony and the risks for dissociation that eyewitnesses are susceptible to. This Web site provides a hands-on introduction to eyewitness memory.

∞ *http://www.exploratorium.edu/memory/index.html*—An extensive Web site on memory from the on-line museum. Try your skills here.

∞ *http://www.learner.org/*—This web site supports *Discovering Psychology: Updated Edition* with a page for each video program featuring an "academic footnote" to further update the content of the videos. The site also offers four special interactive features as well as an extensive webography.

UNIT 10

COGNITIVE PROCESSES

I think; therefore, I am.

René Descartes

The study of mental processes and structures—perceiving, reasoning, imagining, anticipating, and problem-solving—is known as cognition. Unit 10 explores these higher mental processes, offering insight into how the field has evolved and why more psychologists than ever are investigating the way we absorb, transform, and manipulate knowledge.

Objectives

After viewing the television program and completing the assigned reading, you should be able to:

1. Compare inductive and deductive reasoning.

2. Define the concept, "problem," in information processing terms and describe some ways to improve problem-solving abilities.

3. Discuss the "historical roots of methods for revealing mental processes."

4. Describe the study of language production.

5. Explain how ambiguity in language can be resolved.

6. Give several examples of how context influences language understanding.

7. Explain the role of visual imagery in cognition.

8. Discuss the importance of prototypes and schemas in cognition.

9. Describe what we know about the relation between cognition and brain activity.

Reading Assignment

After viewing Program 10, read pages 232-269 in *Psychology and Life*.

Key People and Terms

As you watch the program and read the assignment, pay particular attention to these people and terms. People and terms defined in the text will be found on the given page numbers.

algorithm (251)
audience design (237)
automatic processes (236)
belief bias effect (254)
cognition (233)
cognitive processes (233)
cognitive science (233)
controlled processes (236)
deductive reasoning (253)
functional fixedness (253)
heuristics (251)
inductive reasoning (255)
inferences (243)
language production (237)
mental set (255)
parallel processes (234)
problem solving (250)
problem space (250)
reasoning (250)

serial processes (234)
think aloud protocols (251)

Dorothy Cheney (244)
Herbert Clark (238)
F.C. Donders (234)
H. Paul Grice (237)
Sue Savage-Rumbaugh (244)
Robert Seyfarth (244)
Herbert Simon (257)
Benjamin Lee Whorf (245)

The following people are referred to in Program 10 but are not introduced in the text.

∞ *Robert Glaser*-studies learning.

∞ *Michael Posner*-uses brain imaging techniques to explore what parts of the brain are used in accomplishing specific cognitive tasks.

Program Summary

Cognition includes knowing, remembering, reasoning, imagining, anticipating, planning, problem solving, and communicating. In Program 10, we learn how psychologists study these mental processes and what they have discovered about how people think.

In 1958, British psychologist Donald Broadbent used a flowchart to demonstrate how people receive, process, and store information as words, pictures, and patterns in memory. His model interpreted the workings of the mind as if it were a computer. Using the information-processing model, many cognitive psychologists today, including Nobel Prize-winner Herbert Simon, are beginning to answer questions about how our experiences are transformed into knowledge that guides our actions.

One of the basic functions the mind performs is categorizing. We sort, label, and store stimuli based on common features, similar functions, and other similarities. The categories we form in our minds are called concepts. Although some concepts are simple and some complex, our minds link virtually all elements into coherent relationships.

Scientists have speculated that we organize our concepts around the representation of the most typical category member: the prototype. For example, most people in our culture have in mind a prototype of a bird that looks like a robin, rather than a turkey or flamingo. Using this prototype allows us mentally to organize objects in an efficient way.

Schemas are a type of complex concepts that allow us to organize a body of knowledge around prior experience, related events, and expectations. When we hear the word *picnic,* for example, we can imagine immediately what items go into a picnic basket, what to wear to a picnic, and in what environment the picnic is likely to take place. The more something fits into an established schema, the more it will make sense to us. If something doesn't fit our knowledge or expectations, we may not even notice it.

Our concepts are formed not only as words or labels, but also as mental pictures. Evidence of visual thinking comes from laboratory experiments in which participants' delayed responses indicate that they are mentally rotating or scanning images. Psychologists can also measure changes in brain activity to show how the brain reacts to surprising events.

Visual thought builds on our experience of spatial or geographical relationships. We use mental maps to give directions, decide on an alternate route to work, and get around the house without turning the lights on. But cognitive maps may also be distorted. For example, our mental map of the rest of the world might enlarge nearby or familiar regions and shrink faraway regions.

While some researchers try to understand how the mind functions, others examine the brain's chemistry and architecture in an effort to find out how we reason, learn, and remember. Psychologist Michael Posner uses sophisticated brain scanning equipment to look at the chemical and electrical processes that occur when a person is reading or solving a problem. Scientists, like Robert Glazer, try to understand how we learn, and such research may help to improve formal education and everyday learning in the years to come.

Program Review Questions

NOTE: Review Questions for Units 10 and 11 are provided in Unit 11.

Questions to Consider

1. Where does the poem "Jabberwocky," by Lewis Carroll, get its meaning? Read the excerpt below and consider the concepts and rules of language and underlying structure that help you make sense of it. Can you paraphrase it?

> 'Twas brillig, and the slithy toves
> Did gyre and gimble in the wabe;
> All mimsy were the borogoves,
> And the mome raths outgrabe.
>
> Beware the Jabberwock, my son!
> The jaws that bite, the claws that catch!
> Beware the Jubjub bird, and shun
> The frumious Bandersnatch!

2. Think of all the ways you can categorize people (e.g., by their gender, their age, their ethnicity, their intelligence, their taste in music). Do you have different schemas for people who belong to these various groups? How does your schema influence your behavior toward people?

3. Can language and knowledge be separated? How do children acquire knowledge before they are able to use verbal labels?

4. Where does "meaning" come from? How much of the meaning that we draw from objects and events is actually generated from our own inferences and expectations?

5. Why can you be so confident that when you say something sarcastically, the person you're talking to will understand your meaning? Under what circumstances are you less sure?

Optional Activities

1. There are many variations on the game, "Ghost." This version challenges players to manipulate concepts by using words in different contexts. Players may find it easier to think up new word pairs as time goes on. What might explain the change? How would you measure it?

    To play: The first player starts off by offering a pair of words that are commonly used together. They may be compounded, hyphenated, or entirely separate. The next player must come up with another pair of words using the last word of the previous pair as the first word of the new pair. (Example: Baseball, ball game, game show, show girl, girlfriend, friendship.) Players keep the chain going until someone cannot come up with a word pair. He or she gets the letter "g." The game resumes. A player is out of the game when he or she gets all the letters of the word "ghost."

2. All of us tend to categorize the world into convenient units and to use common labels for our categories. Often those labels become permanent, and we tend to view our world in a rigid or stereotypical way. When this stops us from producing new ideas, it is called functional fixedness. Can you overcome it?

    Try this: How many uses can you think of for an empty milk carton, a brick, a sock with a hole in it, a paper clip, a bandanna, or another ordinary household object? After you feel you've exhausted all possibilities, list as many attributes of the object as possible. Draw a picture of the object from various points of view. Then see if you can generate any new uses.

3. Draw a map of the United States from memory, in as much detail as possible. Then compare it to a real map of the U.S. Where is your map systematically distorted or simplified?

Additional Resources

Books and Articles

Kosslyn, S. M. (1983). *Ghosts in the mind's machine.* New York: Norton. Good introduction to the issues of cognitive psychology.

Simon, H. (1992). *Economics, bounded rationality, and the cognitive revolution.* Brookfield, CT: E Elgin Pub. Co.

Medin, D. (1999). *Cognitive psychology.* New York: Harcourt College Publishers.

Reisberg, D., Pearson, D. G., and Kosslyn, S. M. (2003). Intuitions and introspections about imagery: The role of imagery experience in shaping an investigator's theoretical views. *Applied Cognitive Psychology, 17,* 147-160.

Films

Many film heroes show an impressive ability to solve problems by overcoming functional fixedness. The films featuring James Bond and directed by Albert Broccoli are among the classics.

Web Sites

∞ *http://www.infoplease.com/ipa/A0004638.html* —The National Inventors Hall of Fame introduces extraordinary problem solvers who have shown insight in identifying human needs and finding clever solutions to them.

∞ *http://www.uml.edu/dept/psychology/aasmi/*—The American Association for the Study of Mental Imagery is dedicated to advances in the science and application of mental imagery.

∞ *http://www.learner.org/*—This web site supports *Discovering Psychology: Updated Edition* with a page for each video program featuring an "academic footnote" to further update the content of the videos. The site also offers four special interactive features as well as an extensive webography.

UNIT 11

If you have to make a choice and don't make it, that in itself is a choice.

William James

Unit 11 explores the decision-making process and the psychology of risk-taking, revealing how people arrive at good and bad decisions. It also looks at the reasons people lapse into irrationality and how personal biases can affect judgment.

Objectives

After viewing the television program and completing the assigned readings, you should be able to:

1. Describe contrasting views of why human thinking is irrational and prone to error.

2. Explain the notions of heuristic thinking and analytical thinking.

3. Compare definitions of problem solving and decision making.

4. Describe the anchoring bias, availability heuristic, and representativeness heuristic.

5. Discuss why the way a problem is framed can influence a decision.

6. Define *decision aversion.*

7. Describe how risk affects decision making.

8. Describe at least one way in which memory and decision making can affect each other.

Reading Assignment

After viewing Program 11, read pages 256-263 in *Psychology and Life.*

Key People and Terms

As you watch the program and read the assignment, pay particular attention to these people and terms. People and terms defined in the text will be found on the given page numbers.

anchoring heuristic (260)
availability heuristic (258)
decision aversion (263)
decision making (257)
frame (261)
heuristics (251)
judgment (257)
representativeness heuristic (259)

Daniel Kahneman (257)
Amos Tversky (257)

To review textbook terms, refer to the Key People and Terms in Unit 10. The following terms and people are referred to in Program 11 but are not defined in the text.

∞ *dread factor*—the fear of unfamiliar or potentially catastrophic events that make us judge these to be riskier than familiar events.

∞ *framing*—the way information is presented, which tends to bias how it is interpreted.

∞ *invariance*—the principle stating that preferences between options should be independent of different representations.

∞ *similarity heuristic*—an error based on the tendency to see a connection between belonging to a certain category and having the characteristics considered typical of members of that category.

∞ *Max Bazerman*—discusses the five most common cognitive mistakes that negotiators make.

∞ *Leon Festinger*—developed cognitive dissonance theory.

∞ *Irving Janis*—studied the Cuban Missile Crisis and looked at distorted "groupthink" reasoning.

Program Summary

No matter how uncertain life is, we all have to think and act decisively. Every day, we assess situations, take risks, and make judgments and decisions. In Program 11, we'll get a chance to participate in experiments that illustrate the psychology of making decisions and taking risks. And we'll find out what psychologists are discovering why people make bad decisions and irrational judgments.

There are several explanations for human error and irrationality. Social psychologists point to the influence of the crowd; Freudians claim that animal passions and emotions tend to overpower our better judgment.

Amos Tversky (now deceased, formerly of Stanford University) and Daniel Kahneman (now of Princeton University) have studied how and why people make illogical choices. They have argued that irrationality is based on the same processes that enable us to form concepts and make inferences. But we often make irrational decisions, because these same mental strategies are not appropriate in all cases. Confronted with uncertainty or ambiguity, we tend to think that the most easily recalled events are the most likely. For example, when news reports are full of vivid accounts of plane crashes and hijackings, we overestimate the likelihood of these events and may avoid traveling altogether.

We make some decisions based on other mental shortcuts, often using prototypes to represent classes of objects, events, and people. These assumptions can mislead us into making poor judgments, because we may mistakenly categorize something based on one feature. How information is "framed," or presented, can also influence our decision making in mathematics, geography, politics—virtually any subject area.

Recently, the science of risk assessment has also been attracting a lot of interest. Researchers are discovering that most people avoid risks when seeking gains. But they also choose risks to avoid sure losses. Prolonged wars are a good example of loss avoidance; it's extremely difficult for one side to accept a sure loss and admit that there's no chance of winning. So both sides end up fighting longer and losing even more.

How people perceive a risk may also depend on complex psychological factors, such as the "dread" factor. For example, we may be terrified of a nuclear accident but never think twice about jaywalking. That's because jaywalking is familiar, while a nuclear accident is unfamiliar and, therefore, seems more potentially catastrophic. Yet the odds of a nuclear accident are a tiny fraction of the odds of getting hurt while jaywalking.

Psychologists also study group decision making and have found that rationality often turns out to have little to do with intelligence, because decision making changes in groups. Psychologist Irving Janis studied the records of John F. Kennedy's cabinet meetings, where the disastrous decision was made to invade the Bay of Pigs. He found many examples of distorted reasoning, which he has labeled *groupthink*. Janis has also outlined some procedures that decision makers can implement in order to prevent irrational group decision making.

Another new field is the psychology of negotiation. It attempts to avoid the negative effects of bad decisions among individuals, groups, and institutions. Many people, especially government and business professionals, are taking a great interest in this area in an effort to improve their own negotiating skills.

The act of making a decision can set other processes in motion. Psychologists have found that whenever we decide something that conflicts with our prior beliefs, a state of "cognitive dissonance" results. We often try to reduce the tension and discomfort of cognitive dissonance by changing our attitude toward the decision or changing how others think about it.

Although bright, reasonable people often make irrational decisions and take unacceptable risks, the field of psychology is helping to shed light on our behavior and even provide guidelines for helping us catch ourselves before we go astray—or redirect ourselves if we do.

Program Review Questions

1. Michael Posner's work on brain imaging showed

    a.   major differences between the brains of young and old adults, with cognitive processes more localized in brains of the elderly.

    b.   that blood flow decreases in the brain as thinking becomes more efficient.

    c.   that electrical stimulation of the brain can enhance performance on logic puzzles reliably.

    d.   that patterns of brain activity differ in predictable ways when people see words, vs. read them aloud, vs. name the function of the objects to which they refer.

2. The movement in psychology, known as cognitive psychology, developed primarily

    a.   at the turn of the century.

    b.   in the 1920s.

    c.   after World War II.

    d.   during the last five years.

3. What analytic tool did Donald Broadbent use to model the process by which information is perceived and stored in memory?

    a.   statistical analysis on a computer

    b.   a flow chart

    c.   a set of categories

    d.   an analogy to a steam engine

4. A cognitive psychologist would be most interested in which one of the following issues?

    a.   how you decide which answer is correct for this question

    b.   how pain stimuli are processed

    c.   maturation of the efferent system

    d.   how to distinguish mania from schizophrenia

5. When we distinguish between groups of letters on the basis of the kinds of lines that form them, we are performing the mental process of

    a. relating.
    b. categorizing.
    c. creating prototypes.
    d. activating schema.

6. Concepts are mental representations. Which is a concept of an attribute?

    a. bed
    b. jumping
    c. slow
    d. courage

7. What is our prototype of a tree most likely to be similar to?

    a. a maple tree
    b. a palm tree
    c. a Christmas tree
    d. a dead tree

8. According to the program, why do we assume that Montreal is farther north than Seattle?

    a. because we have learned it
    b. because we are less familiar with Montreal than with Seattle
    c. because Canada is north of the United States in our mental maps
    d. because we are not good at making such judgments

9. When Steve Kosslyn asked people about the picture of a motorboat, he was primarily interested in

    a. how they scanned a mental image.
    b. how much detail they noted.
    c. how they compared a new picture with a prototype.
    d. how sure they felt about what they had seen.

10. What is one way in which human problem solving appears to be quite different from the way computers solve problems?

    a. Humans can solve problems that don't involve numbers.
    b. Humans are more logical in their approach to problems.
    c. Humans have trouble when content is unfamiliar.
    d. Humans are less likely to be misled by bias.

11. What did Michael Posner find when he conducted PET scans of people reading a word and associating it with a function?

    a.   Localized activity occurred, but the location varied widely.
    b.   Similar localized activity was seen in all the participants.
    c.   Brain activity was general, rather than localized.
    d.   No general pattern of activity was observed.

12. According to Robert Glaser, what is the general purpose of the research at the University of Pittsburgh's Learning and Research Development Center?

    a.   to create new types of computers
    b.   to model the organic functions of the brain
    c.   to classify errors and mistakes
    d.   to improve the way people use their intelligence

13. What is a cognitive illusion?

    a.   a mental map that we can scan for information
    b.   a biased mental strategy
    c.   a concept formed on the basis of a perceptual illusion
    d.   a decision motivated by emotion

14. How did Freud explain the fact that human beings sometimes make irrational decisions?

    a.   They are driven by primitive needs.
    b.   They are influenced by the emotions of the crowd.
    c.   They are basing their decisions on availability.
    d.   They are using standard human mental processes.

15. Why did the people questioned assume that there were more words beginning with "k" than with "k" as the third letter?

    a.   There is a general tendency to favor the initial position.
    b.   The anchoring effect biased their answers.
    c.   It's easier to find examples of words beginning with "k."
    d.   It seems less risky as an answer.

16. A heuristic is a kind of

    a.   mistake.
    b.   meaning.
    c.   mathematical model.
    d.   shortcut.

17. A researcher asks two groups of students to estimate the average price of a new car. One group is asked if the price is more or less than $9,000. The other group is asked if the price is more or less than $18,000. Each group is asked to estimate the actual average price. How will the two averages compare?

    a. The first group will take longer to answer.
    b. The second group will take longer to answer.
    c. The first group will have a higher average.
    d. The second group will have a higher average.

18. When people were confronted with a choice of a sure loss of $85 or an eighty-five percent chance of losing $100, how did most people react?

    a. They chose the loss.
    b. They chose the chance.
    c. They pointed out the statistical equivalence of the alternatives.
    d. They revised to make the choice.

19. Why would smokers be likely to underestimate the chance of developing lung cancer?

    a. They do not dread the disease.
    b. It is an unfamiliar risk.
    c. It is not representative.
    d. It represents a delayed consequence.

20. Irving Janis studied how the decision to invade Cuba was made during the Kennedy administration. What advice does Janis offer to promote better decision making?

    a. Encourage groupthink by team-building exercises.
    b. Appoint one group member to play devil's advocate.
    c. Restrict the size of the group.
    d. Assume that silence means consent on the part of all group members.

21. Imagine that you are a business leader who has been to a negotiating workshop led by Max Bazerman and Lawrence Susskind. Which statement shows something you should have learned from the experience?

    a. "I will escalate conflict."
    b. "I know this is a zero-sum game."
    c. "I will enlarge my frame of reference."
    d. "I am confident that I am right and will prevail."

22. How does cognitive dissonance make us feel?

    a. We are so uncomfortable that we try to reduce the dissonance.
    b. We enjoy it so much that we actively seek dissonance.
    c. Our reaction to dissonance depends largely on personality.
    d. It creates boredom, which we try to overcome.

23. In Festinger's experiment, which students felt dissonance?

    a. both the students who got $20 and those who got $1
    b. the students who got $20 but not those who got $1
    c. the students who got $1 but not those who got $20
    d. neither the students who got $1 nor those who got $20

24. You read the following sentences: "Mary heard the ice cream truck. She remembered her birthday money and ran into the house." What allowed you to understand how these sentences are related?

    a. a cognitive illusion
    b. reasoning by analogy
    c. a schema
    d. the anchoring heuristic

25. When people believe that Linda is more likely to be a bank teller and active in the feminist movement than she is likely to be a bank teller, their error is due to

    a. the availability heuristic.
    b. the representativeness heuristic.
    c. the anchoring heuristic.
    d. groupthink.

26. Which of the following is true of groupthink?

    a. Groupthink is characterized by people's strong motivation to provide their colleagues with information that will change their minds.
    b. To avoid groupthink, a company should hire people who were all trained in the same business philosophy.
    c. Groupthink occurs only in the political world, but not in other domains.
    d. Groupthink is characterized by a self-censorship of one's doubts.

27. According to Howard Gardner, which popular approach to psychology did the field of cognitive science overthrow?

    a. functionalism
    b. structuralism
    c. behaviorism
    d. evolutionism

28. All of the following are true about our representation of schema, *except* that

    a. memory errors can stem from activating inappropriate schema.
    b. schema are complex concepts.
    c. they can be used to understand language.
    d. their use is limited to decision making.

29. According to Robert Glaser, intelligence

    a. is a skill and can be developed.
    b. is genetically determined.
    c. is a myth.
    d. is no higher in humans than it is in chimpanzees and bonobos.

30. Greg is visiting a foreign country that is known for its current political unrest, and he has seen news reports over the past week about tourists being kidnapped. Although his chances of being killed in a car accident during his vacation are higher than his chances of being killed by terrorists, he believes the opposite. What cognitive process is behind his error?

    a. representativeness heuristic
    b. availability heuristic
    c. anchoring and adjustment heuristic
    d. framing heuristic

31. Jim has greater dread of the possible consequences for him of a small meteorite impact on the earth than of the consequences of jaywalking across a busy street. According to the program, this difference is likely because

    a. the consequences of the meteorite impact are less familiar.
    b. the consequences of the meteorite impact are less immediate.
    c. the consequences of jaywalking are smaller for him than of a meteorite impact somewhere on Earth.
    d. the anchoring heuristic leads to greater attention for perceptual events.

32. According to Max Bazerman, all of the following are mistakes commonly made during negotiation, *except*

    a. being willing to compromise on points of lesser importance.
    b. failure to consider the judgments made by one's counterpart.
    c. limiting one's thinking to the specific points of conflict.
    d. assuming that whenever one side wins, the other must lose.

33. Which of these is a likely consequence of cognitive dissonance?

    a. becoming more entrenched in one's beliefs
    b. increasing the behavior that is causing dissonance
    c. becoming more sociable
    d. changing an attitude

34. Al's parents are paying for his college tuition. Joe is working two jobs to put himself through college. Both are taking a fairly dry chemistry course together. Who is more likely to say he likes the course, and why?

    a. Al, because of cognitive dissonance
    b. Joe, because of cognitive dissonance
    c. Al, because of the availability heuristic
    d. Joe, because of the availability heuristic

35. Why is the normative approach to decision making different from the descriptive approach?

    a. because people are not rational
    b. because the normative approach is interested in cross-cultural effects, while the descriptive approach is not
    c. because the normative approach studies framing effects, while the descriptive approach does not
    d. because the descriptive approach is a less scientifically rigorous study of human cognition than the normative approach

Questions to Consider

1. According to the *Journal of the American Medical Association,* strep throat is one of the most common reasons that children and young adults visit the doctor. It is difficult to diagnose by history or examination only. Ten doctors working in a university health center overestimated the incidence of strep throat by eighty-one percent. Of the 308 patients in the study, only fifteen—about five percent—actually had strep throat. What might explain the doctors' overestimation?

2. Knowing about problem-solving strategies and using them are two different things. Based on the information in the program and in your text, what are some of the pitfalls you need to avoid

in both day-to-day problem solving and decision making about major life changes? How optimistic are you that you can really learn to consistently avoid these pitfalls?

3. Creative people often have such qualities as nonconformity, curiosity, a high degree of verbal fluency, flexibility with numbers, concepts, a sense of humor, a high energy level, impatience with routine tasks, and a vivid imagination that may take the form of wild stories or fibs. What would be the implications for this type of child in the typical school classroom?

4. How does the framing effect, which shows how the description of a situation can heavily influence decision making, jibe with the evidence encountered in the previous chapter that the limitations inherent in one's native language only weakly limits one's thinking?

5. How might cognitive heuristics, like representativeness and availability, perpetuate ethnic stereotypes?

Optional Activities

1. Go to a busy intersection and observe pedestrian street-crossing behavior. Observe the kinds of risks people take crossing the street. What do you consider risky behavior? Who is most likely to engage in it? Why do you suppose certain people take more risks than others?

2. Interview people of different economic statuses and ages about their approaches to the stock market. How do their approaches differ with respect to the assessment of risk and their willingness to accept various forms of risk? Find out how much of their behavior is determined by memories, heuristics, and decision aversion.

Additional Resources
Books and Articles

Bazerman, M. (1994). *Judgment in managerial decision making.* 3rd Ed. New York: Wiley.

Gilovich, T, Griffin, D and Kahneman, D. (Eds.) (2002). *Heuristics and biases: The psychology of intuitive judgment.* New York: Cambridge University Press.

Hunink, M., Glaszious, P., Siegel, J., Weeks, J., Pliskin, J., Elstein, A., & Weinstein, M. (2001). *Decision making in health and medicine.* New York: Cambridge University Press.

Kahneman, D., Slovic, P. & Tversky, A. (Eds.) (1982). *Judgment under uncertainty: Heuristics and biases.* Cambridge: Harvard University Press.

Plous, S. (1993). *The psychology of judgment and decision making.* New York: McGraw-Hill.

Rachlin, H., Brown, J., & Cross, D. V. (2000). Discounting in judgments of delay and probability. *Journal of Behavioral Decision Making. Special Issue: Time and Decision, 13,* 145-159.

Films

M*A*S*H. Directed by Robert Altman, 1970. Medical personnel need to make decisions about diagnoses and treatments based on incomplete or masked information and under time pressure. In emergency situations like those encountered in mobile army surgical units, decisions are complicated by the need to determine who requires more immediate treatment.

Apollo 13. Directed by Ron Howard, 1995. This film, based on the true story of the Apollo 13 astronauts, shows how innovative problem solving can save lives.

Web Sites

∞ *http://www.sjdm.org/links.html* —This site for the Society for Judgment and Decision Making has links to many other sites of interest, including decision theory, game theory, risk, systems analysis, and medical and economic decision making.

∞ *http://www.learner.org/*—This web site supports *Discovering Psychology: Updated Edition* with a page for each video program featuring an "academic footnote" to further update the content of the videos. The site also offers four special interactive features as well as an extensive webography.

UNIT 12

*We may affirm absolutely that nothing great in the world
has been accomplished without passion.*
Georg Wilhelm Friedrich Hegel

What moves us to act? Why do we feel the way we do? Unit 12 shows how psychologists study the continuous interactions of mind and body in an effort to explain the enormous variety and complexities of human behavior.

Objectives

After viewing the television program and completing the assigned reading, you should be able to:

1. Compare emotion and motivation and describe their interrelationships.

2. Describe three theories concerning the sources of motivation.

3. Discuss some of the forces that drive the motivation to eat.

4. Describe some of the factors behind the motivation for sex.

5. Define the need for achievement.

6. Outline the attributions for success and failure in terms of a locus of control orientation.

7. Describe the major theories of emotion and the universality of its expression.

7. Describe the relationship between physical states and the experience of emotions.

Reading Assignment

After viewing Program 12, read pages 339-379 in *Psychology and Life*.

96

Key People and Terms

As you watch the program and read the assignment, pay particular attention to these people and terms. People and terms defined in the text will be found on the given page numbers.

amygdala (356)

anorexia nervosa (348)

attributions (359)

bulimia nervosa (348)

Cannon-Bard theory of emotion (375)

cognitive appraisal (375)

cognitive appraisal theory of emotion (376)

drives (341)

emotion (342, 353)

equity theory (361)

expectancy theory (361)

hierarchy of needs (343)

homeostasis (341)

incentives (342)

instincts (342)

James-Lange theory of emotion (374)

motivation (340)

need for achievement (358)

organizational psychologists (361)

social-learning theory (343)

thematic apperception test (TAT) (358)

Philip Bard (375)

Daryl Bem (356)

Ruth Benedict (342)

Gordon Bower (230)

Walter Cannon (344)

Paul Ekman (371)

Sigmund Freud (366)

Fritz Heider (343)

Peter Herman (346)

Clark Hull (341)

William James (342)

Virginia Johnson (352)

Richard Lazarus (376)

Abraham Maslow (343)

William Masters (352)

David McClelland (358)

Margaret Mead (342)

Henry Murray (358)

Janet Polivy (346)

Julian Rotter (343)

Stanley Schachter (346)

Martin Seligman (360, 367)

Robert Zajonc (376)

The following terms and person are referred to in Program 12 but are not introduced in the text.

∞ *arousal*—a heightened level of excitation or activation.

∞ *optimism*—the tendency to attribute failure to external, unstable, or changeable factors and to attribute success to stable factors.

∞ *pessimism*—the tendency to attribute failure to stable or internal factors and to attribute success to global variables.

∞ *Norman Adler*—studies the physiological and behavioral mechanisms of sexual behavior.

Program Summary

What moves people to act? What makes someone jump into freezing water, risking his or her own life, to save a stranger? Why do exhausted marathon runners stagger relentlessly toward the finish line, determined to complete a punishing race?

To explain the enormous variety and complexity of behavior, psychologists study the environment as well as the individual, and the mind as well as the body, to find what moves people to take action. They have observed that we move toward some things and away from others.

When we can't help moving toward something, we may have an addiction. When we have an unnatural aversion to something, we may have a phobia. Between the two extremes of approach and avoidance, psychologists infer motives by noting what we choose, how intensely we involve ourselves, and how long we keep at it.

Seeking pleasure and avoiding pain explain many of our actions. But this same principle can also work against us. For example, alcohol and drugs may be pleasurable, but they are bad for us. And studying may be extremely difficult, but it can be good for us. As we grow older, we learn to do the things that will pay off in the future. But our true desires may never go away.

Freud theorized that behavior was based on our motivation to seek sexual satisfaction and to express aggressive urges against those who restrain our pursuit of pleasure. He explained that our basic sexual and aggressive desires are hidden from our conscious awareness but that they still influence our behavior and sometimes reveal themselves in dreams, fantasies, or slips of the tongue.

In contrast to Freud, Carl Rogers and Abraham Maslow, who studied normal, healthy people, saw a different side of human nature. They theorized that our lives are shaped by a basic tendency toward growth and mastery.

Sexual behavior is a good example of the complex interaction of psychological and biological forces. In contrast to the motivation of other animals, whose sexual mating behavior patterns promote the survival of the species, human sexual motivation is a readiness to experience intense pleasure and, often, romantic love. It combines physical arousal, strong emotion, and an intense attraction to another person. Human sexual behavior is highly diverse and subject to a mixture of personal, social, situational, and cultural influences.

A related area of psychological interest is emotion, the complex pattern of changes involving feelings, thoughts, behavior, and physical arousal. Psychologist Robert Plutchik has proposed that there are eight basic emotions made up of four pairs of opposites, such as joy and sadness, and anger and fear, which we combine when we feel other emotions.

Psychologist Paul Ekman's cross-cultural studies reveal a remarkable universality in the way facial expressions communicate basic emotions. In fact, people all over the world decode emotions in much the same way. And they show similar changes in the brain, muscles, thoughts, and behavior.

Theorists, such as Martin Seligman, emphasize the role of cognitive appraisal in motivation and emotion. He suggests that what people do and how hard they try are influenced by basic optimism and pessimism. Our motivations and emotional states depend on how we view failure and success. An optimist failing a test would attribute the poor performance to external causes ("The test was too hard.") or changeable factors ("I'll try harder and do better next time."). The pessimist would feel doomed by stable, unchangeable factors ("I guess I'm dumb and unlucky.") and out of control

("Nothing I do will make a difference; I'll always be this way."). On the other hand, optimists take full credit for their successes, while pessimists see only luck or chance in anything good that happens to them. A person's explanatory style can influence performance in school and work and even his or her physical and mental well-being.

Program Review Questions

1. What is the general term for all the physical and psychological processes that start behavior, maintain it, and stop it?

    a. explanatory style
    b. repression
    c. addiction
    d. motivation

2. Phoebe has a phobia regarding cats. What is her motivation?

    a. environmental arousal
    b. overwhelming fear
    c. repressed sexual satisfaction
    d. a need for attachment to others

3. What is the role of the pleasure-pain principle in motivation?

    a. We repress our pleasure in others' pain.
    b. We seek pleasure and avoid pain.
    c. We persist in doing things, even when they are painful.
    d. We are more intensely motivated by pain than by pleasure.

4. Which activity most clearly involves a "reframing" of the tension between desire and restraint?

    a. eating before you feel hungry
    b. seeking pleasurable physical contact with others
    c. working long hours for an eventual goal
    d. getting angry at someone who interferes with your plans

5. Freud thought there were two primary motivations. One of these is

    a. expressing aggression.
    b. seeking transcendence.
    c. fulfilling creativity.
    d. feeling secure.

6. Compared with Freud's view of human motivation, that of Abraham Maslow could be characterized as being more

    a. negative.
    b. hormonally based.
    c. optimistic.
    d. pathologically based.

7. Behaviors, such as male peacocks displaying their feathers or male rams fighting, are related to which part of sexual reproduction?

    a. providing a safe place for mating
    b. focusing the male's attention on mating
    c. selecting a partner with good genes
    d. mating at the correct time of year

8. In Norman Adler's research on mating behavior in rats, what is the function of the ten or so mountings?

    a. to trigger hormone production
    b. to prepare the male for ejaculation
    c. to cause fertilization
    d. to impress the female

9. What kinds of emotions tend to be involved in romantic love?

    a. mainly intense, positive emotions
    b. mainly intense, negative emotions
    c. a mixture of intense and weak emotions that are mainly positive
    d. a mixture of positive and negative emotions that are intense

10. Darwin cited the similarity of certain expressions of emotions as evidence that

    a. all species learn emotions.
    b. emotions are innate.
    c. emotions promote survival of the fittest.
    d. genetic variability is advantageous.

11. Pictures of happy and sad American workers are shown to American college students and to Italian workers. Based on your knowledge of Paul Ekman's research, what would you predict about how well the groups would identify the emotions?

    a. Both groups will identify the emotions correctly.
    b. Only the Americans will identify the emotions correctly.
    c. Only the Italians will identify the emotions correctly.
    d. Neither group will identify the emotions correctly.

12. Theodore has an explanatory style that emphasizes the external, the unstable, and the specific. He makes a mistake at work that causes his boss to become very angry. Which statement is Theodore most likely to make to himself?

    a. "I always make such stupid mistakes."
    b. "I was just distracted by the noise outside."
    c. "All my life, people have always gotten so mad at me."
    d. "If I were a better person, this wouldn't have happened."

13. Why does Martin Seligman believe that it might be appropriate to help children who develop a pessimistic explanatory style?

    a. These children are unpleasant to be around.
    b. These children lack contact with reality.
    c. These children are at risk for depression.
    d. Other children who live with these children are likely to develop the same style.

14. What other outcome will a pessimistic explanatory style likely affect, according to Seligman?

    a. health
    b. artistic ability
    c. reasoning skills
    d. language competence

15. All of the following are possible origins of a pessimistic explanatory style, *except*

    a. assessments by important adults in our lives.
    b. the reality of our first major negative life event.
    c. our mother's pessimism level.
    d. our level of introversion/extraversion.

16. Which theorist is best known for positing a hierarchy of needs that humans strive to meet?

    a. Freud
    b. Rogers
    c. Maslow
    d. Seligman

17. Although motivation can lead to unpleasant states (e.g., hunger, frustration), it seems to have evolved because of its benefits to
    a. survival.
    b. propagation of the species.
    c. health.
    d. all of the above.

18. What has Robert Plutchik argued about emotions?

    a. There are three basic types of emotions: happiness, sadness, and anger.
    b. There are eight basic emotions, consisting of four pairs of opposites.
    c. Love is not a universal emotion; some cultures do not show signs of having it.
    d. Emotional experience is determined by physiology alone.

19. Four people have been obese for as long as they can remember. Their doctors tell all of them that their obesity is putting them at risk for several illnesses. Who is most likely to join a gym, go on a diet, and get in shape?

    a. Al, whose explanatory style includes an internal locus of control
    b. Bob, who has a pessimistic explanatory style
    c. Chuck, whose explanatory style includes an unstable locus of control
    d. Dwayne, who is depressed about his obesity

20. Wolves and squirrels are most likely to show which of the following in their mating patterns?

    a. romantic love
    b. competition by females for males
    c. competition by males for females
    d. a preference for mating in the autumn so that the offspring will be born during the winter

Questions to Consider

1. Human sexual motivation expresses itself in sexual scripts that include attitudes, values, social norms, and expectations about patterns of behavior. Consider how males and females might develop different sexual scripts. How might lack of synchronization affect a couple? How might sexual scripts change as the bad news about sexually transmitted diseases and AIDS increases?

2. Do you consider yourself an optimist or a pessimist? Pick a recent success and a recent failure or disappointment and consider how an optimist and a pessimist would explain each experience. How did you handle each situation?

3. If degree of self-restraint and stress determine how likely it is that people will "cheat" on their diets, what sorts of psychological supports would you build into a diet plan?

4. Consider how eating disorders, such as anorexia and bulimia, contradict the pain-pleasure principle.

5. If you could choose between taking this course pass/fail (credit only) or getting a letter grade, which would you choose? How would your decision affect your study time, motivation, and test-taking behavior?

6.   How do the relative priorities of motivators change for you when you are hungry or sick?

7.   Imagine you were to move to a country whose culture you aren't familiar with. Describe some of the social problems you might encounter because you don't know the cultural norms regarding expression of emotion.

Optional Activities

1.   Are we sad because we cry, or do we cry because we are sad? Can making a sad face make us feel sad? Does going through the motions trigger the emotion?

Try this: Set aside from ten to fifteen minutes for this experiment. Write down the words, *happy, sad, angry*, and *fearful,* on slips of paper. In front of a mirror, select one of the slips, and watch yourself as you create the facial expression for it. Hold the expression for at least a minute. Note the thoughts and physical reactions that seem to accompany your facial expression. Then relax your face and repeat the exercise with another slip of paper. Which theories does your experience support or challenge?

2.   Observe the activities on which you need to concentrate when your hunger has been satisfied, compared with when you are very hungry. How well can you focus on more abstract motivations when your biological motivations have been left unmet?

Additional Resources

Books and Articles

Ekman, P. (1994). *The nature of emotion.* New York: Oxford University Press.

Ekman, P. & Friesen, W. (1975). *Unmasking the face: A guide to recognizing emotions from facial cues.* Englewood Cliffs, N.J.: Prentice-Hall, 1975

Freud, S. (1914). *The psychopathology of everyday life.* New York: Macmillan.

Fromm, E. (1946). *The art of loving.* New York: Harper & Row.

Maslow, A.(1968). *Toward a psychology of being.* New York: Van Nostrand.

Miller, G. F. (2001). *The mating mind: How sexual choice shaped the evolution of human behavior.* Vintage Anchor Publishing.

Zimbardo, P.(1990). *Shyness: What it is, what to do about it*, 2d ed. Reading, MA.: Addison-Wesley.

Films

Fire, 1996. Directed by Deepa Mehta.

Alive, 1993. Directed by Frank Marshall.

Touching The Void, 2004. Directed by Kevin MacDonald.

Web Sites

∞ *http://www.nationaleatingdisorders.org*—This web site gives information and offers resources concerning various forms of common eating disorders.

∞ *http://www.learner.org*—This web site supports *Discovering Psychology: Updated Edition* with a page for each video program featuring an "academic footnote" to further update the content of the videos. The site also offers four special interactive features as well as an extensive webography.

UNIT 13

THE MIND AWAKE AND ASLEEP

One of the most adventurous things left us is to go to bed.
For no one can lay band on our dreams.

E.V. Lucas

Unit 13 describes how psychologists investigate the nature of sleeping, dreaming, and altered states of conscious awareness. It also explores the ways we use consciousness to interpret, analyze, even change our behavior.

Objectives

After viewing the program and completing the reading assignment, you should be able to:

1.   Describe the functions of consciousness.

2.   Describe the different levels of consciousness and the kinds of processing that occur at each level.

3.   Define *circadian rhythms* and describe their relation to the 24-hour day cycle.

4.   Describe the stages of sleep.

5.   Identify the major sleep disorders and the effects of sleep deprivation.

6.   Discuss the difference between night dreaming and day dreaming, and describe lucid dreaming.

7.   Explain Freud's theory of dreaming and contrast it with the Hobson-McCarley theory and the information-processing theory.

8.   Give examples of the difference between a dream's manifest content and latent content.

9.   Describe the issues concerning sleep that will arise as people's lives become more driven and as world travel becomes easier.

Reading Assignment

After viewing Program 13, read pages 135-162 in *Psychology and Life*. This textbook reading covers Units 13 and 14.

Key People and Terms

As you watch the program and read the assignment, pay particular attention to these people and terms. People and terms defined in the text will be found on the given page numbers.

addiction (152)

circadian rhythm (141)

consciousness (136)

dream work (147)

experience-sampling method (138)

hallucinations (153)

hypnosis (149)

hypnotizability (149)

insomnia (145)

latent content (147)

lucid dreaming (148)

manifest content (147)

meditation (151)

narcolepsy (146)

nonconscious (137)

non-REM (NREM) sleep (142)

physiological dependence (152)

preconscious memories (137)

psychoactive drugs (152)

psychological dependence (152)

rapid eye movement (REM) (142)

sleep apnea (146)

somnambulism (146)

think-aloud protocols (138)

tolerance (152)

William Domhoff (148)

Sigmund Freud (137)

J. Allan Hobson (143, 148)

Stephen LaBerge (148)

Robert McCarley (148)

Barbara Tedlock (147)

The following term and person are referred to in Program 13 but are not introduced in the text.

∞ *hypnagogic state*—a period of reverie at the onset of the sleeping state.

∞ *Ernest Hartmann*—an expert on sleep who believes that it serves a restorative function.

Program Summary

Throughout the day, we experience changes in our biological processes and states of consciousness. Body temperature, blood pressure, pulse rate, blood sugar, and hormone levels fluctuate over the course of a day. As we will see in Program 13, these fluctuations affect our moods, motivations, energy level, and performance.

We are rarely aware of our body's automatic "housekeeping" functions. Nor are we aware of processing sensory input. But we are able to walk down the street without bumping into things because our brains automatically estimate distances and detect obstacles. Once we have mastered the routine tasks, we no longer need to direct and monitor our efforts.

Just as some cognitive psychologists use the metaphor of the computer to describe human cognition, William James used the stream, with its constantly changing flow, to explain the concept of consciousness. He also noted that the mind is selective and is able to reduce the continual bombardment of sensory input, freeing us to attend to what is most relevant to our survival.

Interest in the conscious mind has waxed and waned throughout the history of psychology. In nineteenth-century Germany, Wilhelm Wundt conducted studies of consciousness. He looked for an underlying structure of the mind by performing experiments in which people reported their sensations. In the United States, Edward Titchener also explored the contents of consciousness—the "what" instead of the "how and why." This approach became known as *structuralism*. William James rejected the attempts of the structuralists to reduce consciousness to component parts, focusing instead on how the mind adapts to the environment. His approach was known as *functionalism*.

Then, in the 1920s, a leading behaviorist named John B. Watson declared the study of consciousness worthless and called for an objective science that studied behavior. He influenced the focus of American psychology for the first half of the twentieth century.

The study of consciousness was reintroduced in the late 1950s by a new breed of cognitive psychologists who took an interest in how and why we pay attention to some things and not to others. One of them, British psychologist Donald Broadbent, demonstrated that our attention has a limited capacity.

Further research showed the selective aspects of attention. For example, if someone mentions your name across a crowded, noisy room, it will probably catch your attention, whereas you probably wouldn't notice other names or words that were being spoken. This demonstrates mental activity at a preconscious level. Just outside of conscious awareness, ideas and feelings that are stored in memory and external stimuli are continuously processed or filtered.

Another state of consciousness is daydreaming. Although some people consider daydreaming a waste of time, psychologists believe daydreams are quite useful. They can be a source of creativity, a way of coping with problems and overcoming boredom, and a way of stimulating the brain.

In contrast, sleep helps reduce stimulation. But until the first half of this century, we knew relatively little about it. In 1937, research revealed that brain waves change in form during the entire sleep cycle. In the early 1950s, studies led to the discovery of rapid eye movements, known as *REM*. When REM was limited to dreaming, researchers had a reasonably objective index of the dream.

But what do dreams tell us about ourselves and our world? Freud claimed that they revealed the presence of deep secrets buried in the unconscious and that dreams protected the dreamer from disturbing wishes and thoughts. He believed that dreams were the key to understanding unconscious sexual and aggressive desires and fears.

Researchers Alan Hobson and Robert McCarley explain the controversial theory that dreams arise from spontaneous discharges of electrical impulses in the brain stem. They assert that REM sleep promotes brain development and does not have a psychological purpose. The electrical discharges activate the memories that appear in dreams as coherent images, but the psychological meaning is added afterward by the dreamer.

The middle view is that dreams are the result of the interplay of the physiological triggering of brain activity and the psychological function of its imaginative, interpretative parts. Electrical impulses activate concepts stored in memory, and the cerebral cortex helps to shape recall.

Stephen LaBerge of Stanford University explores the power of the cerebral cortex to influence dreamers. He trains his study participants to report aloud their dreams without waking. They can also be given suggestions for directing their dreams. Some people claim this can enhance creativity and control of the unconscious, while others object, because such directed dreaming tampers with the unconscious. Psychologists find it fascinating, because it represents a way of intentionally altering consciousness.

Program Review Questions

NOTE: Review Questions for Units 13 and 14 are provided in Unit 14.

Questions to Consider

1. Donald Broadbent conceived of attention as a selective filter that acts like a tuner on a radio, selecting one message from all the others. According to Broadbent, the unattended sensory information is sent to a buffer, where it either receives attention and gets processed or is ignored and lost. How is this buffer similar to the concept of the sensory memory? What role might it play in subliminal perception?

2. What are the benefits and drawbacks of mindlessness?

3. Consider the role of culture and language in structuring consciousness or focused perception. In what ways is awareness culturally determined?

4. How do you experience REM rebound effects when you have been deprived of sleep? Do you begin dreaming soon after falling asleep? Do you experience vivid visual imagery when you are awake?

Optional Activities

1. Keep a pad and pencil by your bed and start a dream journal. Just before you fall asleep, remind yourself to remember your dreams. Immediately upon awakening, record what you remember: images, actions, characters, emotions, events, and settings. Does your ability to recall your dreams improve over time? Does this change if you set your alarm for different times during the sleep cycle? Does your recall become more vivid or more organized? Can you shape your dreams by telling yourself at bedtime what you want to dream about?

2. Make a list of common examples of dissociation and divided consciousness. Do these examples support the concept of mini-minds or different areas of the brain operating

independently? What other explanations might account for your ability to divide your consciousness?

Additional Resources

Books and Articles

Borbely, A. A., & Tononi, G. (2001). The quest for the essence of sleep. In G. M. Edelman and J.-P. Changeux (Eds.), *The brain.* New Brunswick, NJ: Transaction Publishers.

Cicogna, P., & Bosinelli, M. (2001). Consciousness during dreams. *Consciousness & Cognition: An International Journal. Special Issue, 10,* 26-41.

Coleman, R. (1986). *Wide awake at 3:00 A.M. By Choice or by chance?* New York: Freeman.

Domhoff, G. W. (2001). A new neurocognitive theory of dreams. *Dreaming: Journal of the Association for the study of dreams. Special Issue, 11,* 13-33.

Ellman, S. & Antrobus, J. (Eds.) (1991). *Mind in sleep: Psychology and psychophysiology.* New York: Wiley.

Gazzaniga, M., et al. (Ed.) (2000). *Mind matters: How brain and mind interact to create our conscious lives.* Boston: Houghton Mifflin.

Guezeldere, G., et al. (2000). Consciousness. In M. S. Gazzaniga et al. (Eds.), *The new cognitive neurosciences* (2nd ed.). Cambridge, MA: MIT Press.

Films

Fight Club, 1999. Directed by David Fincher. As the film progresses, your experience of reality will change.

Wizard of Oz, 1939. Directed by Victor Fleming. Almost the entire film exists inside a dream.

Web Sites

∞ *http://www.sleepnet.com/*—The Stanford School of Sleep Medicine's Web site provides, among other things, a test you can take to find out if you show symptoms of various kinds of sleep disorders. Although it is not intended as a source for medical advice, this site provides a wide range of information about sleep and sleep disorders.

∞ *http://www.learner.org*—This web site supports *Discovering Psychology: Updated Edition* with a page for each video program featuring an "academic footnote" to further update the content of the videos. The site also offers four special interactive features as well as an extensive webography.

UNIT 14

The mind is the most capricious of insects—flitting, fluttering.

Virginia Woolf

Unit 14 considers the evidence that our moods, behavior, and even our health are largely the result of multiple mental processes, many of which are out of conscious awareness. It also looks at some of the most dramatic phenomena in psychology, such as hypnosis and the division of human consciousness into "two minds" when the brain is split in half by surgical intervention.

Objectives

After viewing the program and completing the assigned reading, you should be able to:

1. Describe hypnotic techniques, experiences, and applications.

2. Explain the difference between psychological dependence and physical addiction.

3. Define the major drug categories, and compare the effects of specific drugs, such as stimulants and depressants.

4. List and describe the characteristics of the various extended states of consciousness, such as lucid dreaming, hypnosis, meditation, hallucinations, and drug use.

5. Describe the three levels of consciousness.

6. Explain the phenomenon of "discovered memory."

Reading Assignment

After viewing Program 14, review pages 135-162 in *Psychology and Life*.

Key People and Terms

To review textbook terms, refer to Key People and Terms in Unit 13.

The following term and people are referred to in Program 14 but are not defined in your text.

∞ *posthypnotic amnesia*—forgetting selected events by suggestion.

∞ *Michael Gazzaniga*—conducts research on the psychological study of split brain phenomena.

∞ *Jonathan Schooler*—studies discovered memories in people who had previously had no memory of major, traumatic events in their lives.

Program Summary

Is it possible to "know thyself?" Evidence suggests both that a lot of important mental activity occurs outside our conscious awareness and that unconscious experiences can significantly alter our moods, behavior, and health. This is the subject of Program 14.

In one experiment, patients under anesthesia were given negative and positive information about their conditions. Patients who received positive messages felt better, required less medication, and were discharged earlier than those who overheard upsetting news. This suggests that the unconscious brain processes stimuli and receives messages. Although the patients claimed not to be aware of what was said, some did recall the messages under hypnosis.

How does unconscious processing influence our thoughts, moods, and behavior? Neuroscientists theorize that our brains are organized into separate functional units. Each is designed to do a specific job, such as speaking or reading; there is really no single, all-powerful command center.

Since the earliest times, people have been fascinated with the idea that human behavior could be taken over by hidden identities or unknown parts of themselves. The transformation of identity is one of the major themes in world literature and myth; recall Robert Louis Stevenson's famous story, *The Strange Case of Dr. Jekyll and Mr. Hyde,* and Franz Kafka's *The Metamorphosis.*

We do know that there are many ways the mind can be transformed. Psychoactive drugs can change how the mind functions and how personality is expressed. Studies of different cultures reveal rituals and many other forms of altering consciousness, including drugs, fasting, and meditation.

According to Freud, our most traumatic feelings are bound and gagged in the unconscious. Unacceptable desires, urges, and painful memories are hidden by a process he called repression. Freud interpreted anxiety as the alarm that warns when these feelings are about to break through into consciousness. Dreams, errors, and slips of the tongue reveal some of these otherwise repressed aspects of unconscious activity.

Jonathan Schooler of the University of Pittsburgh has studied cases in which people suddenly become aware of previously unavailable memories. These "discovered memories" are often for major events in one's life, such as one involving sexual molestation or violence. Schooler finds that many of these memories can be confirmed by consulting other witnesses or documents, and he studies how such memories can be blocked from conscious awareness.

Hypnosis is another window into the unconscious. Under hypnosis, some people act unconsciously on ideas, thoughts, and feelings. Suggestions can direct behavior afterward, altering memory, the perception of pain, even influencing decisions about smoking and eating.

The idea that part of the mind can function separately is difficult for many people to accept. But we can't deny the evidence. Supporting data about the behavior of the divided brain come from studies of patients whose corpus callosum, the connecting nerves between the two hemispheres of the brain, has been cut to prevent epileptic seizures from spreading across both hemispheres. Although the behavior of these patients appears normal, tests of eye-hand coordination show that each hemisphere receives and processes only certain information. The right brain is better at solving perceptual problems, pattern recognition, and spatial relationships; the left excels in language and logical analysis (see figure on previous page).

Other research suggests that the left brain is the "social brain" and that each person's unique consciousness is a product of this interpretive left hemisphere. The idea that the brain has many semi-independent modules or highly specialized multiminds is supported by research with split-brain and brain lesion patients. Modularity has a real anatomical base.

Program Review Questions

1. Which of the following is an example of a circadian rhythm?

    a. eating three meals a day at approximately the same time
    b. experiencing alternate periods of REM and non-REM sleep
    c. having systematic changes in hormone levels during twenty-four hours
    d. having changes in fertility levels during a month

2. How normal is it to experience alternate states of consciousness?

    a. It happens to most people, mainly in times of stress.
    b. It is something we all experience every day.
    c. It is rare and generally indicates a mental disorder.
    d. It is common in childhood and becomes rarer with age.

3. In the program, the part of the brain that is identified as the "interior decorator" imposing order on experience is the

    a. pons.
    b. hippocampus.
    c. limbic system.
    d. cerebral cortex.

4. Which of the following is an example of the lower-level processing of sensory input that is nonconscious?

   a. recognizing a friend's face
   b. detecting edges
   c. working on an assembly line
   d. noticing something tastes good

5. Edward Titchener was the leader of structuralism in the United States. What aspect of the concept of consciousness interested him?

   a. the contents of consciousness
   b. the material repressed from conscious awareness
   c. the uniqueness of consciousness
   d. He viewed consciousness as a scientifically worthless concept.

6. In Donald Broadbent's research, what happened when people heard two stories but were asked to attend to only one?

   a. They comprehended both stories.
   b. They comprehended only the attended story.
   c. They wove bits of the unattended story into the attended story.
   d. They were not able to follow either story.

7. What is a positive function of daydreaming?

   a. It focuses attention on a task.
   b. It reduces demands made on the brain.
   c. It enables us to be mentally active when we are bored.
   d. It provides delta wave activity normally received only in sleep.

8. Ernest Hartmann points out the logic behind Shakespeare's description of sleep. According to Hartmann, a major function of sleep is that it allows the brain to

   a. process material too threatening to be dealt with consciously.
   b. integrate the day's events with previously learned material.
   c. make plans for the day ahead.
   d. discharge a buildup of electrical activity.

9. According to Freud, dreams are significant because they

   a. permit neurotransmitters to be regenerated.
   b. reveal unconscious fears and desires.
   c. forecast the future.
   d. supply a story line to patterns of electrical charges.

10. According to McCarley and Hobson's activation synthesis theory of dreams, what activates dreams?

    a. the needs of the dreamer's unconscious
    b. the sending of electrical charges to the forebrain
    c. the memories contained in the cerebral cortex
    d. the synthesis of chemicals needed for brain function

11. According to McCarley and Hobson, what is true about REM sleep?

    a. Adults spend more time in REM sleep than infants.
    b. REM sleep is an unnecessary physiological function.
    c. The random burst of brain activity occurs first, followed by the dreamer's attempt to make sense of it.
    d. The subconscious expresses its deepest desires during REM sleep.

12. In his work on lucid dreaming, why does LaBerge use a flashing light?

    a. so participants are consciously aware of their dream and can control it
    b. so participants can incorporate the light itself into their dream narrative
    c. so participants get feedback about where they are in the REM sleep cycle
    d. so measurements can be made of physiological response

13. In the experiment described in the program, patients under anesthesia were exposed to a positive or negative message. What effect did getting a positive message have?

    a. It meant less anesthesia was needed.
    b. It shortened patients' hospital stays.
    c. It created more positive attitudes toward surgery.
    d. Positive messages had no effect because patients were unaware of them.

14. Which part of the brain is responsible for conscious awareness?

    a. cerebral cortex
    b. brain stem
    c. limbic system
    d. hypothalamus

15. When societies around the world were studied, what proportion of them practiced some culturally patterned form of altering consciousness?

    a. practically none
    b. about a third
    c. about half
    d. the vast majority

16. Edward Tichener is to structuralism as William James is to

    a. introspection.
    b. functionalism.
    c. lucid dreaming.
    d. discovered memories.

17. According to Freud, how do we feel when painful memories or unacceptable urges threaten to break into consciousness?

    a. relieved
    b. guilty
    c. sad
    d. anxious

18. What are Freudian slips thought to reveal?

    a. what we have dreamed about
    b. how we really feel
    c. who we would like to be transformed into
    d. why we make certain choices

19. What happens if a hypnotized person who expects to smell cologne actually smells ammonia?

    a. The ammonia smell wakes him from the trance.
    b. He recognizes the ammonia smell, but he remains hypnotized.
    c. He interprets the ammonia smell as a musky cologne.
    d. He overgeneralizes and finds the cologne smells like ammonia.

20. All of the following appear to fluctuate based on circadian rhythm, *except*

    a. intelligence.
    b. hormone levels.
    c. blood pressure.
    d. body temperature.

21. Michael Gazzaniga has worked with split-brain, or "broken-brain," patients. What has this led him to believe about our individuality?

    a. It comes from an interpreter in the left hemisphere.
    b. It is an illusion based on our emotional needs.
    c. It derives from our unique set of independent mind-modules.
    d. It is located in the corpus callosum.

22. Consciousness performs all of the following functions, *except*

    a. filtering sensory data.
    b. enabling us to respond flexibly.
    c. allowing us to have a sense of our own mortality.
    d. guiding performance of highly routinized actions.

23. Which of the following people would have the strongest objection to the concept of consciousness?

    a. William James
    b. John Watson
    c. Edward Titchener
    d. Wilhelm Wundt

24. Instances in which people believe they have remembered long-forgotten traumatic events are known as

    a. repression.
    b. suppression.
    c. recovered memories.
    d. fugue states.

25. One of the most important techniques that psychologists commonly use to confirm the validity of a recovered memory is to

    a. have the subject recount the memory under hypnosis.
    b. subject the rememberer to a lie-detector test.
    c. count the number of details in the rememberer's story.
    d. collect confirming evidence from other people who knew about the event.

26. Sigmund Freud is to the unconscious as _____ is to discovered memories.

    a. B.F. Skinner
    b. Jonathan Schooler
    c. Michael Gazzaniga
    d. Stephen LaBerge

27. According to Freud, normal people banish undesirable memories from their conscious minds through

    a. repression.
    b. projection.
    c. anterograde amnesia.
    d. hysteria.

28. According to Freud, the "alarm" that signals that unconscious thoughts or memories are about to break loose to consciousness is

    a. sexual desire.
    b. lethargy.
    c. confusion.
    d. anxiety.

29. Which topic related to human consciousness is conveyed by the story of Dr. Jekyll and Mr. Hyde?

    a. witchcraft
    b. hypnosis
    c. identity transformation
    d. sleep disorders

30. Communication between the two hemispheres of the brain is disrupted when

    a. a person is in deep meditation.
    b. a person is in deep Freudian denial.
    c. a person has just recovered an early memory.
    d. the corpus callosum is severed.

31. What occurs about every ninety minutes throughout sleep?

    a. rapid eye movement
    b. rapid irregular changes in brain activity
    c. dreaming
    d. more than one of the above

Questions to Consider

1. Changes in perceptions, time sense, memory, feelings of self-control, and suggestibility are aspects of an altered state of consciousness. Would you consider illness, love, or grief to be altered states of consciousness?

2. Psychoactive drugs are only partially responsible for the changes in the drug taker's consciousness. Mental sets, expectations, and the context in which the drugs are taken can also have significant influences. What are the implications for alcohol and drug education and treatment?

3. Do you consider television or other electronic media to have mind-altering influence? What do they have in common with other mind-altering substances or experiences? Are children more susceptible to these effects than adults?

4. Do you think you could benefit from hypnosis or meditation? Do you believe you could easily enter these states? If someone finds it difficult to become hypnotized or to meditate, would you advise them that it is worth the effort of learning? And how would you suggest they learn?

Optional Activities

1. Use this visualization technique to achieve a state of relaxation and, perhaps, alter your consciousness. Select a quiet place where you won't be interrupted. Choose a scene in which you have been very relaxed. To help you create a good mental picture, recall all the sensations that enhance in you a feeling of deep calm. Focus on the scene for fifteen to thirty minutes. Practice this visualization exercise several times over a period of a few weeks. With practice, calling up the visual image may trigger a sensation of calm whenever you want it to.

2. Try to think of a time when you surprised yourself by having a very strong feeling in response to an incident that didn't seem to warrant such a strong response. Could nonconscious factors have played a role in your response? What did you think about your response at the time? What did you think about it later?

3. Go on the Internet and look up various cultures, religions, and communities that practice altered states of consciousness. See if you can develop any insights into what aspects of their art, social interaction, and values appear to be influenced by such practices.

Additional Resources

Books and Articles

Dennett, D. (1998). *Brainchildren: Essays on Designing Minds*, MIT Press.

Freud, S. (1923). *The ego and the id.* Edited by Joan Riviere, New York: Norton.

Kabat-Zinn. (1994). *Wherever you go, there you are*. New York: Hyperion.

Schooler, J., & Eich, E. (2000). Memory for emotional events. In E. Tulving, and F.I.M. Craik (Eds.), *The Oxford handbook of memory*. New York: Oxford University Press.

Films

Altered States, 1980. Directed by Ken Russell.

Awakenings, 1990. Directed by Penny Marshall.

Web Sites

∞ *http://www.hypnotherapysociety.com/*—Altered states of consciousness are often sought in order to use them toward some particular end. For example, the heightened suggestibility associated with hypnosis has led to the development of hypnotherapy. You can discover the techniques and practical uses of hypnotherapy at this site, provided by the Hypnotherapy Society of the United Kingdom.

∞ *http://www.meditationcenter.com/connect/mind.html*—This web site provides an introduction to the purpose and methods of mindfulness meditation.

∞ *http://www.learner.org*—This web site supports *Discovering Psychology: Updated Edition* with a page for each video program featuring an "academic footnote" to further update the content of the videos. The site also offers four special interactive features as well as an extensive webography.

UNIT 15

[There is a need] to discover that we are capable of solitary joy and having experienced it, know that we have touched the core of self.

Barbara Lazear Ascher

What makes each of us unique? What traits and experiences make *you*? Unit 15 describes how psychologists systematically study the origins and development of self-identity, self-esteem, and other aspects of our thoughts, feelings, and behaviors that make up our personalities.

Objectives

After viewing the television program and completing the assigned reading, you should be able to:

1. Define *personality.*

2. Compare type and trait theories of personality.

3. List and describe "The Big Five" dimensions of personality.

4. Describe Freud's theory of personality development and the role of the id, ego, and superego in the conscious self.

5. Describe how post-Freudian theories differ from Freudian theories.

6. Describe the major humanistic theories and their contribution.

7. Describe social learning and cognitive theories and their contribution.

8. List the five most important differences in assumptions about personality across theoretical perspectives.

9. Compare the value and accuracy of standardized and projective tests of personality.

Reading Assignment

After viewing Program 15, read pages 406-440 in *Psychology and Life.*

Key People and Terms

As you watch the program and read the assignment, pay particular attention to these people and terms. People and terms defined in the text will be found on the given page numbers.

analytic psychology (420)
anxiety (417)
archetype (419)
collective unconscious (419)
consistency paradox (412)
ego (417)
ego defense mechanisms (417)
five-factor model (410)
fixation (416)
id (417)
independent construals of self (430)
interdependent construals of self (430)
libido (415)
personality (407)
personality inventory (433)
personality types (407)
possible selves (428)
projective test (434)
psychic determinism (416)
psychobiography (422)
psychodynamic personality theories (414)
reciprocal determinism (425)
repression (417)
self-actualization (420)
self-concept (427)
self-efficacy (425)
self-esteem (428)
self-handicapping (429)
shyness (415)
social intelligence (426)
superego (417)
traits (408)
unconditional positive regard (420)
unconscious (416)

Alfred Adler (419)
Gordon Allport (409)
Albert Bandura (424)
Raymond Cattell (409)
Nancy Cantor (426)
Hans Eysenck (410)
Sigmund Freud (414)
Hippocrates (407)
Karen Horney (419)
William James (427)
Carl Jung (419)
Shinobu Kitiyama (430)
Hazel Markus (428)
Walter Mischel (423)
Henry Murray (435)
Carl Rogers (420)
Hermann Rorschach (435)
Frank Sulloway (408)

The following terms and people are referred to in Program 15 but are not discussed in the text.

∞ *reference standard*—a norm or model of behavior that we use to decide how to behave in a situation.

∞ *status transaction*—a form of interpersonal communication in which we establish relative degrees of social status and power.

∞ *Teresa Amabile*—studies the psychology of creativity.

∞ *Mark Snyder*—studies strategic self-presentation and behavioral confirmation

Program Summary

How do you know who you are? Are you the same person when you are alone as you are in public? Who is the real you? In Program 15, we'll find out how we develop our concept of self—the consciousness of our own identities.

Through the ages, philosophers have tried to solve the puzzle of identity—to explain the consistencies and differences in human behavior that result in individual character and personality. In 1890, William James differentiated three aspects of identity: our awareness of the world, our awareness of ourselves as thinkers, and our awareness of the impressions we make on others.

For much of the twentieth century, the concept of the self was considered too "fuzzy" for the behaviorists who dominated American psychology. Even Freud did not consider the conscious self to be as important as either our moral conscience or our primitive unconscious. Today, however, many psychologists are dedicated to explaining our needs, fears, wishes, decisions, and expectations in an attempt to understand how self-concept affects behavior and, conversely, how behavior influences our sense of self.

The humanist movement of the 1940s, led by Carl Rogers, concentrated on the conscious self, characterizing it as a striver for personal fulfillment. Rogers believed that a positive self-image enhanced personal development.

Other psychologists use the term *self-concept* to refer to an individual's awareness of a continuous identity. The self-concept shapes behavior by acting as a self-monitor and regulating behavior according to an inner standard. According to this approach, we organize our knowledge into clusters, or schemas, and make adjustments to match the way we think things ought to be. If our self-concept is good, we try to live up to our ideal standard. If it is bad, we behave and feel badly.

Still other psychologists theorize that we present ourselves so others will see us the way we see ourselves. We act and react to each other, creating and confirming the person we believe ourselves to be. Some research suggests that that's why depressed people are often treated as if they were inadequate and why happy people tend to elicit positive responses from others.

Shy people vividly illustrate this process. Typically, they feel inadequate and anticipate failure and rejection. When they get negative reactions, their self-doubts are reinforced. Their low self-esteem makes them anxious in situations in which they may be judged—in meetings, at parties, or in other social and business settings.

People who fear failure need to protect their self-esteem, so they develop strategies to avoid challenges. They also protect their self-image with cover-ups to avoid blaming themselves for failure. They tend to procrastinate, forget to show up for important appointments, even abuse alcohol or drugs to excuse poor performance or to dull the pain caused by it.

Although people sometimes handicap themselves, society can be a handicapper too. Racism, sexism, and social prejudice discourage and inhibit a positive self-image and good behavior. Consider the high rate of alcoholism and suicide among Native Americans and the perpetual despair and rage in our urban ghettos.

On a more hopeful note, another element of personality—the creative self—testifies to our ability to invent new realities. In every civilization, men and women have left their stamp of individuality on anything that can be shaped, decorated, colored, or rearranged. Just as Carl Rogers believed that people naturally move toward fulfillment, Alfred Adler has called this phenomenon our inner striving for superiority.

But social evaluation can undermine creativity. Researcher Teresa Amabile has found that children from ages seven to eleven were less creative when they expected their work to be judged by others. To be truly creative, people need a sense of self-esteem independent of social approval. They need the freedom to experience the world in new, unusual, and unconventional ways.

Hazel Markus argues that the very basis of one's self is, in fact, socially derived. Although we usually think of individuals creating and shaping culture, Markus argues that cultural ideas and cultural practices shape who we are, and shaping a person is a social endeavor. This *mutual constitution* of individual and culture can be seen in the artifacts of all societies.

Program Review Questions

1. What name did William James give to the part of the self that focuses on the images we create in the mind of others?

   a. the material self
   b. the spiritual self
   c. the social self
   d. the outer self

2. Gail is a toddler who is gradually separating from her mother. This process is called

   a. identification.
   b. individuation.
   c. self-presentation.
   d. self-consciousness.

3. In Freudian theory, the part of the person that acts as a police officer restraining drives and passions is called the

    a. superego.
    b. ego.
    c. id.
    d. libido.

4. Which statement reflects the humanistic view of the self, according to Carl Rogers?

    a. Our impulses are in constant conflict with society's demands.
    b. We have a capacity for self-direction and self-understanding.
    c. We form an image of ourselves that determines what we can do.
    d. Our views of ourselves are created by how people react to us.

5. When we characterize self-image as a schema, we mean that

    a. we use it to organize information about ourselves.
    b. other people see us in terms of the image we project.
    c. it is a good predictor of performance in specific situations.
    d. we rationalize our behavior to fit into an image.

6. In Albert Bandura's research, people were given the task of improving production at a model furniture factory. They performed best when they believed that performance

    a. depended on their intelligence.
    b. related mainly to how confident they felt.
    c. would be given a material reward.
    d. was based on learning an acquirable skill.

7. Which of the following behaviors signals low status in a status transaction?

    a. maintaining eye contact
    b. using complete sentences
    c. moving in slow, smooth way
    d. touching one's face or hair

8. According to the principles of behavioral confirmation, what reaction do people generally have to a person who is depressed?

    a. People sympathetically offer help to the person.
    b. People regard the person as inadequate.
    c. People act falsely cheerful to make the person happy.
    d. People treat a depressed person the same as anybody else.

9. What was referred to in the film as a type of psychological genocide?

    a. drugs
    b. falling emphasis on education
    c. prejudice
    d. immigration

10. What is the relevance of schemas to the self?

    a. We try to avoid schemas in constructing our sense of self.
    b. We organize our beliefs about ourselves in terms of schemas.
    c. Schemas are what makes us individuals.
    d. Schemas are always negative, since they underlie prejudice.

11. In Teresa Amabile's work on creativity, how did being in a competitive situation affect creativity?

    a. It reduced creativity.
    b. It increased creativity.
    c. Its effects varied depending on the person's innate creativity.
    d. There was no effect.

12. According to Hazel Markus, culture is what you

    a. think.
    b. see.
    c. do.
    d. hate.

13. The phrase, "mutual constitution," refers to which two components, according to Hazel Markus?

    a. parent and child
    b. art and scholarship
    c. religion and society
    d. self and culture

14. In which culture are you most likely to find a definition of the person as a part of the group?

    a. Japanese
    b. American
    c. Portuguese
    d. Russian

15. The high rate of alcoholism among Native Americans was cited as an example of

    a. individualism.
    b. social handicapping.
    c. mutual constitution.
    d. striving for superiority.

16. According to William James, which part of the self serves as our inner witness to outside events?

    a. the material self
    b. the spiritual self
    c. the social self
    d. the outer self

17. Of the following psychologists, who is considered to be the least optimistic about the human condition?

    a. Freud
    b. Adler
    c. Rogers
    d. Maslow

18. Which of the following refers to how capable we believe we are of mastering challenges?

    a. self-efficacy
    b. self-handicapping
    c. confirmatory behavior
    d. status transaction

19. Amabile is to creativity as _____ is to behavioral confirmation.

    a. Alfred Adler
    b. Patricia Ryan
    c. Mark Snyder
    d. Albert Bandura

20. Who is credited as being responsible for psychology's return to the self?

    a. William James
    b. B. F. Skinner
    c. Patricia Ryan
    d. Carl Rogers

Questions to Consider

1. Different kinds of standardized tests have been criticized over the years because they may not apply equally well to people of different genders, socioeconomic status, or cultural backgrounds. Speculate on what sorts of problems might arise when standardized personality tests (such as the MMPI-2) are used. Think about what sorts of items might lead to problems, and think about what sorts of consequences might arise from the use of a biased instrument.

2. How is Seligman's concept of pessimism related to shyness?

3. What are some of the positive and negative aspects of the id, according to Freud?

4. Do you have higher self-esteem in some situations than in others? How do different environments and conditions affect you? Do you think that self-esteem is constant or variable?

5. Compare the social skills of your friends and yourself to people who did not grow up with computers and the internet playing a central role in their lives. Do you see systematic differences in sociability, shyness, and apparent self-concept?

Optional Activities

1. How do you recognize extroverts and introverts? Observe people on television, in a public place, or at home. Rate their behavior on a continuum between the opposites of extrovert and introvert. How helpful is the distinction? Do these qualities seem to be a primary dimension of personality?

2. Describe yourself by highlighting your special abilities, admirable qualities, and accomplishments. Write a brief description of your parents, spouse, children, or a close friend. Consider how often you appreciate the positive aspects of your own or another's personality and how often you focus on the negatives. How does your focus affect your own self-esteem and your relationships?

3. Take some characteristic about yourself that you have never liked (e.g., the tendency to interrupt, or the tendency to become tongue-tied around people of higher status than you). Spend the next month seeing if you can completely rid yourself of that characteristic. If you are successful, how would you describe the shift? Was it a change in your personality, or was it a change in behavior despite the underlying traits that used to produce it?

4. Interview a new parent and find out how his or her attitudes and behavior toward small children have changed.

Additional Resources

Books and Articles

Bandura, A. (1997). *Self-Efficacy in Changing Societies*. Cambridge: Cambridge University Press.

Dweck, C.S. (1999). *Self-Theories: Their role in motivation, personality and development*. Philadelphia: Taylor and Francis/Psychology Press

Goleman, D.(1992). *Creative spirit*. New York: Dutton.

Green, Alan, (2003), *Celebrating diversity: Building self-esteem in today's multicultural classroom*, Netherlands: Kluwer Academic Publishers

Films

Single White Female, 1992. Directed by Barbet Schroeder.

Zelig, 1984. Directed by Woody Allen.

Web Sites

∞ *http://www.gires.org.uk/*—Home page of the Gender Identity Research & Education Society (GIRES). A lot of our sense of self derives from schema, and one of the most important is our gender schema. Organizations like GIRES address issues of gender identity for people who have adopted nontraditional gender schema. Because gender schema contribute in such a major way to self, adoption of gender identity belonging to the opposite sex can lead to serious social and mental challenges.

∞ *http://www.emory.edu/EDUCATION/mfp/bandurabio.html*—Web site for Albert Bandura of Stanford University. This Web site provides a history of Bandura's theoretical contributions, showing how the theory of self relates to other important areas in personality, social, and clinical psychology.

∞ *http://www.learner.org*—This web site supports *Discovering Psychology: Updated Edition* with a page for each video program featuring an "academic footnote" to further update the content of the videos. The site also offers four special interactive features as well as an extensive webography.

∞

UNIT 16

> *Intelligence is not something possessed once and for all. It is in constant process of forming, and its retention requires constant alertness in observing consequences, an open-minded will to learn and courage in readjustment.*
>
> John Dewey

Just as no two fingerprints are alike, no two people have the same set of abilities, aptitudes, interests, and talents. Unit 16 explains the tools psychologists use to measure these differences. It also describes the long-standing controversy over how to define intelligence and how IQ tests have been misused and misapplied.

Is it wise, accurate, or fair to reduce intelligence to a number? Researchers are currently debating the value of intelligence and personality tests.

Objectives

After viewing the television program and completing the assigned reading, you should be able to:

1. Define *assessment.*

2. Describe several ways to measure the reliability and validity of a psychological test.

3. Identify the contributions of Galton, Binet, Terman and Weschler to the science of measuring intelligence.

4. Explain how IQ is computed.

5. Summarize Howard Gardner's theory of multiple intelligences.

6. Describe the evidence for the genetic and environmental bases of intelligence.

7. List the four methodological techniques used to gather information on a person.

8. Discuss the links among intelligence, creativity, and madness.

9. Explain the function of vocational interest tests.

10. Discuss the controversies surrounding intelligence assessment.

Reading Assignment

After viewing Program 16, read pages 270-296 in *Psychology and Life*.

Key People and Terms

As you watch the program and read the assignment, pay particular attention to these people and terms. People and terms defined in the text will be found on the given page numbers.

chronological age (275)
creativity (288)
criterion validity (273)
crystallized intelligence (279)
divergent thinking (289)
emotional intelligence (281)
fluid intelligence (279)
formal assessment (272)
g (279)
heritability estimate (283)
intelligence (274)
intelligence quotient (IQ) (275)
internal consistency (272)
learning disorders (278)
mental age (275)
mental retardation (277)
norms (274)
parallel forms (272)
predictive validity (273)
psychological assessment (271)
psychometrics (279)
reliability (272)

split-half reliability (272)
standardization (274)
stereotype threat (287)
test-retest reliability (272)
validity (272)

Alfred Binet (274)
Raymond Cattell (279)
Sir Francis Galton (271)
Howard Gardner (281)
Henry Goddard (283)
Charles Spearman (279)
Claude Steele (287)
Robert Sternberg (279)
Lewis Terman (275)
David Wechsler (275)
Robert Weisberg (290)

The following person is used in Program 16 but is not described in the text.

∞ *W. Curtis Banks*—an expert on psychological testing.

Program Summary

From nursery school through college, in business and the military, tests are used to label and classify each of us. Information about our academic achievements and failures, personality traits, and mental health is collected in an effort to predict how we will perform in the classroom, on the job, or in society.

Defining and measuring intelligence is perhaps the best-known but most elusive goal of psychometricians, the scientists who specialize in psychological testing. Since the turn of the century, when the Englishman Sir Francis Galton devised a set of mental tests, there has been an ongoing debate about what intelligence is, how to measure it, and how much heredity and environment contribute to it.

In 1905, in France, Alfred Binet set out to replace teachers' subjective opinions with an objective way to identify children who needed special help in school. His procedure included testing children individually on various reasoning tasks, then comparing each child to the average performance of children in the same age group.

In 1916, Lewis Terman of Stanford University adapted Binet's test for American schools and introduced the concept of the intelligence quotient. Terman came to believe that intelligence was an inner quality reflecting inherited differences and an unchangeable aspect of a person's makeup.

Terman's test became popular in the United States. The time was ripe for an efficient and inexpensive way to test and categorize large numbers of children. There were millions of new immigrants to be educated and a flood of army recruits enlisting for service in World War I. Assessing mental ability seemed a good way to impose order on this social chaos. Many people accepted the idea that intelligence tests could identify special abilities. Test results seemed to support the idea that there were racial and ethnic differences in intelligence.

But critics protested that intelligence tests depended too much on language ability and could not measure the competencies of non-English speakers and young children. In 1939, David Wechsler developed test problems that did not depend on English skills, a major milestone in intelligence testing.

Psychological testing has become big business. The late William Curtis Banks, of Howard University, explained the criteria used to judge whether a test does what it is supposed to do. First, a test must predict what it was designed to predict. That is, it must be valid. If it helps to identify those who will get the highest grades in the future, then it is valid as a grade predictor. Second, the test must demonstrate over time that its results are consistent. Third, everyone taking or scoring the test must do it according to the same rules. But how objective are these tests? Are they the unbiased, objective assessment device that Binet had imagined?

Banks points out that tests and testing practices can be used to discriminate against minorities in school and in the workplace. Cultural biases in many tests overlook important differences in experience and only measure attributes, such as verbal ability or social conformity without acknowledging the importance of creativity, common sense, and other important skills. Some personnel screening tests are used to reject or exclude people although the tests have nothing to do with skills required for success on the job. The most serious misuse of tests is rooted in the mistaken belief that an intelligence test can somehow reveal basic unchanging qualities of mind and character. Some people have even used test results to claim that entire races are inferior.

In addition to challenging how tests are constructed and how results are used, psychologists define intelligence in different ways. Some psychometricians believe they are measuring a single ability or trait called intelligence. But recently, cognitive psychologists have provided alternative views on the subject. Howard Gardner of Harvard University theorizes that there are at least seven different kinds of abilities and that it is society or culture that decides the value of a particular ability (see figure 3). Western cultures prize verbal skills and logical thinking; in Bali, physical grace and musical talent are highly coveted skills.

Some neurologists completely bypass the complications of mind and culture. They measure brain waves to detect differences in how people react and adjust to surprises. They assume that the smart brain has characteristic reaction patterns. Whether these measures are valid and what purpose they serve is not yet known.

1. Linguistic ability

2. Logical-mathematical ability

3. Spatial ability—navigating in space; forming, transforming, and using mental images

4. Musical ability—perceiving and creating pitch patterns

5. Bodily-kinesthetic ability—skills of motor movement, coordination

6. Interpersonal ability—understanding others

7. Intrapersonal ability—understanding one's self, developing a sense of identity

Figure 3: Gardner's Seven Intelligences
According to cognitive psychologist Howard Gardner, intelligence can be identified as seven different classes of abilities, the value of which are culturally determined.

One of the more serious current controversies concerns "teaching for tests." Although students' scores can increase on standardized assessment measures if teachers concentrate on the skills and content that they know will be tested, it's not clear whether that is the optimal way to educate our children. One concern is that, although students may perform well on the assessment measure, they may not be very good at anything else. And this would render the test invalid.

Another very important concern is that of labeling. Claude Steele, of Stanford University, has discovered that the social aspects of one's situation may cause self-labelling that affects one's performance. For example, being reminded of the stereotype that girls are bad at math and being reminded that she is a girl may cause a student's math score to fall.

Intelligence seems to be similar to how Alfred Binet originally conceptualized it. It is a dynamic, complex cognitive construct. Because of this, its assessment can be very tricky. The controversies surrounding it will likely continue far into the future.

Program Review Questions

1. What is the goal of psychological assessment?

    a. to derive a theory of human cognition
    b. to see how people vary in ability, behavior, and personality
    c. to measure the stages of growth in intellectual abilities
    d. to diagnose psychological problems

2. You are taking a test in which you are asked to agree or disagree with statements, such as "I give up too easily when discussing things with others." Which test would this be?

    a. the Scholastic Aptitude Test
    b. the Rorschach test
    c. the Strong Interest Inventory
    d. the Minnesota Multiphasic Personality Inventory

3. What was Binet's aim in developing a measure of intelligence?

    a. to identify children in need of special help
    b. to show that intelligence was innate
    c. to weed out inferior children
    d. to provide an empirical basis for a theory of intelligence

4. How were the results of Binet's test expressed?

    a. in terms of general and specific factors
    b. as an intelligence quotient
    c. as a mental age related to a norm
    d. as a percentile score

5. What formula did Terman create to express intelligence?

    a. MA/CA = IQ
    b. MA □ CA = IQ
    c. CA/MA □ 100 = IQ
    d. MA/CA □ 100 = IQ

6. In 1939, David Wechsler designed a new intelligence test. What problem of its predecessors was the test designed to overcome?

    a. bias in favor of minority groups
    b. unreliable scores
    c. dependence on language
    d. norms based on a restricted population

7. A test for prospective firefighters has been shown to predict success on the job. Which statement about the test is true?

    a. the test is reliable.
    b. the test is valid.
    c. the test is standardized.
    d. the test is unbiased.

8. Cultural biases in tests can lead to the overvaluing of some attributes and the undervaluing of others. Which of the following is likely to be overvalued in the U.S.?

    a. common sense
    b. motivation
    c. creativity
    d. verbal ability

9. Imagine that anyone who wants a job as a hospital orderly has to take a test. The test is valid for its norm group, white men. Imagine a black woman is taking the test. Which statement about the woman's score is most likely to be accurate?

    a. It will accurately predict her job performance.
    b. It will be lower than that of white men.
    c. It may indicate she is not capable when she in fact is capable.
    d. It cannot indicate anything about her because there were no blacks or women in the norm group.

10. What new perspective did Howard Gardner introduce to the study of intelligence?

    a. He redefined intelligence as "practical intelligence."
    b. He expanded intelligence to include other types.
    c. He argued for a biological basis for describing intelligence in terms of brain waves.
    d. He argued that the term, *intelligence,* should be abolished.

11. Robert Sternberg has devised a test for managers. How does its prediction of success compare with predictions from a standard IQ test?

    a. They predict equally well and are not correlated.
    b. They predict equally well, probably because they are measuring the same thing.
    c. Sternberg's test predicts twice as well as IQ and is not correlated with IQ.
    d. Sternberg's test predicts twice as well as IQ and is moderately correlated with IQ.

12. The attempt by neuroscientists to find biologically based measures of intelligence rests on the assumption that intelligence involves

    a. multiple factors.
    b. cultural learning.
    c. speed of adaptation.
    d. high excitability.

13. Standardized intelligence tests typically

    a. overvalue verbal ability.
    b. give too much value to creative problem solving.
    c. are biased to give exceptionally high scores to people from other cultures.
    d. are the best available predictors of life success.

14. Which of these is a self-fulfilling prophesy that can be based on age, race, or gender?

    a. test-retest reliability
    b. stereotype threat
    c. crystallized intelligence
    d. criterion validity

15. The growing practice of "teaching for tests" creates the possibility of

    a. lessened ecological validity.
    b. eliminating stereotype threat.
    c. lowered reliability.
    d. eliminating genetic influences on intelligence.

16. Which of the following is an innovation in intelligence assessment that David Wechsler introduced?

    a. displaying physical coordination
    b. demonstrating social sensitivity
    c. producing appropriate verbal metaphors
    d. putting pictures in a logical sequence

17. William Curtis Banks argued for the importance of all of the following, *except*

    a. correlating intelligence measures with vocational success.
    b. ensuring validity of intelligence tests.
    c. being confident that our assessment measures are reliable.
    d. standardizing assessment measures with respect to the larger population.

18. Which is the most effective way to break the influence of stereotype threat?

    a. Assure the test-taker that the test cannot discriminate between members of their own group and members of other groups.
    b. Provide the test-taker with a visualization exercise ahead of time to enhance his or her self-esteem.
    c. Provide the test-taker with a very simple task beforehand in order to boost confidence.
    d. Suggest that the test-taker should try to make their minority group proud.

19. Stereotype threat requires that the test-taker

    a. believe in the stereotype.
    b. be of relatively high intelligence.
    c. know that others believe in the stereotype.
    d. be of relatively low intelligence.

20. What we have learned about intelligence over the years is that it is *not*

    a. complex.
    b. influenced by environment.
    c. a singular process.
    d. culturally defined.

Questions to Consider

1. Does evidence of a genetic basis for intelligence mean that intelligence is unchangeable?

2. What would happen if everyone knew everyone else's IQ scores? How might it affect decisions about whom to marry or hire?

3. Would you rather score high on a standardized test of intelligence or a test of creativity?

4. What are some of the ethical questions related to intelligence testing and psychological assessment?

5. Does it seem reasonable that you can score very high on one type of intelligence and very low on others? Does that change your view of what it means to be "intelligent?"

Optional Activities

1. Pick a special interest of yours, such as cooking, baseball, woodworking, dancing, or traveling. Design a test that includes both questions and tasks that would measure knowledge and ability in that area. How would you ensure the test's validity?

2. Consider the possibility that intelligence could be improved. Design a one-year plan to improve your intelligence. What would be the most important components of your plan? Would the plan you devised work equally well for someone else?

3. Talk to an elementary school teacher about his or her experience with children's intellectual development under different kinds of teaching conditions. In his or her view, is it a good idea to "teach to the test" when they know their students will be given standardized tests later on that will determine whether they are "advanced," "average," or "below average?" In his or her experience, what happens to students with respect to educational opportunities and attention after they are categorized in these different ways?

Additional Resources

Books and Articles

Fraser, S. (Ed.) (1995). *Bell curve wars: Race, intelligence and the failure of America.* New York: Basic Books.

Gardner, H. (1983). *Frames of mind: The theory of multiple intelligences.* New York: Basic Books.

Gould, S. J. (1981). *The mismeasure of man.* New York: Norton.

Herrnstein, R. & Murray, C. (1995). *The bell curve.* New York: Free Press.

Sternberg, R. & Grigorenko, E. (2001). *Dynamic testing: The nature & measurement of learning potential.* New York: Cambridge University Press.

Films

Stand and Deliver. Directed by Ramon Menendez, 1987.

Web Sites

∞ *http://www.ets.org/*—The Educational Testing Service probably played or will play an important role in your educational career. It is responsible for the SAT, the GRE, the Advanced Placement Tests, the Test of English as a Foreign Language, and many other standardized tests that are used to compare candidates for various kinds of programs. You can find out more about this company and how it develops its assessment instruments by visiting its Web site.

∞ *http://www.learner.org*—This web site supports *Discovering Psychology: Updated Edition* with a page for each video program featuring an "academic footnote" to further update the content of the videos. The site also offers four special interactive features as well as an extensive webography.

UNIT 17

Different though the sexes are, they intermix. In every human being a vacillation from one sex to the other takes place, and often it is only the clothes that keep the male or female likeness, while underneath the sex is the very opposite of what it is above.

Virginia Woolf

Unit 17 looks at the similarities and differences between the sexes resulting from the complex interaction of biological and social factors. It contrasts the universal differences in anatomy and physiology with those learned and cultural, and it reveals how roles are changing to reflect new values and psychological knowledge.

Objectives

After viewing the television program and completing the assigned readings, you should be able to:

1. Define and compare the difference among these terms: *sex, gender, gender identity,* and *gender role.*

2. Explain the role of pheromones in sexual arousal.

3. Describe evolutionary theory as it applies to sexual behavior.

4. Describe the similarities in and differences between males and females in the sexual response cycle and mating.

5. Summarize current research on homosexuality.

Reading Assignment

After viewing Program 17, read pages 327-329 and pages 350-357 in *Psychology and Life.*

Key People and Terms

As you watch the program and read the assignment, pay particular attention to these people and terms. People and terms defined in the text will be found on the given page numbers.

date rape (355)
parental investment (353)
sexual arousal (352)
sexual scripts (354)

David Buss (353)
Virginia Johnson (352)
Alfred Kinsey (354)
Eleanor Maccoby (329)
William Masters (352)

The following terms and person are referred to in the program but are not defined in the text.

∞ *androgynous*—having both masculine and feminine traits.

∞ *cognitive developmental theory*—the theory stating that children use male and female as fundamental categories and actively sex-type themselves to achieve cognitive consistency.

∞ *developmental strategies*—behaviors that have evolved to conform to the sex roles typical of the adult members of a species.

∞ *sex typing*—the psychological process by which boys and girls become masculine or feminine.

∞ *social learning theory*—the theory stating that children are socialized by observing role models and are rewarded or punished for behaving appropriately.

∞ *stereotype*—the belief that all members of a group share common traits.

∞ *Michael Meaney*—developmental neuroscientist who studies the interaction of biology and psychology in the development of sex differences.

Program Summary

From the first breath a baby takes, sex determines how he or she will be treated throughout life. Being male or female means we inhabit very different biological, psychological, and social environments. Program 17 looks at sex, the biologically based characteristic that distinguishes males from females, and gender, the cultural category that includes the psychological and social characteristics of being male or female.

From birth, life is full of gender messages and lessons that shape behavior. Boys and girls learn which behaviors are appropriate for their gender group and act accordingly. In our culture, they also dress differently, act differently, and often develop different interests and goals. These categories exist in the home, in school, in social situations, and in the workplace.

Although gender roles are often portrayed as polar opposites, psychologist Sandra Bem argues that people have both masculine and feminine characteristics, and, in fact, this blend of traits she calls psychological androgyny often results in greater behavioral adaptiveness.

Scientists have discovered that there are some universal behavioral differences between the sexes. Male children tend to engage in more rough play and gross motor activities. Female children are more likely to play mother, groom baby dolls, and engage in fine motor activities. The latter is true of people, as well as other animals.

Neuroscientist Michael Meaney explains that these sex differences in social play are evidence of how biology and psychology influence each other. Sex-role behaviors have evolved because different activities stimulate different brain regions. And the hormones affect the brain during prenatal development, causing sex-linked preferences to certain social activities. Another example of the interaction of biology and psychology in sex differences is physical health. Because men are more likely to drink, smoke, use weapons, and work in hazardous environments, they are more vulnerable to certain diseases, such as lung cancer, bronchitis, emphysema, and heart disease.

One example of sex-role behavior that has no biological basis is crying. It is acquired as part of the socialization process. Of course, both male and female babies cry. But as they grow, boys learn to hold back their tears while girls learn that crying is acceptable.

According to psychologist Jeanne Block, social gender messages affect the way children think about themselves and the world. Girls' activities are more supervised, structured, and restricted. They are raised to stay close to home, while boys are typically given more freedom to roam and discover the world.

But children also participate in shaping their own social environment. Eleanor Maccoby has studied how young boys and girls use sex as a basic category to sort themselves. In the classroom and on the playground, each group seems to have a distinct culture and style, including different language patterns. Gender identification serves as a powerful organizer of their social lives. Girls play house and boys play army. Girls play with dolls and boys play with trucks. These differences are apparent as early as nursery school.

There are positive and negative consequences to gender differences. Males have the freedom to innovate and explore, but their independence may cost them a sense of family intimacy or the security of belonging to a community. Females have the freedom to express their feelings and build a social support network, but they suffer social constraints on their intellectual and individual development. And a greater focus on their feelings and moods makes them more susceptible to depression.

Despite traditional gender stereotypes, researchers have never been able to link different social roles to innate sex differences. Any differences are more a matter of degree than a difference in kind. For example, in physical ability and sports, male and female performances overlap when their training is comparable.

It is important to recognize that our gender categories heavily influence our expectations, judgments, and behavior. These gender stereotypes narrow the options available to us. In fact, women and men are more similar than different in almost all psychological traits and abilities.

Program Review Questions

1. According to research by Zella Lurin and Jeffrey Rubin, the difference in the language parents use to describe their newborn sons or daughters is primarily a reflection of

    a. actual physical differences in the newborns.
    b. differences in the way the newborns behave.
    c. the way the hospital staff responds to the babies.
    d. the parents' expectations coloring their perceptions.

2. Which set of adjectives best characterizes the feminine gender role in the United States?

    a. gentle, emotional, dependent
    b. creative, intelligent, attractive
    c. aggressive, independent, dominant
    d. industrious, nurturing, ambitious

3. Which difference between the ways in which boys and girls play seems linked to sex hormones?

    a. Girls play with dolls.
    b. Boys engage in rough and tumble play.
    c. Boys play in larger groups than girls do.
    d. Girls build rooms, and boys build towers.

4. Michael Meaney attributes the differences in the behavior of male and female rats to the fact that these behaviors "feel good" to the animals. The reason for this is that the behaviors

    a. increase hormone production.
    b. prepare the organism for its life tasks.
    c. stimulate certain brain regions.
    d. fit the preferred pattern of motor activity.

5. How does the health of men compare with the health of women throughout the life cycle?

    a. Men are more vulnerable throughout the life cycle.
    b. Women are more vulnerable throughout the life cycle.
    c. Women are more vulnerable only during their childbearing years.
    d. There is no consistent sex difference in health.

6. Which learned behavior associated with the masculine gender role poses a health risk?

    a. having recessive genes
    b. relying on social networks
    c. being assertive
    d. drinking alcohol

7. What is the likeliest source of the behavioral difference between the sexes regarding crying?

    a. It is an innate difference.
    b. Initial innate differences are reinforced by parents.
    c. It is learned during the socialization process.
    d. We do not know the source.

8. What typically happens when a girl behaves in gender-inappropriate ways?

    a. She feels uncomfortable.
    b. She is praised.
    c. She is scolded.
    d. The behavior is not noticed.

9. According to Jeanne Block, the sociopsychological contexts for boys and girls tend to be different. One such difference is that the context for girls tends to be more

    a. home-centered.
    b. achievement-oriented.
    c. filled with risk.
    d. involved with same-sex peers.

10. According to Jeanne Block, the sociopsychological context typically provided to boys is

    a. less protective than for girls.
    b. more supervised than for girls.
    c. less likely to provide opportunities for inventing and discovering than for girls.
    d. more restricted in the network of friends they come into contact with.

11. What is one of the negative consequences of the masculine gender role?

    a. It makes men more vulnerable to depression.
    b. It imposes limits on intellectual development.
    c. It provides little sense of belonging.
    d. It encourages risk-taking behaviors.

12. According to Eleanor Maccoby, at about what age do children begin to prefer same-sex playmates?

    a. two years old
    b. three years old
    c. four years old
    d. five years old

13. Which statement about sex differences in psychological traits and abilities is best supported by research?

    a. There are no identifiable differences.
    b. The differences that exist are more a matter of degree than a difference in kind.
    c. The differences are the result of differences in brain chemistry and organization.
    d. The differences are arbitrary, because they are the result of social learning.

14. Which is true about gender roles in children?

    a. Girls tend to be the first to segregate themselves and play among members of their own gender.
    b. Girls are more aggressive in their physical behavior.
    c. Boys and girls will develop strong gender role stereotypes and will segregate themselves based on gender only if adults strongly encourage that.
    d. None of the above.

15. The term, *androgynous*, would best apply to which of the following people?

    a. a macho man who participates in body-building competitions
    b. a dainty woman who belongs to a sewing club
    c. a young boy who never talks in class because he feels shy
    d. a male rock star who wears heavy make-up, long hair, and feminine clothing.

16. According to the film, boys' greater propensity for rough-and-tumble play is likely the result of

    a. biological differences between boys and girls.
    b. different cultural treatment of boys and girls.
    c. both of the above.
    d. none of the above.

17. Boys tend to have _____ friends than girls and tend to be _____ intimate with their friends than girls are.

    a. more; more
    b. more; less
    c. less; more
    d. less; less

18. Because of the way we socialize our children, men tend to experience more freedom to _____, while women tend to experience more freedom to _____.

    a. explore; criticize
    b. withdraw; invent
    c. discover; express themselves
    d. express themselves; explore

19. Which of the following appears in children by six years of age?

    a. gender role-related depression
    b. sexual desire
    c. secondary sexual characteristics
    d. extreme gender-based segregation

20. Imagine that a set of parents avoids using gender role stereotypes in the house and that they encourage their son to play with other neighborhood children of both genders. What can we expect will happen?

    a. The boy will show no signs of gender role stereotypes and will be happy playing with both trucks and dolls.
    b. The boy will develop cooperative play patterns that are typical of little girls.
    c. Through social pressure, the boy will develop male gender role-stereotypic behavior.
    d. The boy will be about ten percent less competent in physical tasks than his male peers.

Questions to Consider

1. People organize their perceptions, expectations, and judgments around social schema and scripts. How are sexual scripts related to gender roles?

2. How does gender-typing influence perceptions?

3. How do young children show that they are aware of their gender identity?

4. Research suggests that androgynous people are better adjusted than those who are traditionally sex-role stereotyped. But critics contend that the masculine traits lead to higher self-esteem and better adjustment than a combination of masculine and feminine traits. How can having masculine traits enhance a woman's self-esteem?

5. Many women writers, including J. K. Rowling, have published under masculine-sounding or gender-ambiguous names. Does the sex of the writer make a difference? Should it?

6. If you tried to raise a child without exposing him or her to any gender-typing biases, how extensively would you need to change the social and physical environments that the child would normally encounter? How big of a job would this be? Could you ultimately be successful?

Optional Activity

1. Pick three close relatives or friends. How would your relationship with them be different if you were of the opposite sex? Which aspects of your personal identity and behavior would change? Which would stay the same?

Additional Resources

Books and Articles

Bem, S. (2001). *An unconventional family*. New Haven, CT: Yale University Press.

Buss, D.(1994). *The evolution of desire: Strategies of human mating*. New York: Basic Books.

Masters, W., Johnson, V., & Kolodny., R. (1997). *Human sexuality*. New York: Addison-Wesley.

Nicholson, I. A. M., (2001), *"Giving up maleness": Abraham Maslow, masculinity, and the boundaries of psychology.* Washington, D.C.: American Psychological Association/Educational Publishing Foundation.

Riger, S. (2000), *Transforming psychology: Gender in theory and practice. Oxford:* Oxford University Press

Gunnoe, J., & DiBaise, R, (2004), *Gender and culture differences in touching behavior.* Washington, D.C.: Heldref Publications.

Films

Boys Don't Cry. Directed by Kimberly Peirce, 2000.

Kiss of the Spider Woman. Directed by Hector Babenco, 1985.

Victor/Victoria. Directed by Blake Edwards, 1982.

Web Sites

∞ *http://www.kinseyinstitute.org/*—This is the Web site of the famous Kinsey Institute for Research in Sex, Gender, and Reproduction, named for the pioneering researcher in sexual behavior, Alfred Kinsey. They offer clinics, special events, and exhibitions. The home page includes links to other sexology sites, if you would like to explore these further.

∞ *http://www.rider.edu/~suler/psycyber/genderswap.html*—One of many sites that discuss interesting issues in gender identity and gender role-playing available in an internet age.

∞ *http://www.learner.org*—This web site supports *Discovering Psychology: Updated Edition* with a page for each video program featuring an "academic footnote" to further update the content of the videos. The site also offers four special interactive features as well as an extensive webography.

UNIT 18

As a man advances in life he gets what is better than admiration—judgment to estimate things at their own value.

Samuel Johnson

Thanks to growing scientific interest in the elderly, research on aging has replaced many myths and fears with facts. Unit 18 focuses on what scientists are learning about life cycle development as they look at how aging is affected by biology, environment, and lifestyle.

Objectives

After viewing the television program and completing the assigned readings, you should be able to:

1. Describe Erikson's eight psychosocial stages.

2. List the physical changes associated with aging.

3. Summarize the tasks of adolescence.

4. Discuss the central concerns of adulthood.

5. List the strengths and weaknesses of Kohlberg's cognitive approach to moral development, describe the controversies around the issues of gender and cultural differences in moral judgment, and discuss the distinction between moral behavior and moral judgment.

6. Identify cultural factors that place youth at risk for unhealthy development.

7. Discuss the importance of attachment in social development.

8. List the biological and social factors that can affect health and sexuality in later life.

9. Describe the risk factors for an elderly person in a nursing home.

Reading Assignment

After viewing Program 18, read pages 311-313 and 324-327 in *Psychology and Life*.

Key People and Terms

As you watch the program and read the assignment, pay particular attention to these people and terms. People and terms defined in the text will be found on the given page numbers.

attachment (319)
contact comfort (321)
imprinting (319)
intimacy (324)
parenting practices (321)
parenting style (320)
psychosocial stages (317)
socialization (319)

Mary Ainsworth (320)
Ruth Benedict (322)
John Bowlby (320)

Laura Carstensen (327)
Erik Erikson (317)
Anna Freud (317)
G. Stanley Hall (322)
Henry Harlow (321)
Konrad Lorenz (319)
Margaret Mead (322)
Alison Clarke-Stewart (323)
Steven Suomi (336)

The following term and people are referred to in Program 18 but are not introduced in the text.

∞ *senile dementia*—biochemical and neuronal changes in the brain that lead to a gradual reduction in mental efficiency.

∞ *Daniel Levinson*—studies the life course as a sequence of developmental experiences.

∞ *Pat Moore*—reporter who disguised herself as an eighty-five-year-old woman to find out more about the experience of being old in America.

∞ *Werner Schaie*—studies long-term effects of aging.

∞ *Sherry Willis*—uses new educational training methods to help the elderly function more effectively.

Program Summary

Until recently, many psychologists believed that there were few important developmental changes after adolescence. However, beginning in the 1950s, research on aging began to expose many myths about the extent of deterioration and despair among the elderly.

Psychologist Erik Erikson created the concept of life-cycle development. His framework describes eight psychosocial developmental stages in which individuals face specific conflicts that require balancing two opposite demands. Failure to resolve these conflicts can lead to isolation, feelings of unfulfillment, even despair (see Figure 4).

Dan Levinson, another developmental psychologist, studies the life course of adults as a sequence of developmental stages. He has identified age-linked developmental periods and transition periods that coincide with specific age ranges.

Approximate Age Crisis		Adequate Resolution	Inadequate Resolution
0–1½	Trust vs. mistrust	Basic sense of safety	Insecurity, anxiety
1½–3	Autonomy vs. self-doubt	Perception of self as agent capable of controlling own body and making things happen	Feeling of inadequacy to control events
3–6	Initiative vs. guilt	Confidence in oneself as initiator, creator	Feelings of lack of self-worth
6–puberty	Competence vs. inferiority	Adequacy in basic social and intellectual skills	Lack of self-confidence, feelings of failure
Adolescent	Identity vs. role confusion	Comfortable sense of self as a person	Sense of self as fragmented; shifting, unclear sense of self
Early adult	Intimacy vs. isolation	Capacity for closeness and commitment to another	Feeling of aloneness, separation; denial of need for closeness
Middle adult	Generativity vs. stagnation	Focus of concern beyond oneself to family, society, future generations	Self-indulgent concerns; lack of future orientation
Later adult	Ego-integrity vs. despair	Sense of wholeness, basic satisfaction with life	Feelings of futility, disappointment

Figure 4: Erikson's Psychosocial Stages
According to Erik Erikson, certain conflicts must be resolved at each stage in the life cycle in order for people to meet the demands of the next life stage. *(Based on Erikson, 1963; from Zimbardo* Psychology and Life, *Addison Wesley Longman., 16th ed., 2001.)*

Until we are old, most of us will have little understanding of what it is like to be old, and we rarely consider how society treats its elderly citizens. Social responses to the elderly range from indifference to fear to hostility. But although the processes of biological aging are inevitable, variables, such as life-style, diet, and exercise, can influence when and how fast they occur. Whether or not a person lives in a supportive community or has a sense of control over his or her life can also influence self-concept and attitude toward aging. Mental strategies may also increase an individual's self-worth and optimism.

Recent studies have shown that psychological deterioration is the exception, not the rule, of old age when there is no physical illness. Specialists have developed new strategic training methods to teach the elderly to recover earlier levels of inductive reasoning, spatial orientation, and attention.

Though some problems can be overcome with training, brain injury and dementia are often permanent disabilities with devastating consequences. But they occur much less frequently than people generally think. Contrary to another popular myth, depression and anxiety are not more common among the elderly. In fact, the elderly do not show an increase in stress-related disorders, despite an increase in stressful life events. As a group, they tend to be less lonely than college-aged people. And, if a person remains in good health, there is no decline in the ability to enjoy sex, either.

If the latest research findings are generally optimistic about the state of the elderly, why does the stereotype of deterioration and despair persist? It may be because of the availability heuristic. Dramatic or vivid negative images are overrepresented in our memory so that we get a falsely exaggerated picture, despite many examples of outstanding accomplishment and self-satisfaction among the elderly and despite general improvement in such skills as emotional problem solving and the processing of emotional complexity.

Laura Carstensen, of Stanford University, examines how aging differs from person to person and how the elderly become more selective in making the best life choices and rearranging the priorities in their social environment as they age.

There is also a very sad side of growing old in the United States. Our society, including our physical environment, does not always accommodate the physical limitations of the elderly, who may find walking, seeing, and hearing difficult. As the number of older people in the population increases, the percentage of those living in nursing homes will increase, too. In many nursing homes, unfortunately, people suffer significant losses and are subjected to conditions that accelerate their physical deterioration, even death.

As we learn more about the elderly, we discover that many of those problems can be ameliorated by education, training, and environmental changes. We can also work on improving our attitudes toward aging and the elderly.

The first step is dispelling the myths and changing our culture's negative stereotypes about the elderly. Second, it is important to redesign the environment and health care delivery systems to make them more accessible and accommodating to the needs of those with limitations. Third, an early intervention program that identifies those with psychological and behavioral problems and provides psychotherapy and behavioral therapy is needed.

As older people become an increasingly powerful force in the population, we can expect the "Graying of America" to bring about many positive changes.

Program Review Questions

1. How has research on life-span development changed our idea of human nature?

    a. We see development as a growth process of early life.
    b. We see that a longer life span creates problems for society.
    c. We view people as continuing to develop throughout life.
    d. We regard development as a hormonally based process.

2. What does the term *psychological adolescing* mean?

    a. coming into conflict with parents
    b. entering into a senile state
    c. being swept up by emotional conflicts
    d. developing to our full potential

3. What personal experience does Erik Erikson cite as leading to his redefinition of himself?

    a. having a religious conversion
    b. being an immigrant
    c. surviving a major illness
    d. getting married

4. According to Erikson, the young adult faces a conflict between

    a. isolation and intimacy.
    b. heterosexuality and homosexuality.
    c. autonomy and shame.
    d. wholeness and futility.

5. Which statement sounds most typical of someone in the throes of a midlife crisis?

    a. "I enjoy my connections with other people."
    b. "I'd like to run off to a desert island."
    c. "My work is my greatest source of satisfaction."
    d. "I accept the fact that I've made some bad decisions."

6. During which period of life does Erikson argue that people face the issue of wholeness vs. futility?

    a. old age
    b. middle adulthood
    c. adolescence
    d. toddlerhood

7. Daniel Levinson divides the life cycle into a series of eras. For which era is a major problem the hazard of being irrelevant?

    a. childhood
    b. early adulthood
    c. middle adulthood
    d. late adulthood

8. What has happened to the life expectancy of the average American over the past fifty years?

    a. It has lessened.
    b. It has remained stable.
    c. It has risen very slowly.
    d. It has nearly doubled.

9. When Pat Moore transformed herself into an eighty-five-year-old woman, she was surprised by the

    a. compassion with which others treated her.
    b. lack of facilities designed to accommodate the aged.
    c. extent of ageism in our society.
    d. poverty faced by many older people.

10. How do psychosomatic symptoms tend to change with age?

    a. People develop more of them.
    b. The ones people develop are more severe.
    c. They tend to be more related to sleeping and less related to eating.
    d. They are less common.

11. What has Sherry Willis found about the abilities of older people with regard to spatial orientation tasks?

    a. Irreversible decline is inevitable.
    b. Training programs yield improved skills.
    c. Skills can be maintained but not improved.
    d. If memory loss occurs, other skills deteriorate.

12. About what percent of people over age sixty-five suffer from senile dementia?

    a. five percent
    b. fifteen percent
    c. twenty-five percent
    d. forty percent

13. There is a(n) _____ in paranoid disorders with age largely because _____ .

    a. decrease; people have become more at peace with their lives.
    b. decrease; life becomes more sheltered and more predictable during retirement.
    c. increase; life becomes more chaotic during retirement.
    d. increase; of hearing and vision losses that make the world harder to process.

14. Assuming that a person remains healthy, what happens to the ability to derive sexual pleasure as one ages?

    a. It does not change.
    b. It gradually diminishes.
    c. It abruptly ceases.
    d. It depends on the availability of a suitable partner.

15. In general, how does the view of the elderly among the population at large compare with the actuality?

    a. It is more negative.
    b. It is more positive.
    c. It is generally accurate.
    d. It is more accurate for men than for women.

16. The results of the long-term study by Werner Schaie suggest that the people who do best in the later stages of life are people with

    a. high incomes.
    b. advanced degrees.
    c. flexible attitudes.
    d. large, close-knit families.

17. In nursing homes, the staff often behave in ways that treat the elderly like children. What is the effect of this treatment on most older people?

    a. It makes them feel more secure.
    b. It makes them behave in dependent, childlike ways.
    c. It increases their sense of autonomy and control.
    d. It improves their health by reducing their stress levels.

18. In which of the following areas do the elderly typically have an advantage over college students?

    a. The elderly are better able to climb stairs.
    b. The elderly generally have higher short-term memory capacity.
    c. The elderly are less lonely.
    d. The elderly have a more developed sense of humor.

19. Cognitive agility in the elderly

    a. is considered to have completely disappeared in the average eighty-five-year-old person.
    b. tends to improve radically in the years just before death.
    c. is one of the most predictable outcomes of the aging process.
    d. does not necessarily decline.

20. The elderly are particularly adept at processing information with

    a. emotional content.
    b. spatial content.
    c. mathematical content.
    d. folkloric content.

Questions to Consider

1. Define normal aging. How has science helped to differentiate between the normal processes of aging and the effects of illness?

2. What are the psychological themes unique to the middle years, sometimes called the midlife crisis?

3. How does cognitive capability change in the later adult years?

4. Is the increased divorce rate over the last few decades related to patterns of attachment and parent-child relationships developed early in life? How could such a hypothesis be tested?

5. How do social conditions help create the characteristics of adolescence and adulthood in the human life cycle?

6. How does becoming a parent help define the developmental stages of adulthood? What other sorts of roles might accomplish a similar end?

Optional Activities

1. At what age will you consider yourself to be "old?" Define your personal concept of old age, and describe what you expect your life to be like. Describe the health status, activities, satisfactions, and concerns you anticipate in your late adult years.

2. Keep track of the images of people over sixty, over seventy, and over eighty that you encounter during an average day. Notice how older adults are depicted in television programs and advertisements. What stereotypes persist? Is there evidence that images are changing?

3. Make a list of the labels used to describe people at various stages of life from infancy to old age. Which age group has the most labels? Compare the synonyms and modifiers for childhood to the words that help define adulthood. What might explain the difference?

4. Take a close look at your own generation. Identify ways in which that generation has attempted to distinguish itself as a sub-culture. Does the "retro" style serve to create any links to previous generations?

Additional Resources

Books and Articles

Carstensen, L.L., Charles, S.T., Isaacowitz, D. & Kennedy, Q. (2003). Life-span personality development and emotion. (pp. 726-746). In R.J. Davidson, K. Scherer & H.H. Goldsmith (Eds.), Handbook of Affective Sciences. Oxford: Oxford University Press.

Erikson, E. (1981). *The life cycle completed: A review.* New York: Norton.

Kübler-Ross, E. (1981). *Living with death and dying.* New York: Macmillan.

Moore, P. (1985). *Disguised.* Waco, TX: Word Books.

Whitbourne, S. K. (2000). *Adult development & aging: Biopsychosocial perspectives.* New York: John Wiley & Sons.

Films

The following popular films illustrate the diversity and vitality of older people:

Cocoon. Directed by Ron Howard, 1985.

Harold and Maude. Directed by Hal Ashby, 1972.

On Golden Pond. Directed by Mark Rydell, 1981.

The Trip to Bountiful. Directed by Peter Masterson, 1985.

The Whales of August. Directed by Lindsay Anderson, 1987.

Driving Miss Daisy. Directed by Bruce Beresford, 1989.

Web Sites

∞ *http://www.nih.gov/nia/*—Home page for the National Institute On Aging. This is a branch of the National Institutes of Health and is dedicated to improving the health and lifestyle of the elderly in America. The Institute is a primary national resource for training, information, funding, and research concerning the elderly.

∞ *http://www.aghe.org*—a membership organization of colleges and universities that offer education, training, and research programs in the field of aging. The purpose of AGHE is to foster the commitment of higher education to the field of aging through education, research, and public service.

∞ *http://www.learner.org*----This web site supports *Discovering Psychology: Updated Edition* with a page for each video program featuring an "academic footnote" to further update the content of the videos. The site also offers four special interactive features as well as an extensive webography.

UNIT 19

THE POWER OF THE SITUATION

This man is dangerous. He believes what he says.
Joseph Goebbels on Adolf Hitler

Is everyone capable of evil? Unit 19 investigates the social and situational forces that influence our individual and group behavior and how our beliefs can be manipulated by other people.

Objectives

After viewing Program 19 and completing the assigned reading, you should be able to:

1. Describe Philip Zimbardo's prison experiment and his conclusions about how people's behavior is constrained by social situations.

2. Describe Solomon Asch's experiment and his conclusions on the conditions that promote conformity.

3. Compare the major leadership styles in Lewin's experiment and describe their effects on each group of boys.

4. Describe Stanley Milgram's obedience experiments and his conclusions about conditions that promote blind obedience.

5. Describe the phenomenon of bystander intervention and how it reflects another aspect of situational forces.

6. Describe Serge Moscovici's work on the influence of the minority on the majority.

7. Discuss the Bennington study and how its findings might help develop strategies to promote more responsible decision making.

8. Discuss various factors that contribute to aggressive behavior.

9. Explain why experimental research is necessary for understanding social influences on behavior.

Reading Assignment

After viewing Program 19, read pages 508-548 in *Psychology and Life*.

Key People and Terms

As you watch the program and read the assignment, pay particular attention to these people and terms. People and terms defined in the text will be found on the given page numbers.

attitude (523)
bystander intervention (541)
cognitive dissonance (526)
compliance (527)
conformity (516)
elaboration likelihood model (525)
group dynamics (494)
group polarization (520)
groupthink (520)
informational influence (516)
norm crystallization (516)
normative influence (516)
persuasion (524)
prejudice (528)
reciprocity norm (527)
rules (513)
self-perception theory (527)
social categorization (529)
social norms (516)
social role (513)

Elliot Aronson (546)
Solomon Asch (516)
Daryl Bem (527)
John Darley (541)
Leon Festinger (526)
Irving Janis (520)
Bibb Latané (541)
Kurt Lewin (546)
Karl Lorenz (319)
Stanley Milgram (520)
Serge Moscovici (519)
Richard Nisbett (510)
Muzafer Sherif (531)

The following terms are referred to in Program 19 but are not introduced in the text.

∞ *autocratic*—governed by one person with unlimited power.

∞ *democratic*—practicing social equality.

∞ *laissez-faire*—allowing complete freedom, with little or no interference or guidance.

∞ *legitimate authority*—a form of power exercised by someone in a superior role such as a teacher or president.

Program Summary

During the 1930s and 1940s, evil seemed to have taken over much of the world. Millions of ordinary people became willing agents of fascist governments dedicated to genocide. The Holocaust took place more than fifty years ago, but accounts of massacres, terrorism, torture, and cruelty are still in the news every day. Are these horrors the work of sadists and madmen? Or are they perpetrated by ordinary people like us? Program 19 attempts to provide some answers to these questions.

While most of psychology tries to understand the individual, social psychology looks at human behavior within its broader social context. Efforts to understand how dictators mold the behavior of individuals gave birth to this field. Its practitioners began to analyze how leaders, groups, and culture shaped individual perceptions, attitudes, and actions.

One group of social psychologists began by studying the power of persuasive speeches. Another group looked at the nature of prejudice and the authoritarian personality. A third team, headed by Kurt Lewin, studied how leaders directly influence group dynamics. Lewin's team trained men to lead groups of boys, using one of three styles of leadership: autocratic, laissez-faire, and democratic. The results suggested that the leader's style, not personality, determined how the boys behaved.

Understanding conformity is another important goal of social psychologists. In a series of visual perception tests, Solomon Asch discovered that nearly a third of the participants were willing to go along with the majority's wrong judgment to avoid seeming "different."

Another researcher, Stanley Milgram, concluded that virtually all of us are capable of blind obedience to authority. In various versions of an experiment, hundreds of people—men and women, young and old—delivered what they believed were severe shocks to innocent people, rather than disobey authority. Milgram demonstrated that anyone has the capacity for evil if the situation is powerful enough.

Philip Zimbardo's Stanford prison experiment also demonstrated the effect of social situations on human behavior. In the study, college students were assigned to play the roles of either prison guards or prisoners. The situation was so powerful that these bright, healthy students actually took on the personalities of sadistic guards and despondent prisoners. In fact, the experiment, which was meant to last two weeks, had to be terminated after six days because of the extremely disturbing results.

Social influence can be positive as well. Researcher Tom Moriarity showed how apathy can be turned into action simply by asking for assistance from another person, even a total stranger.

Clearly, manipulating even small or seemingly minor aspects of social situations can bring out the best or worst in human nature. But most of us are too quick to blame people for their problems and to give them credit for their successes. We tend to overemphasize the importance of personality traits and to discount how easily people are influenced by the power of situations.

The experiments in Program 19 reveal much about human nature, but they also raise an important ethical question: How far can researchers go when a study calls for deceiving, manipulating, or humiliating research participants? Research goals and procedures must meet ethical standards to protect study participants from distress or unnecessary deception. They must also maintain the integrity of psychological research. Many of the experiments in this program would not be permitted under today's strict guidelines.

Program Review Questions

NOTE: Review Questions for Units 19 and 20 are provided in Unit 20.

Questions to Consider

1. Some psychologists have suggested that participants in Milgram's research must have suffered guilt and loss of dignity and self-esteem, although they were told later that they hadn't actually harmed the learner. Follow-up studies to the prison experiment revealed that the participants had not suffered long-term ill effects. What psychological principle might explain these outcomes? Did the value of the research outweigh the risks for participants? Was Milgram in a position to weigh the relative value and risks ahead of time? Would you participate in such experiments?

2. In emerging democracies like Iraq, people are faced with freedoms that they previously had not known. When the situation shifts so dramatically and being in a position of submission to power is suddenly removed, what sorts of new risks also emerge?

3. In Zimbardo's prison experiment, students were randomly assigned the role of guard or prisoner. All participants in the study were surprised when the true identities of the guards and prisoners were erased during the course of the experiment. Each of us plays many roles: child, spouse, friend, student, parent, boss, employee, citizen, consumer, sibling. Do you feel that any of the roles you play conflict with your "true identity?" How do you know what your true identity is?

4. Think about your own experiences in school, at work, and in group situations. Consider which factors bring out the best and worst in you. Recall and compare examples of how teachers, bosses, or leaders brought out positive and negative aspects of your personality.

5. What is the difference between respect for authority and blind obedience? How do you tell the difference? How would you explain the difference to a child?

6. Imagine that you are on vacation in New York City and that you have dropped your keys in the pond in Central Park. What could you do to counteract people's tendency toward diffusion of responsibility? Using what you know about social psychology, how might you increase the odds of actually getting people to help you?

Optional Activities

1. Architects and interior designers use specific elements—furnishings, lighting, color, seating arrangements—to encourage certain behaviors and to discourage others. Compare the comfort

level of chairs in various public places. Which chairs are designed to encourage lingering or to discourage loitering? What types of people use the spaces? What physical changes would influence who uses the space and how they behave there?

2. Norms of social behavior include "social distances" that we place between ourselves and friends, acquaintances, and strangers. Observe and compare the social distance you maintain between yourself and family members, friends, and strangers. Purposely change how close to them you would normally stand. Observe their responses. Does anyone mention it? Do others adjust their positions to achieve normal distances?

3. Observe the interactions of several different kinds of pairs of people: for example, a boss speaking with an employee, a minister speaking with a church member, a customer speaking with a clerk, or two close friends speaking with each other. Compare how those conversations differ (e.g., in terms of how often each has the floor, how often polite requests vs. direct requests are made, and how often each looks the other directly in the eye or physically touches the other person). If you can, observe the same person in many different kinds of situations in which they do or do not have the more powerful position. How does their behavior differ?

Additional Resources

Books and Articles

Aronson, E. (1997). Back to the future: Retrospective review of Leon Festinger's "A theory of cognitive dissonance." *The American Journal of Psychology, 110*, 127-137.

Aronson, E. (1998). *The social animal*. New York: W.H. Freeman and Co.
Festinger, L. (1983). *The human legacy*. New York: Columbia University Press.

Cialdini, R. B. (2000), *Influence: Science and practice*. 4th Edition. Boston: Allyn & Bacon.

Festinger, L., H. Riecken, & Schachter, S. (1956). *When prophecy fails*. Minneapolis: University of Minnesota Press.

Jones, M. (2001). *Social psychology of prejudice*. Upper Saddle River, NJ: Prentice Hall.

Kumkale, G., T., & Albarracin, Dolores. (2004) The Sleeper effect in persuasion: A meta-analytic review. *Psychological Bulletin. 130*, 143-172.

Lewin, K. (1951). *Field theory in social science*. New York: Harper.

Milgram, S. (1974). *Obedience to authority*. New York: Harper & Row.

Ross, L. & Nisbett, R. (1991). *The person and the situation: Perspectives of social psychology.* New York: McGraw-Hill.

Sanchez-Burks, J., Nisbett, R. E., & Ybarra, O. (2000). Cultural styles, relational schemas, and prejudice against out-groups. *Journal of Personality and Social Psychology, 79,* 174-189.

Films

Fog of War. Directed by Errol Morris, 2003.

Lacombe Lucien. Directed by Louis Malle, 1974.

Schindler's List. Directed by Steven Spielberg, 1993.

Trading Places. Directed by John Landis, 1983.

West Side Story. Directed by Robert Wise and Jerome Robbins, 1961.

Remember the Titans. Directed by Boaz Yakin, 2000.

Web Sites

∞ *http://www.psych.upenn.edu/sacsec/*—The Solomon Asch Center is dedicated to understanding and reducing ethnopolitical conflict. Social psychologists often find themselves addressing issues of worldwide and immediate importance. The psychologists at the Asch Center extend and put into practice all we know about the social psychological principles underlying prejudice and aggression. Armed with an understanding of how it starts and is perpetuated, we can begin to reduce conflict.

∞ *http://www.stanleymilgram.com*—A Web site dedicated to Stanley Milgram and his research, hosted by Thomas Blass. You can find out about the people, devices, and methods of the original studies, and you can learn interesting facts about Milgram's own scholarly history (including the fact that he never took a psychology course during his undergraduate career at Queens College).

∞ *http://www.learner.org*—This web site supports *Discovering Psychology: Updated Edition* with a page for each video program featuring an "academic footnote" to further update the content of the videos. The site also offers four special interactive features as well as an extensive webography.

UNIT 20

Everything that deceives may be said to enchant.

Plato

Unit 20 explores our subjective view of reality and how it influences social behavior. It reveals how your perceptions and reasoning ability can be influenced in positive and negative ways, and it increases our understanding of how psychological processes govern interpretation of reality.

Objectives

After viewing the television program and completing the assigned reading, you should be able to:

1. Explain the fundamental attribution error.

2. Describe attribution theory.

3. Explain self-perception theory.

4. Summarize Rosenthal's experiment that demonstrates the Pygmalion effect and explain its relation to self-fulfilling prophecies.

5. Describe the effect of cognitive dissonance on behavior and attitude change.

6. Describe the techniques used by cults to maintain control over their members.

Reading Assignment

After viewing Program 20, read pages 508-548 in *Psychology and Life.*

Key People and Terms

attitude (523)
attribution theory (510)
behavioral confirmation (530)
contact hypothesis (531)
covariation model (510)
fundamental attribution error (510)
in-group bias (529)
in-groups (529)
jigsaw classrooms (546-547)
out-group (529)
self-fulfilling prophecies (512)
self-serving bias (511)
social cognition (509)
social perception (509)
social psychology (509)
stereotypes (530)

Elliot Aronson (546)
Leon Festinger (526)
Fritz Heider (510)
Harold Kelley (510)
Thomas Pettigrew (531-532)
Robert Rosenthal (512)
Lee Ross (510)
Muzafer Sherif (531)
Mark Snyder (530)
Claude Steele (287)

To review additional textbook terms, refer to the Key People and Terms in Unit 19. The following terms and people are referred to in Program 20 but are not defined in the text.

∞ *cognitive control*—the power of beliefs to give meaning to a situation.

∞ *Pygmalion effect*—the effect of positive and negative expectations on behavior.

∞ *thought-stopping*—a technique employed by cults to suppress critical thinking by its members.

∞ *Elliot Aronson*—helped change the way students saw themselves and others in terms of cooperation and not competition through creating the "Jigsaw classroom" with *Alex Gonzalez*.

∞ *Jane Elliot*—conducted an experiment where she induced prejudice in third graders based on blue-eyed versus brown-eyed children.

∞ *Steven Hassan*—once a high-ranking member of the Sun Myung Moon Unification Church, he has devoted twenty-five years to understanding and counseling people on the manipulative techniques used by cults to recruit and retain their members.

Program Summary

Our beliefs can be so powerful that they can influence our perceptions and interpretation of reality. The power to create subjective realities is known to psychologists as cognitive control. When individuals and nations believe that their own perception is the only valid one, hostility and prejudice can result in an "us versus them" mentality.

Even our most minor differences can trigger prejudice, as we see in Jane Elliot's fourth-grade classroom experiment. Elliot demonstrated how easy it is to alter reality by providing an arbitrary reason to think in adversarial terms. She divided the children into two groups: the "inferior" brown-eyed students and the "superior" blue-eyed ones. This superficial difference provided the basis for institutionalizing discrimination. Those who were seen as inferior began to feel and act that way. And the blue-eyed students took on superior airs.

Another classroom experiment demonstrated that positive expectations can dramatically influence perceptions and behavior. When psychologist Robert Rosenthal and school principal Lenore Jacobson randomly labeled some students as academically superior, those students were given more attention, support, and praise by their teachers. They had created a climate of approval and acceptance that transformed ordinary kids into extraordinary students. The teachers' expectations became a self-fulfilling prophecy.

Both classroom experiments illustrate how social feedback influences the way we see ourselves and the way we behave. In another school, Elliot Aronson and Alex Gonzales created the "Jigsaw Classroom," a class divided into several expert groups that reported on specific topics. Aronson and Gonzales wanted to test their theory that cooperation, not competition, increases achievement and instills self-esteem in all students. The Jigsaw Classroom proved to be a great success, demonstrating that situational forces include not only objective characteristics, but also the participants' subjective realities.

Manipulating our perceptions is also the specialty of advertising professionals. They are experts in manipulating the decisions we make as consumers and voters. Their goal is to get us to say yes to their products without thinking or critically evaluating what we are doing.

Psychologist Robert Cialdini has studied tactics used by salespeople, fund-raisers, public relations practitioners, and advertisers. These tactics fall into categories, each governed by a basic psychological principle (see figure 5). Cialdini's research shows how easy it is for us to behave in conforming, prejudiced, or competitive ways. Social psychologists hope to use these same principles of influence to develop new strategies that will help people become more independent, more tolerant, and more cooperative.

Techniques of persuading, when taken to an extreme, can be used for dangerous purposes. Steven Hassan, once a high-ranking member of the Sun Myung Moon Unification Church, left the church and became a cult counselor. In his role, he has a unique understanding of how social psychological principles can be employed to maintain power over other people's behavior and thinking. The average person may assume that someone who joins a cult is particularly weak or flawed in some way, but Hassan argues that people who join cults are quite normal but have been caught at a particularly vulnerable period in their lives. In cults, people are not allowed to think for themselves. The cult leaders may use suggestive questioning, hypnosis, sleep deprivation, and thought-stopping techniques to maintain control over their members. This extreme sort of phenomenon shows how subjective reality can be dictated by the very powerful situation in which people find themselves.

---

1. *Commitment–Consistency*—Public commitment engages the need to be or appear consistent with and/or oneself.

2. *Authority–Credibility*—Conferring authority status on others by virtue of their roles and appearances simplifies information processing by increasing credibility.

3. *Obligation–Reciprocity*—When someone does us a favor or gives us a gift or compliment, a context of obligation is created which induces a social need to respond politely to reciprocate.

4. *Scarcity–Competition*—When anything is perceived as scarce, demand for it escalates, and individuals will compete against potential rivals to get it.

5. *Social Validation–Consensus*—We use the behavior of similar others or the majority as guidelines for what we do, especially in novel or ambiguous situations.

6. *Friendship–Liking*—Contexts that encourage the perception of familiarity and similarity increase liking and effectiveness.

Figure 5: Cialdini's Six Influence Strategies
Psychologist Robert Cialdini of Arizona State University spent three years examining advertising strategies and tactics as a professional in the field. He found six central categories of influence strategies, each based on a basic psychological principle.

Program Review Questions

1. What do social psychologists study?

   a. how people are influenced by other people
   b. how people act in different societies
   c. why some people are more socially successful than others
   d. what happens to isolated individuals

2. What precipitated Kurt Lewin's interest in leadership roles?

   a. the rise of social psychology
   b. the trial of Adolf Eichmann
   c. Hitler's ascent to power
   d. the creation of the United Nations after World War II

3. In Lewin's study, how did the boys behave when they had autocratic leaders?

    a. They had fun but got little accomplished.
    b. They were playful and did motivated, original work.
    c. They were hostile toward each other and got nothing done.
    d. They worked hard but acted aggressively toward each other.

4. In Solomon Asch's experiments, about what percent of participants went along with the group's obviously mistaken judgment at least once?

    a. seventy percent
    b. fifty percent
    c. thirty percent
    d. ninety percent

5. Before Stanley Milgram did his experiments on obedience, experts were asked to predict the results. The experts

    a. overestimated people's willingness to administer shocks.
    b. underestimated people's willingness to administer shocks.
    c. gave accurate estimates of people's behavior.
    d. believed most people would refuse to continue with the experiment.

6. Which light did Milgram's experiment shed on the behavior of citizens in Nazi Germany?

    a. Situational forces can bring about blind obedience.
    b. Personal traits of individuals are most important in determining behavior.
    c. Cultural factors unique to Germany account for the rise of the Nazis.
    d. Human beings enjoy being cruel when they have the opportunity.

7. Which statement most clearly reflects the fundamental attribution error?

    a. Everyone is entitled to good medical care.
    b. Ethical guidelines are essential to conducting responsible research.
    c. People who are unemployed are too lazy to work.
    d. Everyone who reads about the Milgram experiment is shocked by the results.

8. Why did the prison study conducted by Philip Zimbardo and his colleagues have to be called off?

    a. A review committee felt that it violated ethical guidelines.
    b. It consumed too much of the students' time.
    c. The main hypothesis was supported, so there was no need to continue.
    d. The situation that had been created was too dangerous to maintain.

9. How did Tom Moriarity get people on a beach to intervene during a robbery?

    a. by creating a human bond through a simple request
    b. by reminding people of their civic duty to turn in criminals
    c. by making the thief look less threatening
    d. by providing a model of responsible behavior

10. Which leadership style tends to produce hard work when the leader is watching but much less cooperation when the leader is absent?

    a. authoritative
    b. autocratic
    c. democratic
    d. laissez-faire

11. Typically, people who participated in Milgram's study

    a. appeared to relish the opportunity to hurt someone else.
    b. objected but still obeyed.
    c. refused to continue and successfully stopped the experiment.
    d. came to recruit others into shocking the learner.

12. Psychologists refer to the power to create subjective realities as the power of

    a. social reinforcement.
    b. prejudice.
    c. cognitive control.
    d. the Pygmalion effect.

13. When Jane Elliot divided her classroom of third-graders into the inferior brown-eyed people and the superior blue-eyed students, what did she observe?

    a. The students were too young to understand what was expected.
    b. The students refused to behave badly toward their friends and classmates.
    c. The boys tended to go along with the categorization, but the girls did not.
    d. The blue-eyed students acted superior and were cruel to the brown-eyed students, who acted inferior.

14. In the research carried out by Robert Rosenthal and Lenore Jacobson, what caused the performance of some students to improve dramatically?

   a. Teachers were led to expect such improvement and so changed the way they treated these students.
   b. These students performed exceptionally well on a special test designed to predict improved performance.
   c. Teachers gave these students higher grades, because they knew the researchers were expecting the improvement.
   d. The students felt honored to be included in the experiment and so were motivated to improve.

15. Robert Rosenthal demonstrated the Pygmalion effect in the classroom by showing that teachers behave differently toward students for whom they have high expectations in all of the following ways, *except*

   a. by punishing them more for goofing off.
   b. by providing them with a warmer learning climate.
   c. by teaching more to them than to the other students.
   d. by providing more specific feedback when the student gives a wrong answer.

16. What happens to low-achieving students in the Jigsaw Classroom?

   a. They tend to fall further behind.
   b. They are given an opportunity to work at a lower level, thus increasing the chance of success.
   c. By becoming "experts," they improve their performance and their self-respect.
   d. By learning to compete more aggressively, they become more actively involved in their own learning.

17. When Robert Cialdini cites the example of the Hare Krishnas' behavior in giving people at airports a flower or other small gift, he is illustrating the principle of

   a. commitment.
   b. reciprocity.
   c. scarcity.
   d. consensus.

18. Salesmen might make use of the principle of scarcity by

   a. filling shelves up with a product and encouraging consumers to stock up.
   b. claiming they have a hard time ordering the product.
   c. imposing a deadline by which the consumer must make a decision.
   d. being difficult to get in touch with over the phone.

19. Nancy is participating in a bike-a-thon next month and is having a large group of friends over to her house in order to drum up sponsorships for the event. She is capitalizing on the principle of

    a. liking.
    b. consensus.
    c. commitment.
    d. authority.

20. An appropriate motto for the principle of consensus would be

    a. "I've reasoned it through."
    b. "I am doing it of my own free will."
    c. "It will be over quickly."
    d. "Everyone else is doing it."

21. All of the following manipulation techniques were described as being used by cults to maintain control over their members, *except*

    a. sleep deprivation.
    b. suggestive questioning.
    c. thought-stopping.
    d. bribery.

22. Which of the following people would be most likely to advise that you try to understand a cult member by adopting his or her perspective?

    a. Hassan
    b. Festinger
    c. Aronson
    d. Cialdini

Questions to Consider

1. How can personal factors interact with social influences to affect behavior?

2. How is nationalism used to structure social reality? Does this become a more powerful force for people's attitudes and interaction during times of actual war or cold war than it is during times of peace? How might it be affected by phenomena like globalized economics and common languages across borders?

3. What do dissonance reduction, the self-serving bias, and the defense mechanism of rationalization all have in common?

4. How do programs on television construct a distorted reality for children? Has this problem gotten better or worse with the introduction of "reality TV?"

5. Many of the socially undesirable aspects of human behavior (e.g., violent crime, rudeness, apathy) seem to be more likely in urban than in suburban or rural environments. How can social psychology help to explain this phenomenon?

Optional Activities

1. Look for editorials, news stories, or political cartoons that portray an international situation. Which words, labels, and images promote "us versus them" thinking? How might someone with opposite views have written the articles or drawn the cartoons differently? Do you find that the tendency to present an "us versus them" view changes over time or that it differs across cultures?

2. Think of norms of proper dress or social behavior that you can violate. For example, what would happen if you wore shorts to a formal gathering? Or asked a stranger an extremely personal question? Or arrived at work in your bedroom slippers? Pay attention to your feelings as you think about carrying out these activities. What fears or inhibitions do you have? How likely is it that you could actually carry out these activities?

3. How are more modern attitudes toward education, such as Montessori-style education, similar to Lewin's democratic leaders? What sorts of outcomes, in school, in the home, and in the children's future social interactions, would you expect from such a teaching style?

Additional Resources

Books and Articles

Bless, H. (1999). *Subjective experience in social cognition and behavior.* Hillsdale, NJ: Erlbaum.

Cialdini, R. (2000) *Influence: Science and practice.* Boston: Allyn & Bacon.

Festinger, L. (1957). *A theory of cognitive dissonance.* Evanston, IL: Row Peterson.

Tabor, J. (1997). *Why Waco?* Berkeley, CA: University of California Press.

Films

Twelve Angry Men. Directed by Sidney Lumet, 1957.

Web Sites

∞ *http://www.freedomofmind.com*—Official Web Site for Steven Hassan's Freedom of Mind Resource Center. Visitors to the site can find information, resources for further study, and opportunities for group support.

∞ *http://www.heavensgate.com/*—Web site for Heaven's Gate. This group became known by the public when several members committed suicide as part of their plan to enter a higher plane of existence.

∞ *http://www.learner.org*—This web site supports *Discovering Psychology: Updated Edition* with a page for each video program featuring an "academic footnote" to further update the content of the videos. The site also offers four special interactive features as well as an extensive webography.

UNIT 21

Life begins on the other side of despair.

Jean-Paul Sartre

Unit 21 describes the major types of mental illnesses and some of the factors that influence them—both biological and psychological. It also reports on several approaches to classifying and treating mental illness and explains the difficulties of defining abnormal behavior.

Objectives

After viewing the television program and completing the assigned readings, you should be able to:

1. Identify the seven criteria commonly used to determine abnormal behavior.

2. Describe the *Diagnostic and Statistical Manual of Mental Disorders* and how it is used.

3. Explain how psychological disorders are classified.

4. List and describe the major types of psychological disorders.

5. List the biological and psychological approaches to studying the etiology of psychopathology.

6. Summarize the genetic and psychosocial research related to the origins of schizophrenia, including subtypes and etiology.

7. Identify sources of error in judgments of mental illness.

8. Discuss stigmas against mental illness and how they can be overcome.

Reading Assignment

After viewing Program 21, read pages 441-476 in *Psychology and Life*.

Key People and Terms

As you watch the program and read the assignment, pay particular attention to these people and terms. People and terms defined in the text will be found on the given page numbers.

abnormal psychology (442)

agoraphobia (450)

anxiety disorders (448)

bipolar disorder (455)

comorbidity (445)

delusions (465)

diathesis-stress hypothesis (469)

dissociative amnesia (463)

dissociative disorder (463)

dissociative identity disorder (DID) (463)

DSM-IV-TR (445)

etiology (446)

fear (450)

generalized anxiety disorder (448)

hallucinations (465)

insanity (446)

learned helplessness (456)

major depressive disorder (454)

manic episode (455)

mood disorder (453)

neurotic disorders (445)

obsessive-compulsive disorder (OCD) (451)

panic disorders (449)

personality disorders (459)

phobia (450)

posttraumatic stress disorder (PTSD) (451)

psychological diagnosis (444)

psychopathological functioning (442)

psychotic disorders (446)

schizophrenic disorders (465)

social phobia (450)

specific phobias (462)

stigma (472)

Aaron Beck (456)

Sigmund Freud (447)

Irving Gottesman (467)

Emil Kraepelin (444)

Susan Nolen-Hoeksema (457)

Philippe Pinel (444)

David Rosenhan (443)

Martin Seligman (456)

Thomas Szasz (444)

The following people are referred to in Program 21 but are not identified in the text:

∞ *Hans Strupp*—argues that psychological factors are of primary importance in the origin of schizophrenia.

∞ *Fuller Torrey*—studies the psychology and biology of schizophrenia.

Program Summary

Hearing voices, fear of public places, and pervasive feelings of inadequacy are just a few examples of how our perceptions, thoughts, and feelings can become distorted. Psychopathology, the subject of Program 21, is the study of these distortions, the mental disorders that affect personality and normal functioning.

One in every five Americans suffers from some form of mental disorder. It is difficult to measure the true extent of the problem because many mental disorders resemble typical everyday problems that we all experience. Mental health specialists trained to make these judgments rely on observations of behavior, diagnostic tests, complaints from the individual who is suffering, and complaints from others.

Mental illnesses need to be classified for many different reasons. When a problem is identified and classified, appropriate treatment can be planned. Mental health and stability can also have important legal implications. For example, a psychiatric diagnosis may determine whether a person is able to stand trial. Classification also aids research, furthering the study of pathology and the effectiveness of various treatments. And insurance companies need classification for economic reasons; they provide payments based on the type of mental disorder and its accepted treatment.

Years ago, people with psychological problems were lumped with society's outcasts and punished without compassion. In the eighteenth century, Philippe Pinel, a French physician, suggested that mental problems should be viewed as sickness. The treatment of people with mental disorders has changed and continues to improve—but not fast enough.

Psychiatrist Thomas Szasz argues that mental illness is a myth used as an excuse for authorities to repress people who violate social norms. It has been used by the Soviet Union to justify imprisoning social and political dissidents. It was also used to justify the treatment of slaves in the United States.

Stanford psychologist David Rosenhan explains that behavior is always interpreted within a context. In an experiment, he and seven other sane people gained admission to mental hospitals, having convinced authorities that they were suffering from hallucinations. Although they behaved normally once they were admitted, virtually everything they did was interpreted as abnormal. His experiment teaches us that virtually anyone can be diagnosed as mentally ill in certain situations.

But mental illness is not simply a social label. Anxiety disorders such as phobias, affective disorders such as depression or mania, and schizophrenia account for an estimated twenty million cases in the United States.

Freud labeled anxiety states *neuroses,* a term considered too general today. He believed that neurotic individuals, unaware of underlying infantile conflicts, showed a pattern of self-defeating behavior. According to his theory, the difference between neurotic and normal behavior is one of degree.

Although almost everyone has been depressed at one time or another, an individual with extreme and chronic depression may require hospitalization and drug therapy. In fact, depression accounts for most mental hospital admissions. But about eighty percent of those suffering from clinical depression never receive any treatment.

The label *psychosis* describes a class of disorders that are not on the continuum of normal behavior. People with psychotic disorders suffer from impaired perception, thinking, and emotional responses. Schizophrenic disorders, a major subclass, are characterized by a break with reality.

The two primary approaches to understanding schizophrenia are biological and psychological. As described by Fuller Torrey in the film, the biological approach traces the disorder to abnormal brain structure or functioning. The psychological approach assumes that the key to understanding lies in the patient's personal experiences, traumas, and conflicts.

Because schizophrenia and depression are so varied, most researchers believe that the disorders are the result of complex interactions between biological and psychosocial factors. Irving Gottesman, a leading expert on the genetics of schizophrenia, concludes that there is a genetic path for some forms of the disease. He has conducted research in collaboration with Fuller Torrey, using pairs of identical twins, one of whom is schizophrenic and the other who is not. They run a battery of tests, including SPECT analyses of the twins' brains, and have found some clear differences in the structure and functioning of normal and mentally ill brains. The results of their research also shed light on other psychosocial factors that may precipitate mental illness, such as family communication patterns and social isolation.

Other scientists, such as Teresa LaFromboise, are trying to understand the origins of psychopathology by looking at cultural factors. LaFramboise explains that because Native American values conflict with those that predominate in the culture around them, mental problems have become common in their culture.

Mental illness may be caused by a combination of physical and psychological variables, and its diagnosis may be biased by cultural or social factors. But the suffering of the afflicted is real.

Program Review Questions

1. Psychopathology is defined as the study of

    a. organic brain disease.
    b. perceptual and cognitive illusions.
    c. clinical measures of abnormal functioning.
    d. mental disorders.

2. What is the key criterion for identifying a person as having a mental disorder?

    a. The person has problems.
    b. The person's functioning is clearly abnormal.
    c. The person's ideas challenge the status quo.
    d. The person makes other people feel uncomfortable.

3. Which is true about mental disorders?

   a. They are extremely rare, with less than one-tenth of one percent of Americans suffering from any form of mental illness.
   b. They are not that uncommon, with about one-fifth of Americans suffering from some form of recently diagnosed mental disorder.
   c. The number of Americans with psychotic disorders fluctuates with the calendar, with more cases of psychosis during the weekends than during weekdays.
   d. The actions of people with mental disorders are unpredictable.

4. Fran is a mental health specialist who has a Ph.D. in psychology. She would be classified as a

   a. psychiatrist.
   b. clinical psychologist.
   c. social psychologist.
   d. psychoanalyst.

5. What happened after David Rosenhan and his colleagues were admitted to mental hospitals by pretending to have hallucinations and then behaved normally?

   a. Their sanity was quickly observed by the staff.
   b. It took several days for their deception to be realized.
   c. In most cases, the staff disagreed with each other about these "patients."
   d. Nobody ever detected their sanity.

6. Olivia is experiencing dizziness, muscle tightness, shaking, and tremors. She is feeling apprehensive. These symptoms most resemble those found in cases of

   a. anxiety disorders.
   b. affective disorders.
   c. psychoses.
   d. schizophrenia.

7. Agoraphobia is one of the most common phobias. What does a person with this condition fear?

   a. being at the top of a tall building
   b. going out in public
   c. being violently attacked
   d. In this condition, people have a generalized fear of experience.

8. When Freud studied patients with anxiety, he determined that their symptoms were caused by

    a. actual childhood abuse, both physical and sexual.
    b. imbalances in body chemistry.
    c. childhood conflicts that had been repressed.
    d. cognitive errors in the way patients viewed the world.

9. What happens to most people who are suffering from serious clinical depression?

    a. They commit suicide.
    b. They are hospitalized.
    c. They receive treatment outside a hospital.
    d. They receive no treatment at all.

10. People lose touch with reality in cases of

    a. neurosis but not psychosis.
    b. psychosis but not neurosis.
    c. both psychosis and neurosis.
    d. all psychoses and some neuroses.

11. When Hans Strupp speaks of the importance of psychological factors in schizophrenia, he specifically cites the role of

    a. feelings of inadequacy.
    b. antisocial personality.
    c. delayed development.
    d. early childhood experiences.

12. Irving Gottesman and Fuller Torrey have been studying twins to learn more about schizophrenia. If the brain of a twin with schizophrenia is compared with the brain of a normal twin, the former has

    a. less cerebrospinal fluid.
    b. larger ventricles.
    c. a larger left hemisphere.
    d. exactly the same configuration as the latter.

13. For Teresa LaFromboise, the major issue in the treatment of mental disorders among Native Americans is

    a. the prevalence of genetic disorders.
    b. alcohol's impact on family structure.
    c. the effect of imposing white American culture.
    d. isolation due to rural settings.

14. According to experts, what proportion of Americans suffer from some form of mental illness?

    a. about one-fifth
    b. less than one in ten thousand
    c. about two-thirds
    d. about one in a thousand

15. Which of the following people would argue that psychopathology is a myth?

    a. Philippe Pinel
    b. Thomas Szasz
    c. Teresa LaFromboise
    d. Sigmund Freud

16. What might a severe viral infection do to a woman who has a genetic predisposition toward schizophrenia?

    a. make her schizophrenic
    b. destroy the genetic marker and make her mentally more stable
    c. redirect the predisposition toward a different class of mental illness
    d. kill her with greater likelihood than if she did not have a predisposition toward mental illness

17. Which of the following has been nicknamed "the common cold of psychopathology" because of its frequency?

    a. phobia
    b. personality disorder
    c. schizophrenia
    d. depression

18. All of the following are typically true about schizophrenia, *except* that

    a. less than one-third improve with treatment.
    b. the people who have it are aware that they are mentally ill.
    c. about one percent of the world's total population is schizophrenic.
    d. it is associated with impaired thinking, emotion, and perception.

19. Who is credited as being the first to introduce the idea that insane people are ill?

    a. Sigmund Freud
    b. Jean Charcot
    c. Emil Kraepelin
    d. Philippe Pinel

20. Which of the following is characterized by boundless energy, optimism, and risk-taking behavior?

    a. a manic episode
    b. paranoid schizophrenia
    c. anxiety disorders
    d. depression

Questions to Consider

1. If a person is mentally ill and has violated the law, under what circumstances should he or she be considered responsible for the criminal actions? Under what circumstances should we consider the person to be rehabilitatable?

2. Why has the DSM been criticized?

3. Is homosexuality a deviant behavior?

4. Are standards for psychological health the same for men and women? Why are most patients women?

5. How can you tell whether your own behavior, anxieties, and moods are within normal limits or whether they signal mental illness?

Optional Activities

1. Collect the advice columns in the daily papers for a week or two (such as "Ann Landers" or "Dear Abby"). What kinds of problems do people write about? How often does the columnist refer people to a psychologist, psychiatrist, or other professional for counseling? Why do people write to an anonymous person for advice about their problems?

2. Ask several people (who are not psychology professionals) to define the terms *emotionally ill, mentally ill, and insane.* Ask them to describe behaviors that characterize each term. Do some terms indicate more extreme behavior than others? How do their definitions compare with the ones in your text? What can you conclude about the attitudes and understanding of mental illness shown by the people you interviewed?

3. Read through the DSM-IV-TR with an eye toward seeing that it is a statistically based manual. The behaviors that define mental illness fall on the same continuum as those that define mental health. Notice whether there are any classifications within the DSM-IV-TR for which some of the criteria are a partial match to you.

Additional Resources

Books and Articles

Adams, H. E., & Sutker, P. B. (Eds.) (2000). *Comprehensive handbook of psychopathology.* Dordrecht, The Netherlands: Kluwer Academic Publishers.

Laing, R.D. (1965). *The divided self.* Baltimore, MD: Penguin Books.

Noyes, R., & Hoehn-Saric, R. (1998). *The anxiety disorders.* Charlotte, NC: Baker & Taylor.

Peterson, C., Maier, S. & Seligman, M. (1993). *Learned helplessness.* New York: Oxford University Press.

Rosenhan, D. L.(1973). On being sane in insane places. *Science, 179,* 250-58.

Szasz, T. (1964). *The myth of mental illness.* New York: Harper & Row.

Vonnegut, M. (1975). *The Eden express.* New York: Praeger.

Woychuk, D. (1996). *Attorney for the damned: A lawyer's life with the criminally insane.* New York: Free Press.

Films

Best Boy. Directed by Ira Wohl, 1979.

I Never Promised You a Rose Garden. Directed by Anthony Page, 1977.

In Cold Blood. Directed by Richard Brooks, 1967.

One Flew over the Cuckoo's Nest. Directed by Milos Forman, 1975.

Rain Man. Directed by Barry Levinson, 1988.

Fisher King. Directed by Terry Gilliam, 1991.

Shine. Directed by Scott Hicks, 1996.

Silence of the Lambs. Directed by Jonathan Demme, 1991.

Web Sites

∞ *http://www.narsad.org/*—The National Alliance for Research on Schizophrenia and Depression is a non-profit organization devoted to supporting scientific research on brain and behavior disorders. You can find out about the research they fund and about the brain bases of various psychological disorders by visiting this site.

∞ *http://www.learner.org*—This web site supports *Discovering Psychology: Updated Edition* with a page for each video program featuring an "academic footnote" to further update the content of the videos. The site also offers four special interactive features as well as an extensive webography.

UNIT 22

To say that a particular psychiatric condition is incurable or irreversible is to say more about the state of our ignorance than about the state of the patient.

Milton Rokeach

Unit 22 looks at psychotherapy and therapists, the professionals trained to help us solve some of our most critical problems. You will learn about different approaches to the treatment of mental, emotional, and behavioral disorders and the kind of helping relationships that therapists provide.

Objectives

After viewing the television program and completing the assigned reading, you should be able to:

1. Describe early approaches to identifying and treating mental illness.

2. Identify the major approaches to psychotherapy.

3. Describe how psychiatrists, psychoanalysts, and clinical psychologists differ in their training and therapeutic orientations.

4. Identify the major features of psychoanalysis and explain the purposes of each.

5. Explain the goals of various behavior therapies.

6. Describe how counterconditioning can be used effectively to treat phobias.

7. Summarize the major rationale behind all types of cognitive therapy.

8. Describe the use of psychosurgery and electroconvulsive shock in the treatment of mental illness.

9. Identify the common forms of drug therapy and how they have changed the mental health system.

10. Summarize research on the effectiveness of psychotherapy.

11. Summarize the main features of client-centered therapy and Gestalt therapy and how these reflect the existential-humanistic perspective.

Reading Assignment

After viewing Program 22, read pages 477-507 in *Psychology and Life*.

Key People and Terms

As you watch the program and read the assignment, pay particular attention to these people and terms. People and terms defined in the text will be found on the given page numbers.

aversion therapy (487)
behavioral rehearsal (489)
behavior modification (484)
behavior therapy (484)
biomedical therapies (478)
catharsis (482)
client (479)
client-centered therapy (493)
clinical psychologist (479)
clinical social worker (479)
cognitive behavioral therapy (491)
cognitive therapy (491)
contingency management (487)
counseling psychologists (479)
counterconditioning (484)
countertransference (483)
dream analysis (483)
electroconvulsive therapy (ECT) (499)
exposure therapy (484)
free association (482)
Gestalt therapy (494)
human potential movement (493)
insight therapy (482)
meta-analysis (500)
participant modeling (489)
pastoral counselor (479)
patient (479)
placebo therapy (500)
prefrontal lobotomy (498)

psychiatrist (479)
psychoanalysis (482)
psychoanalyst (479)
psychopharmacology (496)
psychosurgery (498)
psychotherapy (478)
rational-emotive therapy (RET) (491)
repetitive transcranial magnetic
stimulation (rTMS) (499)
resistance (482)
social-learning therapy (488)
spontaneous remission effect (500)
systematic desensitization (485)
transference (483)

Albert Bandura (489)
Aaron Beck (491)
Albert Ellis (491)
Hans Eysenck (500)
Sigmund Freud (482)
Melanie Klein (483)
Egao Moniz (498)
Fritz Perls (494)
Philippe Pinel (480)
Carl Rogers (493)
Virginia Satir (495)
B.F. Skinner (487)
Henry Stack Sullivan (483)
Joseph Wolpe (485)

The following terms and people are referred to in Program 22 but are not introduced in the text.

∞ *biological biasing*—a genetic predisposition that increases the likelihood of getting a disorder with exposure to prolonged or intense stress.
∞ *genetic counseling*—counseling that advises a person about the probability of passing on defective genes to offspring.
∞ *time-limited dynamic psychotherapy*—a form of short-term therapy.
∞ *Enrico Jones*—investigates which type of treatment is best for which type of problem.
∞ *Hans Strupp*—psychodynamic therapist.

Program Summary

When you have a problem, to whom do you turn for comfort and advice? For most of us, the answer is a family member or a friend. But when problems cause prolonged or severe distress, friends and relatives may not have the interest or skills to help us resolve them. Then it may be time to seek professional help. Program 22 considers the range of treatments available, how they developed, and the types of problems they are effective in treating.

Therapies can be divided into two major groups: biomedical therapies, which focus on physical causes, and psychological therapies, which focus on helping us to change the way we think, feel, and behave.

The biomedical approach looks at mental disorders as the result of biochemical events that disrupt the delicate ecology of the mind. Psychiatrists and neurobiologists specialize in identifying disease states or syndromes believed to underlie the disorders.

One of the most radical biomedical treatments is psychosurgery. The prefrontal lobotomy, used only in extreme cases, cuts the nerve fibers connecting the brain's frontal lobes. Although the operation eliminates agitated schizophrenia or extreme compulsions, many people consider the cure to be worse than the illness. After a lobotomy, the patient cannot remember clearly or plan ahead and may no longer feel the normal range of emotions.

Electroconvulsive shock therapy, which alters the brain's electrical and chemical activity, is also controversial. Its proponents claim that for depressed patients who can't tolerate medication, it can be an effective treatment. But its misuse has prompted legal restrictions in many states.

The real revolution in biomedical therapy began in the 1950s with the use of tranquilizing and antipsychotic drugs. Drug therapies not only relieved suffering but also made psychotherapy possible. The danger with drugs, however, is that they may be misused by overworked or poorly trained hospital staff or by patients overmedicating themselves.

Another great revolution in biomedical therapy is currently underway. Scientists are already making significant breakthroughs in identifying genetic sources of schizophrenia, depression, and Alzheimer's disease. They are also learning how these genetic predispositions interact with environmental influences to affect the development of the disease.

Psychotherapists deal with psychological problems in very different ways. Although there are at least 250 different approaches, they can be divided into four general categories. Psychodynamic (or psychoanalytic) therapy sees all behavior as being driven by inner forces, including early life traumas and unresolved conflicts. Sigmund Freud developed this perspective around the turn of the century. In psychoanalysis (psychotherapy based on the psychodynamic approach), the patient's therapy is based on talking things out. Change comes from analyzing and resolving unconscious tensions by using various techniques, including free association, dream analysis, achieving insight and ultimately catharsis.

Over the years, psychoanalysts have modified Freud's techniques, but the goal has always been to change the patient's personality structure, not just to cure the symptoms. It can take years and requires a lot of participation by the patient. Shorter, time-limited, and less intensive treatment can also be effective in helping many patients.

Another approach, behavior therapy, ignores unconscious motives, the past, and personality; instead, it concentrates on problem behaviors. Behavior therapists apply principles of conditioning and reinforcement in an effort to eliminate symptoms and teach patients new and healthier behaviors.

Cognitive therapists teach their clients how to change problem attitudes, irrational beliefs, and negative thoughts that trigger anxiety or low self esteem. They also teach clients to change the way they perceive significant life events. In rational-emotive therapy, a form of cognitive therapy developed by Albert Ellis in the 1960s, the therapist teaches clients to recognize the "shoulds," "oughts," and "musts" that control them so that they can choose the life they wish to lead.

Program Review Questions

1. What are the two main approaches to therapies for mental disorders?

    a. the Freudian and the behavioral
    b. the client-centered and the patient-centered
    c. the biomedical and the psychological
    d. the chemical and the psychosomatic

2. The prefrontal lobotomy is a form of psychosurgery. Though no longer widely used, it was at one time used in cases in which a patient

    a. was an agitated schizophrenic.
    b. had committed a violent crime.
    c. showed little emotional response.
    d. had a disease of the thalamus.

3. Leti had electroconvulsive shock therapy a number of years ago. She is now suffering a side effect of that therapy. What is she most likely to be suffering from?

    a. tardive dyskinesia
    b. the loss of her ability to plan ahead
    c. depression
    d. memory loss

4. Vinnie suffers from manic-depressive disorder, but his mood swings are kept under control because he takes the drug

   a. chlorpromazine.
   b. lithium.
   c. Valium.
   d. tetracycline.

5. The Silverman family is receiving genetic counseling because a particular kind of mental retardation runs in their family. What is the purpose of such counseling?

   a. to explain the probability of passing on defective genes
   b. to help eliminate the attitudes of biological biasing
   c. to repair specific chromosomes
   d. to prescribe drugs that will keep problems from developing

6. In psychodynamic theory, what is the source of mental disorders?

   a. biochemical imbalances in the brain
   b. unresolved conflicts in childhood experiences
   c. the learning and reinforcement of nonproductive behaviors
   d. unreasonable attitudes, false beliefs, and unrealistic expectations

7. Imagine you are observing a therapy session in which a patient is lying on a couch, talking. The therapist is listening and asking occasional questions. What is most likely to be the therapist's goal?

   a. to determine which drug the patient should be given
   b. to change the symptoms that cause distress
   c. to explain how to change false ideas
   d. to help the patient develop insight

8. Rinaldo is a patient in psychotherapy. The therapist asks him to free associate. What would Rinaldo do?

   a. describe a dream
   b. release his feelings
   c. talk about anything that comes to mind
   d. understand the origin of his present guilt feelings

9. According to Hans Strupp, in what major way have psychodynamic therapies changed?

   a. Less emphasis is now placed on the ego.
   b. Patients no longer need to develop a relationship with the therapist.
   c. Shorter courses of treatment can be used.
   d. The concept of aggression has become more important.

10. In the program, a therapist helped a girl learn to control her epileptic seizures. What use did the therapist make of the pen?

    a. to record data
    b. to signal the onset of an attack
    c. to reduce the girl's fear
    d. to reinforce the correct reaction

11. When Albert Ellis discusses with the young woman her fear of hurting others, what point is he making?

    a. It is the belief system that creates the "hurt."
    b. Every normal person strives to achieve fulfillment.
    c. Developing a fear-reduction strategy will reduce the problem.
    d. It is the use of self-fulfilling prophecies that cause others to be hurt.

12. What point does Enrico Jones make about investigating the effectiveness of different therapies in treating depression?

    a. All therapies are equally effective.
    b. It is impossible to assess how effective any one therapy is.
    c. The job is complicated by the different types of depression.
    d. The most important variable is individual versus group therapy.

13. What is the most powerful anti-depressant available for patients who cannot tolerate drugs?

    a. genetic counseling
    b. electro-convulsive therapy
    c. psychoanalysis
    d. family therapy

14. All of the following appear to be true about the relation between depression and genetics, *except* that

    a. depression has been linked to a defect in chromosome #11.
    b. depression appears to cause genetic mutation.
    c. most people who show the genetic marker for depression do not exhibit depressive symptoms.
    d. genetic counseling allows families to plan and make choices based on their risk of mental illness.

15. For which class of mental illness would Chlorpromazine be prescribed?

    a. mood disorder
    b. psychosis
    c. personality disorder
    d. anxiety disorder

16. Which approach to psychotherapy emphasizes developing the ego?

    a. behavioral
    b. desensitization
    c. humanistic
    d. psychodynamic

17. In behavior modification therapies, the goal is to

    a. understand unconscious motivations.
    b. learn to love oneself unconditionally.
    c. change the symptoms of mental illness through reinforcement.
    d. modify the interpretations that one gives to life's events.

18. Which style of therapy has as its primary goal to make the client feel as fulfilled as possible?

    a. humanistic
    b. cognitive-behavioral
    c. Freudian
    d. social learning

19. Which psychologist introduced rational-emotive therapy?

    a. Carl Rogers
    b. Hans Strupp
    c. Albert Ellis
    d. Rollo May

20. Which type of client would be ideal for modern psychoanalytic therapy?

    a. someone who is smart, wealthy, and highly verbal
    b. someone who is reserved and violent
    c. someone who has a good sense of humor but takes herself seriously
    d. someone who grew up under stressful and economically deprived conditions

Questions to Consider

1. How do the placebo effect and the spontaneous remission effect make evaluating the success of therapy difficult?

2. Why might it be that behavioral and medical approaches to the same psychological problem can result in similar effects on the brain? Does this imply that in the future, effective behavioral treatments can be developed for cases that had been successful only through medical intervention?

3. How does someone decide on an appropriate therapy?

4. Can everyone benefit from psychotherapy, or do you think it is only for people with serious problems?

5. Why is there a stigma sometimes associated with seeking professional help for psychological problems? What might be some effective ways to change that?

6. Should we have any concerns about an overreliance on or abuse of drug therapies?

7. If you found that you had a specific phobia, would you be willing to undergo exposure therapy?

Optional Activities

1. Identify the services and resources available in your community in case you ever need emotional support in a crisis, want to seek therapy, or know someone who needs this information. How much do these services cost? Look for names of accredited professional therapists and counselors, support groups, hotlines, medical and educational services, and in church and community programs. Is it difficult to find information?

2. Do you have any self-defeating expectations? Do you feel that you might benefit from cognitive therapy? Write out statements of positive self-expectations. Then try to use them in situations in which you feel anxious or insecure. Do they have any effect?

3. Run an Internet search with the goal of finding social support groups for various psychological disorders. In what ways do they serve a therapeutic role? How are they helpful, and how might they potentially be counterproductive?

Additional Resources

Books and Articles

Leigh, I. W.(2004), *The power of psychotherapy*. Oxford: Oxford University Press

Nichols, M. P., & Schwartz, R. C. (2001). *Essentials of family therapy: Concepts & methods*. New York: Allyn & Bacon.

Taylor, S. (2000). *Understanding & treating panic disorder: Cognitive-behavioral approaches*. New York: John Wiley & Sons.

Films

Analyze This. Directed by Harold Ramis, 1998.

Analyze That. Directed by Harold Ramis, 2002.

Good Will Hunting. Directed by Gus Van Sant. 1997.

Web Sites

∞ *http://www.nacbt.org/*—Web site for the National Association of Cognitive-Behavioral Therapists. This therapy has become very popular for treating a range of disorders, including depression. You might be particularly interested in their on-line store, which offers books and therapeutic aids.

∞ *http://www.apa.org/*—The American Psychological Association has various divisions that are devoted to research, teaching, practice, and more. You might be particularly interested in exploring Divisions 12, 13, 17, 29, 37, 39, 42, 43, and 53, all of which focus on therapy.

∞ *http://www.learner.org*—This web site supports *Discovering Psychology: Updated Edition* with a page for each video program featuring an "academic footnote" to further update the content of the videos. The site also offers four special interactive features as well as an extensive webography.

UNIT 23

Suffering isn't enabling; recovery is.

Christian Barnard

A profound rethinking of the relationship between mind and body has led to an approach to health that assumes that mental and physical processes are constantly interacting. Unit 23 looks at what health psychologists know about the factors that increase our chances of becoming ill and what we can do to improve and maintain our health.

Objectives

After viewing the television program and completing the assigned readings, you should be able to:

1. Define *stress* and list the major sources of stress.

2. Describe the role of cognitive appraisal in stress.

3. Describe the major physiological stress reactions, including the general adaptation syndrome.

4. Explain the relationship between stress and illness.

5. Describe various kinds of events that can lead to psychological stress.

6. Describe the types of coping strategies in coping with stress.

7. Explain the mind-body relationship in terms of the biopsychosocial model of health and illness.

8. Describe the effects of self-disclosure on health.

9. Describe biofeedback, how it works, and its role in behavioral medicine.

10. Discuss how personality types relate to different health outcomes.

11. List some things you can do to reduce your stress level, promote your health, and protect yourself from job burnout.

Reading Assignment

After viewing Program 23, review pages 379-405 in *Psychology and Life.*

Key People and Terms

As you watch the program and read the assignment, pay particular attention to these people and terms. People and terms defined in the text will be found on the given page numbers.

acute stress (379)
AIDS (395)
anticipatory coping (388)
biofeedback (397)
biopsychosocial model (393)
chronic stress (379)
coping (387)
fight-or-flight response (379)
general adaptation syndrome (GAS) (382)
health (392)
health promotion (393)
health psychology (392)
HIV (395)
hozho (393)
job burnout (400)
life change units (LCU) (383)
perceived control (390)
posttraumatic stress disorder (PTSD) (385)
psychosomatic disorders (383)
relaxation response (396)

social support (390)
stress (379)
stress moderator variables (387)
stressor (379)
tend-and-befriend response (380)
Type A behavior pattern (399)
Type B behavior pattern (399)
wellness (393)
Thomas Coates (395)
Janet Kiecolt-Glaser (398)
Christina Maslach (400)
Donald Meichenbaum (389)
Neal Miller (397)
James Pennebaker (398)
Shelley Taylor (381)
Hans Selye (382)

The following terms and people are referred to in Program 23 but are not defined in the text.

∞ *psychic numbing*—being emotionally unaffected by an upsetting or alarming event.
∞ *psychogenic*—organic malfunction or tissue damage caused by anxiety, tension, or depression.
∞ *Richard Lazarus*—studies cognitive appraisal and the effects of stress.
∞ *Judith Rodin*—through her study of aging and mind-body relationships, Rodin investigates how subtle psychological factors bring about significant physiological change.

Program Summary

Noise, smoke, overcrowding, pollution, divorce, violence—how much can one person tolerate? Program 23 focuses on the work of health psychologists who study the social and environmental conditions that put people at risk for physical and psychological disorders.

The field of health psychology has grown out of a profound rethinking of the mind-body relationship. In contrast to the traditional biomedical model, health psychology is based on a new holistic approach that recognizes each person as a whole system in which emotional, cognitive, and physical processes constantly interact and affect one another.

Mind and body affect each other in a number of ways. Ulcers and hypertension can be caused by anxiety or depression. Headache and exhaustion may be signs of underlying tension. Evidence suggests that psychological factors may suppress or support the body's immune system. And psychological factors certainly contribute to smoking, drinking, and taking drugs.

Judith Rodin of Yale University studies mind-body relationships in the hope of finding ways to improve our health. Her work reveals the link between a person's sense of control and the functioning of the immune system. Rodin has discovered that psychological factors affect complex biological systems that, in turn, can affect health, fertility, and even the life span.

There are many other ways in which the mind can influence the body. Skin temperature, blood pressure, and muscle tension can be influenced by mere thinking. Psychologist Neal Miller discovered that the mind can have a powerful influence on biological systems. Using the psychology of biofeedback, he has helped many people learn to manage chronic pain and to lower their blood pressure.

Another important area of health psychology is stress control. When we feel stressed, our heart beats faster, and our blood pressure and blood sugar levels change. The physical state of alertness, called the fight-or-flight response, is the body's answer to anything that disturbs our equilibrium or taxes our ability to cope. Any change in our lives, good or bad, causes stress, because it demands an adjustment to new circumstances. But even life's little hassles, like sitting in traffic or searching endlessly for a parking space, can create stress (see Figure 6).

As stress accumulates, the chance of becoming ill increases. Some experts believe that stress contributes to more than half of all cases of disease.

The Canadian physician Hans Selye identified two types of stress reactions in animals. One type is a specific response to a specific stressor. Blood vessels constrict in response to cold, for example. The second type is a pattern of responses known as the general adaptation syndrome, which begins with the body's alarm reaction, mobilizing the body's ability to defend itself. In the resistance stage, hormonal secretions are activated, and the body seems to return to normal. Finally, the body may express a state of exhaustion caused by chronic stress.

Selye's work helped point out the role stress plays in the origin of many disorders. However, because he worked mainly with animals, he neglected one factor—how individuals perceive and interpret an event is often more important than the event itself. We know that what one person perceives as a stressful situation another person may consider as a challenge. Richard Lazarus calls this personalized perception of stress "cognitive appraisal."

As relative newcomers to the field, health psychologists help people develop strategies for coping with stress, preventing illness, and promoting good health. They teach behaviors that encourage wellness and help condition our bodies to be less vulnerable to disease.

One illness combines psychological and medical issues in an explosive way: AIDS. Thomas Coates is part of a health psychology team studying the AIDS epidemic from the psychological perspective. He calls for combining medical, epidemiological, psychological, and social knowledge to improve what we know about risk factors, incidence, and progression of the disease. Health psychologists, as scientists and advocates, study how psychological and social processes contribute to disease and then apply their knowledge to the prevention and treatment of illness. Coates emphasizes the need for messages that inform and motivate educational, social, and medical interventions at a variety of levels in the fight against AIDS. It is evident that the role of health psychologists will increase as we acknowledge the importance of psychological factors in health.

Life Event	Life-Change Units
Death of one's spouse	100
Divorce	73
Marital separation	65
Jail term	63
Death of a close family member	63
Personal injury or illness	53
Marriage	50
Being fired at work	47
Marital reconciliation	45
Retirement	45
Change in the health of a family member	44
Pregnancy	40
Sex difficulties	39
Gain of a new family member	39
Business readjustment	39
Change in one's financial state	38
Death of a close friend	37
Change to a different line of work	36
Change in number of arguments with one's spouse	35
Mortgage over $10,000*	31
Foreclosure of a mortgage or loan	30
Change in responsibilities at work	29
Son or daughter leaving home	29
Trouble with in-laws	29
Outstanding personal achievement	28
Wife beginning or stopping work	26
Beginning or ending school	26
Change in living conditions	25
Revision of personal habits	24
Trouble with one's boss	23
Change in work hours or conditions	20
Change in residence	20
Change in schools	20
Change in recreation	19

Life Event	Life-Change Units
Change in church activities	19
Change in social activities	18
Mortgage or loan of less than $10,000*	17
Change in sleeping habits	16
Change in number of family get-togethers	15
Change in eating habits	15
Vacation	13
Christmas	12
Minor violations of the law	11

Figure 6: Scale of Life-Change Units

Researchers Thomas Holmes and Richard Rahe assigned units to both positive and negative life changes. They found that people who accumulated more than 300 units within a year were at greater risk for illness. Source: Holmes and Rahe (1967).

*This figure was appropriate in 1967, when the Life-Change Units Scale was constructed. Today, sad to say, inflation has increased this number substantially.

Program Review Questions

1. How are the biopsychosocial model and the Navaho concept of *hozho* alike?

   a. Both are dualistic.
   b. Both assume individual responsibility for illness.
   c. Both represent holistic approaches to health.
   d. Both are several centuries old.

2. Dr. Wizanski told Thad that his illness was psychogenic. This means that

   a. Thad is not really sick.
   b. Thad's illness was caused by his psychological state.
   c. Thad has a psychological disorder, not a physical one.
   d. Thad's lifestyle puts him at risk.

3. Headaches, exhaustion, and weakness

   a. are not considered to be in the realm of health psychology.
   b. are considered to be psychological factors that lead to unhealthful behaviors.
   c. are usually unrelated to psychological factors.
   d. are considered to be symptoms of underlying tension and personal problems.

4. When Judith Rodin talks about "wet" connections to the immune system, she is referring to connections with the

   a. individual nerve cells.
   b. endocrine system.
   c. sensory receptors.
   d. skin.

5. What mind-body question is Judith Rodin investigating in her work with infertile couples?

    a. How do psychological factors affect fertility?
    b. Can infertility be cured by psychological counseling?
    c. What effect does infertility have on marital relationships?
    d. Can stress cause rejection of in vitro fertilization?

6. When Professor Zimbardo lowers his heart rate, he is demonstrating the process of

    a. mental relaxation.
    b. stress reduction.
    c. biofeedback.
    d. the general adaptation syndrome.

7. Psychologist Neal Miller uses the example of the blindfolded basketball player to explain

    a. the need for information to improve performance.
    b. how chance variations lead to evolutionary advantage.
    c. the correlation between life-change events and illness.
    d. how successive approximations can shape behavior.

8. In which area of health psychology has the most research been done?

    a. the definition of health
    b. stress
    c. biofeedback
    d. changes in lifestyle

9. Imagine a family is moving to a new and larger home in a safer neighborhood with better schools. Will this situation be a source of stress for the family?

    a. No, because the change is a positive one.
    b. No, because moving is not really stressful.
    c. Yes, because any change requires adjustment.
    d. Yes, because it provokes guilt that the family does not really deserve this good fortune.

10. Which response shows the stages of the general adaptation syndrome in the correct order?

    a. alarm reaction, exhaustion, resistance
    b. resistance, alarm reaction, exhaustion
    c. exhaustion, resistance, alarm reaction
    d. alarm reaction, resistance, exhaustion

11. What important factor in stress did Hans Selye *not* consider?

   a. the role of hormones in mobilizing the body's defenses
   b. the subjective interpretation of a stressor
   c. the length of exposure to a stressor
   d. the body's vulnerability to new stressors during the resistance stage

12. Today, the major causes of death in the United States are

   a. accidents.
   b. infectious diseases.
   c. sexually transmitted diseases.
   d. diseases related to lifestyle.

13. When Thomas Coates and his colleagues studying AIDS carry out interview studies, they want to gain information that will help them

   a. design interventions at a variety of levels.
   b. determine how effective mass media advertisements are.
   c. motivate AIDS victims to take good care of themselves.
   d. stop people from using intravenous drugs.

14. The body's best external defense against illness is the skin, while its best internal defense is

   a. the stomach.
   b. the heart.
   c. T-cells.
   d. the spinal cord.

15. In which stage of the general adaptation syndrome are the pituitary and adrenals stimulated?

   a. exhaustion
   b. alarm
   c. reaction
   d. resistance

16. Which stage of the general adaptation syndrome is associated with the outcome of disease?

   a. alarm
   b. reaction
   c. exhaustion
   d. resistance

17. What claim is Richard Lazarus most closely associated with?

    a. The individual's cognitive appraisal of a stressor is critical.
    b. The biopsychosocial model is an oversimplified view.
    c. Peptic ulcers can be healed through biofeedback.
    d. The general adaptation syndrome can account for eighty percent of heart attacks in middle-aged men.

18. Thomas Coates and Neal Miller are similar in their desire to

    a. eradicate AIDS.
    b. outlaw intravenous drug use.
    c. institute stress management courses as part of standard insurance coverage.
    d. teach basic skills for protecting one's health.

19. How should an advertising campaign ideally be designed in order to get people to use condoms and avoid high-risk sexual activities?

    a. It should be friendly, optimistic, and completely nonthreatening.
    b. It should have enough threat to arouse emotion but not so much that viewers will go into denial.
    c. It should contain a lot of humor.
    d. It should feature an older, white, male doctor and a lot of scientific terminology.

20. Neal Miller is to biofeedback as Judith Rodin is to

    a. analgesics.
    b. meditation.
    c. a sense of control.
    d. social support.

Questions to Consider

1. How can you help another person cope with stress?

2. How can a voodoo curse lead to death?

3. How do defense mechanisms help you deal with stress?

4. How can self-deprecating thoughts and behavior increase stress?

5. How might perfectionism lead to stress?

6. What common lifestyle differences might make men or women more susceptible to different kinds of health problems?

7. Is there a likely health benefit to practicing meditation or yoga?

Optional Activities

1. Sort the following behaviors into two categories: Category A, stress warning signals; and Category B, signs of successful coping. (You may add others from your own experience.)

Indigestion	Ability to sleep
Fatigue	Tolerance for frustration
Loss of appetite	Constipation
Indecision	Overeating
Sense of belonging	Overuse of drugs or alcohol
Sense of humor	Adaptability to change
Irritability	Optimism
Reliability	Cold hands
Sexual problems	Ulcers
Frequent urination	Sleep problems
Migraine headaches	Difficulty concentrating
Boredom	Free-floating anxiety
Temper tantrums	Frequent colds

2. Use the Student Stress Scale on page 410 in *Psychology and Life* to rate the stress in your life. Are you at risk for stress-related problems? Do you need to make your life less stressful? What can you do to reduce the amount of stress in your life?

3. Consider three periods in history: Pre-historic cultures, 0 B.C., and twenty-first-century America. Compare these three moments in history for the impact on health of (a) the reigning understanding of illness and health and (b) the demands of everyday living. What trade-offs do you see?

Additional Resources

Books and Articles

Baum, A. W., Revenson, T. A., & Singer, J. E. (Eds.) (2001). *Handbook of health psychology.* Hillsdale, NJ: Erlbaum.

McDonough, P., & Walters, V. (2001). Gender and health: Reassessing patterns and explanations. *Social Science & Medicine, 52,* 547-549.

Monat, A. & Lazarus, R. (1991). *Stress and coping.* New York: Columbia University Press.

Ruehlman, L. S., Lanyon, R. I., & Karoly, P. (1999). Development and validation of the Multidimensional Health Profile, Part I: Psychosocial functioning. *Psychological Assessment, 11,* 166-176.

Seligman, M. E. (1998). *Learned optimism.* New York: Pocket Books.

Films

Ordinary People. Directed by Robert Redford, 1980.

Web Sites

∞ *http://www.stress.org/*—The American Institute of Stress is a non-profit organization based in New York that collects and disseminates information concerning the relationship between stress and health. Among the services it provides, the institute is sometimes called upon to consult in court cases concerning stress and health.

∞ *http://www.health-psych.org/*—Division 38 of the American Psychological Association is devoted to issues in health psychology.

∞ *http://www.healthpsych.com/library/toclinks.html*—Health Psychology and Rehabilitation Library

∞ *http://www.learner.org*—This web site supports *Discovering Psychology: Updated Edition* with a page for each video program featuring an "academic footnote" to further update the content of the videos. The site also offers four special interactive features as well as an extensive webography.

UNIT 24

Peace, peace is what I seek and public calm, Endless extinction of unhappy hates.

Matthew Arnold

Unit 24 concentrates on how psychologists from a variety of fields put their knowledge, research skills, and insights to work in areas concerning human factors, such as sleep research, space travel, child eyewitness testimony, and peace-making.

Objectives

After viewing Program 24 and completing the assigned reading, you should be able to:

1   Describe how psychologists try to improve the human condition through the application of social psychological principles to social problems.

2.   Identify at least three important stress factors for space travelers, and discuss how studying those problems can help people on Earth.

3.   Define *peace psychology* and *conflict negotiation*.

4.   Describe the problems faced by legal professionals when children serve as eyewitnesses.

5.   Identify several signs that people are not getting enough sleep and identify the risks associated with sleep deprivation.

Reading Assignment

After viewing Program 24, review pages 141-146, 221-223, and 520-548 of *Psychology and Life*.

Key People and Terms

As you watch the program and read the assignment, pay particular attention to the following topics, described on the indicated page numbers.

group dynamics (494)

Kurt Lewin (546)
Stanley Milgram (520)

The following terms and people are referred to in Program 24 but are not defined in the text:

∞ *applied psychology*—the practical application of psychological knowledge and principles to concrete problems.

∞ *human factors*—the field of psychology interested in the characteristics of humans that relate to the optimal design of systems and devices.

∞ *narcolepsy*—a sleep disorder, brought on by strong emotion, in which REM sleep occurs suddenly during the day.

∞ *parietal lobe*—a part of the brain that is involved in the performance of math skills.

∞ *sleep apnea*—a sleep disorder characterized by heavy snoring with repetitive pauses in breathing.

∞ *Stephen Ceci*—studies child eyewitness testimony.

∞ *Malcolm Cohen*—NASA AMES researcher who studies the effects of micro-gravity environments on human interaction.

∞ *Jared Curhan*—trains young adults in negotiating skills in order to foster nonviolent conflict resolution.

∞ *Scott Fisher*—develops virtual interactive environmental work stations.

∞ *Nick Kanas*—studies gender and cultural differences and crew relations aboard the shuttle MIR.

∞ *James Maas*—studies sleep deprivation and its effects on cognitive processing.

Program Summary

In the previous programs, we have seen how psychologists study neurons and hormones, motives and needs, perception and decision-making, communication, intelligence, creativity, critical thinking, and stress. In Program 24, we see how psychologists put their insights to work to solve global problems and improve the quality of life for individuals and nations.

One major problem, faced by 40 million Americans and increasing every day, is sleeplessness, and this can have profound consequences for people's health. According to James Maas, the majority of us who believe we are getting enough sleep aren't. As many as 95 percent of high school and college students have some sort of sleep disorder, and most shift workers fall asleep on the job at least once a week. People may forgo sleep in order to be more productive, but fMRI scans of people when they attempt math problems show that sleeplessness interferes with normal brain activity. It is also critical for normal mental functioning. For example, we may fail to consolidate memories effectively if we have disrupted sleep. You should plan your sleep schedule around what you need, rather than what you think you have time for. Adults need about eight hours, and high school students need about nine hours of good, uninterrupted sleep.

One sleep disorder that can lead to sleeplessness is sleep apnea, which affects as many as 30 million Americans and is characterized by heavy snoring with repetitive pauses in breathing. Its cause is an obstruction in the upper airway passage, and it may occur several hundred times per night. Another, much rarer, sleep disorder is narcolepsy, which is an attack of REM sleep during the day, brought on suddenly by a strong emotion.

Although the psychosocial aspects of space travel affect only a handful of people directly, it is important for psychological research to accompany technological research so that we can anticipate and address the problems that will likely face our children and grandchildren. As the duration of space travel lengthens and the crews become larger and more diverse, psychologists will play an increasingly important role in addressing the psychological and physiological dimensions of space flight. There are a variety of stressors in space that could cause medical and psychological problems, such as anxiety, depression, boredom, loneliness, and hostility. These problems threaten the well-being, morale, and performance of astronauts and future space travelers.

The limitations in space are not as much medical as psychological. Taking into account human reactions to the unique features of space travel, psychologists are helping to design the spacecraft environment and to teach personal and group adjustment strategies. Nick Kanas of UCSF and Malcolm Cohen of NASA provide evidence of the many ways that isolation and demands affect astronauts and cosmonauts. There is often a rise in stress hormones, some intellectual impairment, a decline in motivation, an increase in tension and hostility, and social withdrawal.

In order to create a socially comfortable spacecraft environment, psychologists are working on techniques for overcoming the inevitable distortions of voice, facial expression, and movement that affect interpersonal communication. They are also researching techniques to help space travelers overcome boredom. And with larger, more diversified crews on board, they will need to help solve the problems caused by conflicts in professional status, language styles, even cultural differences.

A third area in which psychology makes important contributions is in the courtroom, where three million children serve every year as eyewitnesses. The people who interview these children before and during a trial often have no training in experimental psychology and may be unaware of the ways in which their questioning methods might affect a child's memory. According to Stephen Ceci, of Cornell University, repeated suggestive interviews can lead children to create new memories. Because the children believe that these memories are real, it can often be difficult for us to discriminate them from memories that arise from real events. Although the interviewers might not intend to "plant" false memories, and although the interview techniques they use might sometimes be ideal in a therapeutic setting, they can lead to false convictions in criminal cases.

Like applied psychology related to space travel, the field of conflict resolution incorporates knowledge gleaned from many areas of study, from behavioral and social psychology to biochemistry and environmental engineering. The study of peace demands the involvement of psychologists, sociologists, political scientists, and others concerned with preventing nuclear war and promoting peace among nations. Research ranges from studies of arms negotiations to how people respond to the possibility of nuclear war.

Jared Curhan, of MIT, has developed the Program for Young Negotiators. He teaches young adults to be effective at their goals, including resolving disputes with their peers without resorting to violent measures. He has brought these same skills to courses he has offered in business schools, law schools, and government. One of the major lessons people learn is that negotiation is not about getting what they want; it's about changing what they want.

Program Review Questions

1. Which of the following is true about Americans and sleep?

    a. Most Americans get more sleep than is healthy.
    b. Most Americans have narcolepsy.
    c. Americans with sleep apnea show sudden attacks of REM during the day.
    d. Most Americans get less sleep than they need.

2. Sleep is critical for

    a. formation of long-term memories.
    b. hormonal regulation.
    c. concentration.
    d. all of the above.

3. What will likely happen to a student who stays up all night studying for an exam?

    a. The material will have recently been consolidated in memory and will be highly retrievable.
    b. Although the information will be retrievable the next day during the test, it will not be likely to stay in long-term memory.
    c. He or she will fall asleep during the test.
    d. Brain activity during the test will be seriously decreased.

4. What seems to be the cause of a narcoleptic attack?

    a. low blood pressure.
    b. confusion.
    c. emotion.
    d. viral infection.

5. All of the following are true about sleep apnea, *except* that

    a. it only occurs in infants.
    b. it can lead to 600 interruptions of breathing during a single night.
    c. it is caused primarily by obstruction in the airway passage.
    d. it can, coupled with an alcoholic drink, lead to death.

6. What problems of social psychology arise in space vehicles?

    a. interpersonal conflicts between crew members
    b. cultural conflicts arising from an international crew
    c. conflicts between members of the crew and members of the ground control staff
    d. all of the above

7. What effect does living in close quarters have on the likelihood of interpersonal conflict?

    a. The likelihood increases.
    b. The likelihood decreases.
    c. The likelihood does not change.
    d. It depends on the nationality of the crew.

8. What negative effect does facial edema have on a space flight?

    a. It prevents proper eating.
    b. It hampers communication.
    c. It causes blood clots.
    d. All of the above.

9. The phenomenon, described in the film, of one person being angry at another and taking it out on the ground crew, is referred to as

   a. reaction formation.
   b. repression.
   c. displacement.
   d. lateral conflict.

10. Although having no gravitational field that creates a common "up" and "down" can be interesting, what significant problem have astronauts faced because of it?

    a. problems with their digestion
    b. problems reading each other's facial expressions
    c. problems writing notes
    d. problems using hand tools

11. How did the Little Rascals case begin?

    a. Several children independently told their parents the same story.
    b. One child made allegations of impropriety.
    c. An adult neighbor lied about what his son had told him.
    d. The adults who ran that daycare facility confessed to molesting children.

12. Which of the following was *not* described in the film as a common problem with techniques for interviewing children for court cases?

    a. Children are encouraged with phrases like, "don't be afraid to tell."
    b. Children are encouraged to lie.
    c. Children are encouraged to visualize scenes that they then can't distinguish from reality.
    d. Children are subjected to repeated suggestive interviews.

13. Why is it often so hard to judge the legitimacy of child eyewitnesses?

    a. Because they do not show physiological signs of panic like adults do, they can defeat polygraph tests.
    b. Their vulnerability and angelic demeanor can fool a jury into believing anything they say.
    c. Their testimony rarely makes sense, even when they are telling the truth.
    d. They are not lying.

14. Which of the following researchers is often called in as an expert witness in child eyewitness testimony cases?

    a. Stephen Ceci
    b. Max Bazerman
    c. Jared Curhan
    d. James Maas

15. What is the tell-tale sign that a child is lying during testimony?

    a. facial tension
    b. inconsistencies in their story
    c. use of words that they don't seem to understand
    d. hostility

16. According to the film, what seems to be a primary reason why interviewers ask suggestive questions?

    a. vengeance
    b. a bias to confirm a hypothesis rather than to test alternative explanations
    c. a desire to make the interview as easy as possible for the child
    d. all of the above

17. The Program For Young Negotiators is to adolescent friendships as

    a. economic negotiation techniques are to business.
    b. legal negotiation techniques are to law.
    c. political negotiations are to countries experiencing a cold war.
    d. all of the above.

18. Jared Curhan's goal in working with adolescent conflicts is to eliminate

    a. name-calling.
    b. cooperation.
    c. violence.
    d. unnecessary conversation.

19. In the film, one teenager was able to avoid a fight with her friend by

    a. shrugging and walking away.
    b. explaining her actions.
    c. teasing her friend for being angry.
    d. telling her something secret and embarrassing about herself.

20. Mal Cohen is to space research as James Maas is to

    a. peace research.
    b. space research.
    c. eyewitness testimony research.
    d. sleep research.

Questions to Consider

1. Compare the contributions of basic research with those of applied research. Is either more important?

2. Organizational and industrial psychologists focus on how individuals and organizations influence each other. One of their interests is increasing the compatibility between people and machines. Many computer companies claim their machines and programs are "user friendly." What does that mean? What would be the next great innovation you would like to see?

3. Can psychological principles and knowledge be applied for immoral purposes as well as good?

4. Given your knowledge from the book that historical references can impact people's opinions in very different ways depending on their own personality characteristics, how should a campaign manager go about deciding whether or not to use such references during a campaign?

Optional Activities

1. Collect political cartoons and analyze how individuals, countries, and opposition parties are characterized. Do you see any evidence of stereotyping or dehumanizing?

2. Interview a few people about their attitudes about countries in the news. Ask them to give you two or three adjectives to describe the traits they associate with each. Ask your survey participants how they feel their associations have been shaped by the media and by experience.

3. Interview your friends about their sleeping patterns. Do they get enough sleep? Are there times during the year when they get less sleep than others? Does it affect their health or their ability to concentrate? What gets in the way of their ability to get a full, uninterrupted night's sleep? What can they do to protect their sleep time better?

Additional Resources

Books and Articles

Keen, S. (1986). *Faces of the enemy: Reflections on a hostile imagination.* San Francisco, CA: Harper & Row.

Maas, J. (1998). *Power sleep: The revolutionary program that prepares your mind for peak performance.* New York: Harper Collins.

Powell, M., Thompson, D. M., & Ceci, S. J. (2003). Children's memory of recurring events: Is the first event always the best remembered? *Applied Cognitive Psychology, 17*, 127-146.

Rubin, B., Ginat, J., & Maoz, M. (Eds.) (1994). *From war to peace: Arab-Israeli relations, 1973-1993.* New York: New York University Press.

Stokols, D. & Altman, J. (Eds.) (1987). *Handbook of environmental psychology.* New York: Wiley.

Films

Apollo 13. Directed by Ron Howard, 1995.

The Negotiator. Directed by F. Gary Gray, 1998.

Witness. Directed by Peter Weir, 1985.

Web Sites

∞ *http://human-factors.arc.nasa.gov/*—Web page for NASA's Human Systems Integration Division. Find out about cutting edge research in applying human factors to space-based technologies of the future.

∞ *http://www.learner.org*—This web site supports *Discovering Psychology: Updated Edition* with a page for each video program featuring an "academic footnote" to further update the content of the videos. The site also offers four special interactive features as well as an extensive webography.

UNIT 25

> As he walked along, his brain was busy planning
> hundreds of wonderful things, building hundreds of
> castles in the air.
>
> Carlo Collodi, *The Adventures of Pinocchio*

Unit 25 introduces cognitive neuroscience and the techniques now available for studying mental processes by studying the brain's activities. Cognitive neuroscience is a highly interdisciplinary field that unites psychologists with brain researchers, biologists, and physicists in what has become the most dramatic advance in the last decade of psychological research.

Objectives

After viewing the television program and completing the assigned reading, you should be able to:

1. Describe some of the differences between EEG, ERP, CAT, MRI, PET, and fMRI techniques.

2. Describe how fMRI can be used to study visual pathways.

3. Describe some of the brain structures that underlie face recognition.

4. Support the similarity of imagery and perception by discussing the brain activity they have in common.

5. Explain how brain research can be used to help dyslexics learn to process language stimuli more effectively.

6. Describe how studies of the brain can reveal unconscious stereotypes.

Reading Assignment

After viewing Program 25, review pages 67-89 of *Psychology and Life*.

Key People and Terms

action potential (62)
all-or-none law (64)
amygdala (74)
association cortex (76)
auditory cortex (76)
autonomic nervous system (ANS) (71)
axon (61)
brain stem (72)
Broca's area (68)
central nervous system (CNS) (70)
cerebellum (73)
cerebral cortex (74)
cerebral hemispheres (74)
cerebrum (74)
corpus callosum (74)
dendrites (60)
electroencephalogram (EEG) (69)
endocrine system (81)
estrogen (82)
excitatory inputs (62)
frontal lobe (75)
functional MRI (fMRI) (70)
glia (61)
hippocampus (73)
homeostasis (74)
hormones (81)
hypothalamus (74)
inhibitory inputs (62)
interneurons (61)
ion channels (63)
lesions (68)
limbic system (73)
magnetic resonance imaging (MRI) (69)
medulla (72)
motor cortex (75)
motor neurons (61)
neuromodulator (66)
neuron (60)

neuroscience (60)
neurotransmitters (64)
occipital lobe (75)
parasympathetic division (72)
parietal lobe (75)
peripheral nervous system (PNS) (70)
PET scans (69)
pituitary gland (82)
pons (72)
refractory period (64)
resting potential (63)
reticular formation (72)
sensory neurons (61)
soma (60)
somatic nervous system (71)
somatosensory cortex (76)
sympathetic division (72)
synapse (64)
synaptic transmission (64)
temporal lobe (75)
terminal buttons (61)
testosterone (82)
thalamus (73)
visual cortex (76)
Paul Broca (68)
René Descartes (60)
Michael Gazzaniga (78)
Walter Hess (69)
Sir Charles Sherrington (166)
Roger Sperry (78)

The following terms and people are discussed in Program 25 but are not described in the text.

∞ *ERP*—a measure of event-related potentials of single brain cells.

∞ *IAT (Implicit Attitudes Test)*—uses response time as a means of detecting unconscious prejudice.

∞ *phoneme*—the smallest recognizable unit of speech sound.

∞ *plasticity*—the ability of the brain to restructure itself as a result, for example, of learning.

∞ *priming*—a speeding up in response time as a function of recent exposure.

∞ *Mahzarin Banaji*—studies brain processes that appear to underlie prejudice.

∞ *John Gabrieli*—uses functional MRI to study the brain in action.

∞ *Phineas Gage*—famous brain injury patient whose emotional reactions changed radically after injury.

∞ *David Heeger*—uses functional MRI to study vision.

∞ *Nancy Kanwisher*—studies the brain's processing of faces and scenes.

∞ *Stephen Kosslyn*—studies how mental imagery evokes brain processes similar to those involved in perception.

∞ *Bill Newsome*—studies the brain activity of monkeys during movement perception.

∞ *Paula Tallal*—studies brain activity in children with dyslexia and helps them to learn to read and write.

Program Summary

The most exciting developments in psychology over the past ten years have been in associating the brain's function with the mind's function. The study of how they relate isn't completely new. Throughout human history, unfortunate cases of brain damage, like that of Phineas Gage in 1848, have given some insights into which areas of the brain are responsible for which mental functions.

But the study of the brain through injury is a slow and inexact science. More recently, we have developed the means to study both normal and abnormal brains while a person sits quietly or is engaged in some activity. Of all of these techniques, including EEG, ERP, CAT, MRI, PET, and fMRI, one has emerged as particularly useful for providing high spatial and temporal resolution in brain imaging. This technique, functional magnetic resonance imagining (fMRI), tracks oxygen in the blood that is circulating within the brain. A temporary depletion, followed by a surplus, changes the magnetic properties of the blood, which can then be tracked by using a powerful magnet in the imaging apparatus.

People have used fMRI to study a very wide range of brain structures. For example, David Heeger of Stanford University studies the visual cortex (located in the back of the neocortex) and the 30 to 40 brain structures associated with vision. With the high resolution that fMRI provides, we can, for example, clearly separate the parietal system, which processes object location, from the temporal system, which processes object identity. Others, such as Nancy Kanwisher of MIT, are interested in specialized brain structures, such as those used to discriminate all of the thousands of faces we know from each other.

Psychologists have long wondered how the brain's processing of mental images relates to its processing of objects that are actually perceived. Stephen Kosslyn, of Harvard University, has shown that some brain areas that are associated with vision are also engaged when people imagine. His work on brain imaging, coupled with his behavioral research that showed that people form, inspect, maintain, and transform images in ways that mimic perceptual processes, provides convincing evidence for the argument that imagery makes use of brain's visual system.

There is some promise for the use of imaging techniques to help people whose brains operate below normal levels on certain tasks. For example, Paula Tallal studies the deficits experienced by dyslexic children, who may have damage in the left hemisphere that leads to trouble processing phonemes. Through a combination of behavioral research and brain imaging, psychologists and neuroscientists may be able to close in on answers to some of our most elusive and important problems.

And some of our most insidious problems are the ones that we aren't even aware of. Mahzarin Banaji and Liz Phelps have developed a research program, which also uses both behavioral and brain measures, to detect the presence of unconscious prejudice.

Imaging techniques, particularly fMRI, allows psychologists to examine the normal operation of the brain as we never have been able to before, and psychology can communicate like it never has before with other rapidly developing sciences. These sorts of techniques also encourage us to marvel at ourselves even more than we have in the past. They show us both how brilliantly our brains are organized and how able they are to reorganize and adapt themselves in the face of new information.

Program Review Questions

1. After a rod was shot through Phineas Gage's skull, what psychological system was most strongly disrupted?

   a. his emotional responses
   b. his ability to sleep and wake
   c. his language comprehension
   d. his ability to count

2. Which of the following does *not* provide information about the structure of the brain?

   a. CAT
   b. EEG
   c. MRI
   d. fMRI

3. Which of the following provides the highest temporal and spatial resolution in brain imaging?

   a. ERP
   b. MRI
   c. PET
   d. fMRI

4. The technique of fMRI measures

   a. distribution of radioactivity throughout the brain.
   b. electrical impulses in neurons.
   c. oxygen in the blood vessels of the brain.
   d. neural cellular growth over time.

5. Which of the following accurately identifies how visual information progresses?

   a. from the retina to the thalamus to the primary visual cortex
   b. from the retina to the primary visual cortex to the thalamus
   c. from the thalamus to the retina to the primary visual cortex
   d. from the primary visual cortex to the retina to the thalamus

6. According to David Heeger, about how many separate areas of the brain are involved in vision?

   a. one
   b. four
   c. between thirty and forty
   d. about six hundred

7. All of the following areas are specialized for motion, *except*

    a. V1
    b. right hemisphere
    c. left hemisphere
    d. thalamus

8. The right side of the world is processed by

    a. the left side of the brain.
    b. the front of the brain.
    c. the right side of the brain.
    d. the brain stem.

9. In the visual system, the _____ is to where objects are as the _____ is to what objects are.

    a. temporal lobe; parietal cortex
    b. frontal cortex; occipital lobe
    c. parietal cortex; temporal lobe
    d. occipital lobe; frontal cortex

10. The brain regions that are involved in identifying human faces will also become active when shown

    a. human hands.
    b. animal faces.
    c. a picture of the moon.
    d. a clock.

11. According to Nancy Kanwisher, why is it important to identify faces?

    a. because it allows us to identify other objects, like alphanumeric characters
    b. because we can then identify people who are familiar and friendly from other people
    c. both of the above
    d. none of the above

12. Nancy Kanwisher is to face perception as _____ is to mental imagery.

    a. David Heeger
    b. Paula Tallal
    c. Michael Gazzaniga
    d. Stephen Kosslyn

13. The way that participants move their eyes in Stephen Kosslyn's studies

    a. is diagnostic of whether they may later develop Alzheimer's disease.
    b. indicates whether they harbor unconscious prejudices.
    c. resembles the patterns of eye movements by participants who are looking at real objects.
    d. reveals which part of the brain they are using to view the stimuli.

14. The formation of mental images _____ the construction of real objects, and the transformation of mental images _____ the transformation of real objects.

    a. follows the same pattern as; does not follow the same pattern as
    b. does not follow the same pattern as; does not follow the same pattern as
    c. does not follow the same pattern as; follows the same pattern as
    d. follows the same pattern as; follows the same pattern as

15. The process of learning how to read shows that the brain is plastic. What does this mean?

    a. The brain is rigid in what it is designed to do.
    b. Learning how to read reorganizes the brain.
    c. The brain cannot be damaged simply by attempting new mental feats.
    d. The brain can be damaged when it attempts new mental feats.

16. Dyslexia affects

    a. reading.
    b. speaking.
    c. phoneme manipulation.
    d. all of the above.

17. For dyslexics who have trouble processing phonemes, which area of the brain is most likely to be damaged?

    a. the thalamus
    b. the right hemisphere
    c. the parietal lobe
    d. the left hemisphere

18. The IAT, administered by Mahzarin Banaji, can detect

    a. flaws in the imaginal system.
    b. unconscious prejudice.
    c. sensorimotor malfunctions.
    d. facial processing deficits.

19. Which area of the brain becomes particularly active when prejudice is aroused?

    a.   the hypothalamus
    b.   the amygdala
    c.   the medulla
    d.   the parietal lobe

20. People who show a strong eyeblink response in Banaji's studies also tend to show

    a.   a preference for white faces on the IAT.
    b.   low activation in the amygdala.
    c.   a preference for black faces on the IAT.
    d.   no cultural biases.

Questions to Consider

NOTE: Because these questions are open-ended and require answers based on your own experience and personal opinions, an answer key has not been included in the Appendix.

1.   Will we ever be able to scan someone's brain to find out exactly what they are thinking?

2.   If we have developed techniques that can eventually allow us to fully understand the various pathways of the brain and its neurochemistry, are we close to being able to build a brain from scratch?

3.   What will our scientific study of the brain, including emotion, social interaction, personality, and moral reason, mean for people's religious beliefs? Will the concept of the soul be seriously challenged?

Optional Activities

1.   Check out a textbook for a neuroscience or medical course that shows brain images of normal people and various clinical populations, such as schizophrenics, Alzheimer's patients, or accident victims. Look to see which areas of loss are associated with the loss of which functions.

2.   Go on the Web and look up these terms: *aphasia, agnosia,* and *transient ischemic attack.* Compare the types and durations of the deficits, and see if you can come to understand the functions of different parts of the brain by learning what goes wrong with the loss of tissue in different brain areas.

Books and Articles

Gazzaniga, M. S. (2000). *Cognitive neuroscience: A reader*. Malden, MA: Blackwell.

Sacks, O. (1985). *The man who mistook his wife for a hat and other clinical tales*. New York: Summit Books.

Films

A.I. Directed by Steven Spielberg, 2001.

The Cell. Directed by Tarsem Singh, 2001.

Web Sites

∞ *http://cognet.mit.edu/*—MIT hosts the CogNet Web site, a scholarly community devoted to research in the cognitive and brain sciences. There is a guided tour offered on this site that will allow you to see the diversity and productivity of research in this field. The site offers a news service, a searchable library, ongoing discussions by members, a listing of conferences and symposia, and profiles of individual members.

∞ *http://www.learner.org*—This web site supports *Discovering Psychology: Updated Edition* with a page for each video program featuring an "academic footnote" to further update the content of the videos. The site also offers four special interactive features as well as an extensive webography.

UNIT 26

Society has become dreadfully mixed. One sees the oddest people everywhere.

Oscar Wilde, *An Ideal Husband*

What is culture, and how does it affect who we are? In Unit 26, we explore the mutual interactions between culture, interpersonal interactions, and individual experience. We learn about some of the problems people face when different cultures merge.

Objectives

After viewing the television program, you should be able to:

1. Describe the differences between Eastern and Western cultures in terms of the weight given to individual and group factors to explain behavior.

2. Cite examples of how the Western value on individualism manifests itself.

3. Describe the African cultural values that have benefited African Americans in their struggle against bigotry.

4. List several factors that put Latino immigrants at risk for depression and alienation.

5. Cite evidence that psychology can help solve some of society's most perplexing problems and cite evidence to the contrary.

Reading Assignment

After viewing Program 14, review pages 429-431 and 537-539 in *Psychology and Life*.

Key People and Terms

Key people and terms from Program 26 are listed below.

∞ *independent way of being*—associated with the individual as the focus and locus of action.

∞ *interdependent way of being*—focuses on social relationships and views action as distributed across and caused by a network of people.

∞ *mutual constitution*—the process of culture and individual shaping and being shaped by each other.

∞ *James Jones*—studies the bicultural evolution of African-American culture.

∞ *Shinobu Kitayama*—with Hazel Markus, studies cultural differences that lead to independent and interdependent ways of thinking about the self.

∞ *Hazel Markus*—with Shinobu Kitayama, studies independent and interdependent ways of being.

∞ *Michael Morris*—works with Kaipeng Peng to study how people of different cultures explain the interaction behavior of animated fish.

∞ *Ricardo Munoz*—works with Latino immigrants to screen, prevent, and treat depression.

∞ *Kaipeng Peng*—works with Michael Morris to study how people of different cultures explain the interaction behavior of animated fish.

Program Summary

Culture exerts a complex set of influences on us. There are obvious differences between cultures, such as the fashions, languages, and foods that characterize them. And there are also more subtle differences that shape who we are, how we interpret the world around us, and how we interact with other people. Program 26 considers some of these differences that shape personality, beliefs, values, and emotions.

Culture shapes how we interpret others' behavior. Kaipeng Peng of UC Berkeley and Michael Morris of Stanford University use cartoon figures of fish to examine differences in social perception among people raised in East Asia versus North America. When asked why a lone fish behaved as it did, the Americans focused on the motives of the individual and the Asians focused on the motives of the group. In the film, Peng relates a personal story that illustrates a similar point: Americans tend to focus on stable aspects of an individual's personality when explaining behavior, while Asians give greater weight to the influences of the group.

These differences in social perception extend to cultural differences in self-perception. Hazel Markus of Stanford University and Shinobu Kitayama of Kyoto University investigate how the self and culture continually create each other. Within the context of different cultural settings, this mutual constitution of person and culture can have very different outcomes. Markus and Kitayama describe two possible outcomes as the independent and interdependent modes of being. The independent mode is exemplified by American and other Western cultures and is characterized by personal responsibility, individual control, uniqueness, and a focus on one's positive attributes. In contrast, the interdependent mode is exemplified by East Asian cultures and is characterized by sensitivity to the needs of others, transcendence beyond individual desire, and a focus on areas in which one has to improve. An American host at a party would encourage people to help themselves, while a Japanese host would be attentive to what is good for each guest. The differences between these cultures reflect differences between the Protestant ethic and the Buddhist way of being.

We can find a rich mix of cultures inside American borders as well. James Jones of the University of Delaware studies the influence of West African culture and the culture of slavery on modern African-American culture. He has found profound influences on the conceptualization of time, rhythm, improvisation, orality, and spirituality. The resulting complex approach can help in coping with prejudice, and it can provide the basis for some of the cultural contributions that African-American culture is known for, including its exquisite wordcraft. Similarly, cultural style has allowed Native Americans to adapt to the sometimes brutal treatment endured over several centuries. Joseph Trimble, Fellow at the Radcliffe Institute for Advanced Study at Harvard University, studies how Native Americans have adapted to and been influenced by mainstream American culture. Native American culture has suffered historically because mainstream American culture has taken advantage of and shown disrespect for the generosity and honor it encourages in its people.

We now understand that adapting to a new culture is stressful, particularly when there is little room for the expression of one's original beliefs and ways of being. Ricardo Munoz of UC San Francisco studies the psychology of acculturation in the Latino community. One difference between Latinos and non-Latinos in America is in their willingness to seek mental health services. Because of both cultural opinions about such services and language barriers, Latinos are less likely to make use of psychologists. Particularly given the rapidly rising rates of clinical depression in the Mexican immigrant community, Dr. Munoz advocates for the development of outreach programs. As the trend increases for immigrants to stay in the U.S., separated from their families and social support networks, their level of psychological distress increases. Although social support is important to all of us, it is an especially central component of Latino culture, which revolves around deep familial ties. As these cultural values clash with the mainstream U.S. values of independence and individuality, Mexican immigrants and their children may feel confused, rejected, and depressed.

As the population of the world increases, as people feel freer to settle in different areas around the globe, and as technology brings different cultures into greater contact with each other, we will face new challenges as psychologists and as people in dealing with the interpersonal and intrapersonal conflicts that arise.

Program Review Questions

1. What was Kaipeng Peng investigating when he had people interpret the behavior of cartoon fish?

    a. individuals' tendency toward aggressive language
    b. age-related differences in social perceptions
    c. gender differences in whether the fish were perceived as cooperative
    d. cultural differences in how much attention people paid to personal and group features

2. Who is more likely to say that a lone fish had been kicked out by the group for being bad?

    a. someone raised in East Asia.
    b. someone raised in Los Angeles
    c. someone raised in Mexico who has recently moved to San Francisco
    d. someone raised on a reservation in Wyoming

3. How does the personal story told by Dr. Peng in the film illustrate cultural differences in explaining an individual's behavior?

    a. Americans believed that the man would not have killed anyone if he were raised in a more loving home.
    b. Americans believed that the man was a murderer and that if he were married, he would have killed his wife as well.
    c. The Chinese believed that the man was inherently evil.
    d. The Chinese believed that the man would have been a leader in China.

4. Cultural differences can lead to differences in

    a. our values.
    b. how we view other people's behavior.
    c. how we interpret our own behavior.
    d. all of the above.

5. What is meant by the term *mutual constitution*?

    a. Culture and individual personality shape each other.
    b. Two members of the same small community rely heavily on each other for support.
    c. Individual societies rely on written laws for much of their cultural center.
    d. Two cultures in close proximity will begin to exchange goods and ideas immediately.

6. The United States is a good example of which mode of being, according to Hazel Markus and Shinobu Kitayama?

    a. interdependent
    b. independent
    c. domineering
    d. adaptive

7. Which of the following might be taken as insulting by a Japanese guest in your home?

    a. "May I take your coat?"
    b. "Please try some of this wine."
    c. "Take whichever kind of drink you like."
    d. "Can I offer you a hot towel so you can clean your hands?"

8. According to the film, East Asian culture is to Buddhism as American culture is to

    a. television.
    b. commerce.
    c. the Protestant ethic.
    d. Judaism.

9. Someone who describes himself in terms of the ways he believes he needs to improve is likely to belong to which culture?

    a. lower-class American
    b. Native American
    c. Japanese
    d. Catholic American

10. What is meant by the Japanese term, *gumbaru?*

    a. intelligent and superior
    b. good at adapting to new situations
    c. traitorous to one's cultural heritage
    d. hard-working and modest

11. Kaipeng Peng is to Chinese culture as James Jones is to

    a. Native American culture.
    b. African-American culture.
    c. immigrant Latino culture.
    d. Japanese culture.

12. According to James Jones, "TRIOS" influences are apparent in

    a. African-American Ph.D. dissertation topics.
    b. African-American cuisine.
    c. the implementation of affirmative action programs by the government.
    d. rap music.

13. In West African culture, time is defined

    a. by the seasons.
    b. by the group leaders.
    c. by behavior and feelings.
    d. by none of the above.

14. How can improvisational skills help people to navigate the undercurrents of racism?

    a. Improvisation allows people to assert their unique styles and preferences.
    b. Improvisation allows for flexible problem solving.
    c. Improvisation allows for articulate speaking.
    d. More than one of the above.

15. Three of the components of "TRIOS" are

    a. orality, strength, and thought.
    b. intuition, ownership, and sophistry.
    c. tirelessness, rhapsody, and identity.
    d. time, spirituality, and rhythm.

16. Respect for the earth and all that lives is most closely associated with which culture discussed in the film?

    a. Japanese
    b. Latino
    c. Chinese
    d. Native American

17. What did Columbus risk when he refused a gift from the Native American leaders who greeted him?

    a. insulting the leaders
    b. insulting their families
    c. insulting the entire community
    d. violent retribution

18. The process of adapting to a new, dominant culture

    a. creates safety and comfort for the culture that adapts.
    b. is stressful, particularly when the dominant culture is not welcoming.
    c. has been the goal of Native American societies over the past few centuries.
    d. leads to an easy restructuring of one's goals and values.

19. Which of the following is true about depression among Mexican Americans?

    a. Its rate is growing as the average length of stay in the U.S. increases.
    b. It is relatively rare, because the close-knit family unit of Latino culture buffers against it.
    c. It is relatively rare, because the language barrier protects immigrants from the uglier side of the U.S.
    d. Latino culture actively encourages people who are depressed to seek help from mental health professionals.

20. Who is at particular risk for feelings of confusion and rejection as a result of the conflicting sets of cultural values they encounter?

    a. family members of immigrants to the U.S. who have chosen to stay behind in Mexico
    b. immigrants from Mexico who have been in the U.S. less than a week
    c. first-generation Latinos born in the U.S.
    d. U.S.-born Americans who work with Mexican immigrants

Questions to Consider

NOTE: These questions are designed to promote personal reflection and speculation. Because there are no right or wrong answers, an answer key has not been included in the Appendix.

1. Who will you be in the year 2015? Describe yourself. What personal, family, social, and cultural changes do you anticipate? How will the work of psychologists affect you?

2. Are human beings responsible for their behavior? Or are they victims of environment, their personal history, or biological determinants?

3. American commercial interests have done well over the past century by fostering a sense of competitiveness. How can Japanese cultural values explain Japan's tremendous successes over the past fifty years in the same domains?

4. Some have predicted that the future of psychology will include increasing efforts to prevent psychological problems and enhance human potential. How will this work be carried out? Who should decide who needs preventive intervention?

Optional Activities

1. Imagine that at two years of age, you moved to Italy, Japan, or Peru and grew up there. Make a list of some of your personal habits and values. For each of them, write down how they would have been affected if you had been raised in a very different culture.

2. Study the evolution of large cities, such as New York or Los Angeles. Notice how neighborhoods develop that allow members of the same cultural background to live near each other and create environments that resemble those of home.

Additional Resources

Books and Articles

Paniagua, F. A., O'Boyle, M., & Tan, V. L. (2000). Self-evaluation of unintended biases and prejudices. *Psychological Reports, 87,* 823-829.

Ruiz-Beltran, M., & Kamau, J. K. (2001). The socioeconomic and cultural impediments to well-being along the US-Mexico border. *Journal of Community Health, 26,* 123-132.

Vavrus, M. D. (2001). *American cultural studies.* Champaign: University of Illinois Press.

Films

Goodbye New York. Directed by Amos Kollek, 1984.

Lawrence of Arabia. Directed by David Lean, 1962.

The Gods Must Be Crazy. Directed by Jamie Uys, 1980.

Web Sites

∞ *http://www.iaccp.org/*—Web site for the International Association for Cross-Cultural Psychology. Founded thirty years ago, this organization facilitates communication between people whose interest is in cultural comparison and cultural interaction.

∞ *http://www.lif.org/*—The Latino Issues Forum, based in San Francisco, is concerned with how public policy will affect the social and economic future of the Latino community. The Web site provides information on higher education, health care, and technology and offers links to other sites of interest to Latino concerns.

∞ *http://www.learner.org/*—See previous web descriptions.

ANSWER KEY: REVIEW QUESTIONS

Unit 1

1. c	6. d	11. a	16. c
2. b	7. b	12. c	17. a
3. a	8. b	13. c	18. c
4. c	9. b	14. b	19. b
5. b	10. d	15. d	20. d

Unit 2

1. a	6. b	11. b	16. d
2. c	7. a	12. b	17. c
3. b	8. d	13. a	18. d
4. b	9. a	14. c	19. a
5. d	10. c	15. b	

Units 3 and 4

1. d	6. c	11. a	16. d	21. b	26. b
2. a	7. b	12. d	17. a	22. d	
3. b	8. b	13. a	18. c	23. b	
4. c	9. a	14. b	19. c	24. a	
5. c	10. c	15. c	20. b	25. c	

Unit 5

1. b	6. d	11. d	16. d
2. a	7. b	12. a	17. a
3. c	8. a	13. b	18. b
4. d	9. d	14. d	19. d
5. c	10. c	15. c	20. d

Unit 6

1. c	6. b	11. b	16. a	21. d
2. d	7. c	12. a	17. c	
3. b	8. d	13. c	18. b	
4. a	9. a	14. d	19. d	
5. b	10. a	15. c	20. c	

Unit 7

1. d	6. a	11. b	16. d
2. c	7. a	12. b	17. c
3. c	8. a	13. c	18. a
4. a	9. c	14. b	19. d
5. d	10. c	15. a	20. a

Unit 8

1. b	6. c	11. b	16. d
2. d	7. c	12. d	17. a
3. d	8. a	13. c	18. c
4. a	9. d	14. a	19. b
5. b	10. c	15. b	20. d

Unit 9

1. d	6. a	11. c	16. d
2. c	7. b	12. d	17. a
3. b	8. a	13. d	18. a
4. b	9. b	14. a	19. b
5. d	10. b	15. b	20. d

Units 10 and 11

1. d	6. c	11. b	16. d	21. c	26. d
2. c	7. a	12. d	17. d	22. a	27. c
3. b	8. c	13. b	18. b	23. c	28. d
4. a	9. a	14. a	19. d	24. c	29. a
5. b	10. c	15. c	20. b	25. b	30. b

31. a
32. a
33. d
34. b
35. a

Unit 12

1. d	6. c	11. a	16. c
2. b	7. c	12. b	17. d
3. b	8. a	13. c	18. b
4. c	9. d	14. a	19. a
5. a	10. b	15. d	20. c

Units 13 and 14

1. c	6. b	11. c	16. b	21. a	26. b
2. b	7. c	12. a	17. d	22. d	27. a
3. d	8. b	13. b	18. b	23. b	28. d
4. b	9. b	14. a	19. c	24. c	29. c
5. a	10. b	15. d	20. a	25. d	30. d

31. d

Unit 15

1. c	6. d	11. a	16. b
2. b	7. d	12. c	17. a
3. a	8. b	13. d	18. a
4. b	9. c	14. a	19. c
5. a	10. b	15. b	20. d

Unit 16

1. b	6. c	11. c	16. d
2. d	7. b	12. c	17. a
3. a	8. d	13. a	18. a
4. c	9. c	14. b	19. c
5. d	10. b	15. a	20. c

Unit 17

1. d	6. d	11. c	16. c
2. a	7. c	12. a	17. b
3. b	8. c	13. b	18. c
4. c	9. a	14. a	19. d
5. a	10. a	15. d	20. c

Unit 18

1. c	6. a	11. b	16. c
2. d	7. d	12. a	17. b
3. b	8. d	13. d	18. c
4. a	9. b	14. a	19. d
5. b	10. d	15. a	20. a

Units 19 and 20

1. a	6. a	11. b	16. c	21. d
2. c	7. c	12. c	17. b	22. a
3. d	8. d	13. d	18. c	
4. a	9. a	14. a	19. a	
5. b	10. b	15. a	20. d	

Unit 21

1. d	6. a	11. d	16. a
2. b	7. b	12. b	17. d
3. b	8. c	13. c	18. b
4. b	9. d	14. a	19. d
5. d	10. b	15. b	20. a

Unit 22

1. c	6. b	11. a	16. d
2. a	7. d	12. c	17. c
3. d	8. c	13. b	18. a
4. b	9. c	14. b	19. c
5. a	10. d	15. b	20. a

Unit 23

1. c	6. c	11. b	16. c
2. b	7. a	12. d	17. a
3. d	8. b	13. a	18. d
4. b	9. c	14. c	19. b
5. d	10. d	15. b	20. c

Unit 24

1. d	6. d	11. b	16. b
2. d	7. a	12. b	17. d
3. d	8. b	13. d	18. c
4. c	9. c	14. a	19. b
5. a	10. b	15. b	20. d

Unit 25

1. a	6. c	11. b	16. d
2. b	7. d	12. d	17. d
3. d	8. a	13. c	
4. c	9. c	14. b	
5. a	10. b	15. b	

Unit 26

1. d	6. b	11. b	16. d
2. a	7. c	12. d	17. c
3. b	8. c	13. c	18. b
4. d	9. c	14. d	19. a
5. a	10. d	15. d	20. c

ANSWER KEY: QUESTIONS TO CONSIDER

NOTE: There are not always clear-cut right or wrong answers to these questions, but it may be helpful for students to compare their ideas to the ideas provided in this Answer Key. In addition, the answers given here are brief, of necessity, and sometimes address only some of the components of the question.

Unit 1. Past, Present, and Promise

1. The fundamental issues of psychology include the relationship of mind and body, the role of heredity and environment in determining personality and behavior, the role of the conscious and the unconscious in determining behavior, the influence of individual dispositional and external social and situational forces on behavior, the influence of early experience on later life, and the significance of individual differences and similarities.

2. Many people are not aware of the many different kinds of work that psychologists do. A popular stereotype is that of the slightly nutty Freudian-style analyst depicted in popular movies of the 1930s and 1940s. As you will learn, the treatment of mental illness is only one part of psychology. Psychologists are scientists who can also help people teach more effectively and learn more efficiently. They help people improve their physical and emotional well-being, enhance communication, find the right job, quit smoking, make decisions, improve social relations, understand child development, promote world peace, and fight poverty and prejudice.

3. There is a wide range of reasons people might give for not going to see a therapist. For example, they may feel that therapy cannot help them with their particular problem. There may be issues of limited money or time. They may feel pressure from their cultural tradition to keep problems "in the family" rather than taking them to a stranger. They may not know how to seek out the appropriate therapist for the problems they have. And finally, they may not recognize that they could benefit from therapy, either because they do not recognize the problem themselves or because they believe that it's not until a situation becomes problematic that a therapist would be of value.

4. Observer bias influences our choices about what is relevant and what isn't. Our values, interests, and expectations can even influence our perceptions, leading us to see things that are not there and overlook things that are.

5. Thinking (perceiving, remembering, imagining) is an accepted focus of psychological study. There have been various approaches to studying thinking behavior. People are asked to think out loud while solving problems or to report their reactions to internal or external events. Mental processes can also be inferred from such measurable behaviors as reaction times in decision making, problem-solving strategies, speech patterns, eye movements, and changes in brain activity.

6. We can't know the future, but we're certainly at the dawning of an important era when biological and psychological phenomena can truly be seen to interact with each other. It's unlikely that we'll ever completely know how the brain and body create psychological experience or that we'll ever be able to read the intricate details of someone's thoughts just by looking at the firing patterns of neurons in their brain, but there will certainly be progress even on those fronts. For example, we already know that certain kinds of mental activity are associated with greater brain activity in certain regions. In the year 2500, psychologists will probably have to have training in the neurosciences in order to consider themselves educated in human functioning.

Unit 2. Understanding Research

1. For every person who is supposedly healed, there are many more who are not. Faith healing is big business, and desperate people are deceived purposely in money-making scams. The sick not only lose money to faith healers for empty promises, but also they may not follow proven medical treatments that might help them.

2. Sometimes it's impossible to assign the same person to more than one condition. For example, if we're interested in comparing males and females in their spatial ability, or people of different races for their response to social situations, or people of different intelligence levels in their working memory capacities, we need to run two separate groups of people. Secondly, some research designs would require that participants essentially be run through the same experiment twice, and having been through it once may affect their future behavior in unpredictable ways. In such instances, it would be better to simply compare two groups. If the samples of participants we gather are representative of their groups, and if they're treated similarly in the experiment, our results should be trustworthy.

3. Objections to the study of mental processes (dreams, judgment, perceptions) include the claim that these sometimes rely on self-reports, are too personal, and cannot be verified. Because mental events cannot be observed directly, these are difficult to study scientifically. But psychologists believe that by defining terms carefully, they can draw inferences from measurable behaviors. Personal experiences, such as sensations, emotions, and reactions to internal and external events can be inferred from changes in heart rate, brain activity, eye movements, speech patterns, and other behaviors—all of which can be measured.

4. Some studies cannot be run without keeping participants somewhat in the dark about the purpose of the research, since knowledge of the study's goals would be likely to affect their behavior and make it unlike the actual phenomenon being studied. The goal is always to be as respectful of participants as possible, never to deceive them if it is not necessary to the research, and always to debrief them after their participation is complete so that the deception is removed and any possible distress is dispelled. According to APA Guidelines, which hold the participants' welfare as primary, any likely distress must be consented to before the study begins, and a study involving deception would threaten the opportunity for truly informed consent. Psychologists acknowledge that this disallows some experiments from being

conducted, but we have accepted this limitation and, when possible, we design other, more acceptable studies that address similar questions.

5. Scientists use nonhuman subjects to conduct research that cannot be done with humans, but research involving nonhuman animals also creates ethical dilemmas. You might consider an experiment justified if its findings were of direct benefit to humans, or you might consider it justified only if it concerned matters of life or death. Alternatively, you might consider it unjustifiable under any circumstance. There is wide disagreement among psychologists about the use of animal subjects. The APA's guidelines represent an attempt to prevent mistreatment and to inform the public of its professional standards.

6. People who volunteer are a self-selected group; they are not representative of the general population. Volunteers may be less inhibited or more strongly opinionated about a particular topic. For example, because responding involves going to the trouble of filling out the survey and mailing it in, the results of a magazine survey may depend on a group of readers with specific characteristics not represented in the general population.

7. Psychology experiments depend largely on introductory psychology students as their participants, and there is some concern about how broadly the data gathered from this group of people can generalize to the larger population. Although basic studies on *how* perceptual, biological, and cognitive systems work can generally be applied to humans as a whole, other topics, like cultural values and *what* they know, may be more specific to individual subpopulations.

Unit 3. The Behaving Brain

1. If we know what causes a problem, we can avoid spending a lot of time and money on useless treatments. Even though many conditions are not correctable, knowing the cause gives us a sense of control. For example, some drugs are used to treat depressed and schizophrenic patients. Sometimes the doctors don't even know why the drugs have the desired effect. Nevertheless, these drugs clearly relieve the patients' symptoms. Also, we can move toward building a more complete model of the illness that could eventually allow effective treatment.

2. Although early research by Delgado and others showed that electrical stimulation of the brain could produce certain results, such as initiating or inhibiting aggressive behavior, the explanation for its effects has been questioned by other research. Elliot Valenstein's analysis points out that repeated stimulation to the same spot may not reliably elicit the same feeling or action. Although electrical stimulation has been used to relieve cancer patients of pain by blocking messages in the spinal cord, most doctors consider electrode implants too radical a treatment for healthy patients with weight problems.

3. Techniques such as the fMRI, EEG, CAT, MRI, and PET, provide information that can be used to help distinguish between normal and abnormal brain structures and functions. The process of mapping or imaging the brain promises to help identify the chemical or structural abnormalities

underlying such problems as Alzheimer's disease, schizophrenia, learning disabilities, and depression.

4. When people have catastrophic brain injuries and sudden changes in their functioning, the people who know them best may have trouble adapting. Often this involves a sudden loss of language, spatial ability, or memory, with no real change in what they've come to know as their loved one's personality. In the case of Phineas Gage, not only were the changes he experienced unusual, so that his loved ones did not have a previous model to refer to in learning to relate to him, but his changes were in interpersonal functioning and personality, which people tend to think of as unshakable characteristics. We can only imagine that it was very difficult for them to accept the "new" Phineas and to believe that it had completely replaced the old one.

Unit 4. The Responsive Brain

1. Does an athlete who takes steroids have an unfair advantage over his or her competitors? Most organizations and competitions prohibit competitors from taking drugs to enhance performance. In noncompetitive situations, the issue of taking drugs should involve consideration of the unintended side effects or the individual's long-term health effects.

2. For premature infants, sessions that included touching and movement stimulation caused significant weight gain and advances in organized behavior over the control group of premature infants. You might conclude that in general, infants receiving a lot of contact and stimulation would be more advanced physically, perhaps healthier, and more alert than low-touch infants. (However, there are many other factors that influence later development.) Observation studies of people in different cultures have suggested that some European cultures are more demonstrative and more expressive than that of Americans, for example. You might assume that high-touch families would create more expressive individuals.

3. Federal and state governments sponsor many nutrition programs, as well as drug and alcohol prevention, treatment, and education programs. In some states, legislation has been proposed that would regulate a pregnant woman's behavior if it were judged dangerous to the fetus.

4. Although we are able to determine which areas of the brain are active and may be able to argue that, for example, verbal activity or emotional activity is involved, there is no indication that we can come any closer to reading or controlling the precise thoughts that people experience.

5. Given the health benefits that come with gains in social status and the negative health consequences of various sorts of punishments, a reward-based society would have tremendous value. Needless to say, there are other ethical and practical reasons for increasing the positivity of feedback that people experience. There are at least three factors that work against this happening, however. First, people, like other animals, have a tendency to express negative emotions, which serve as punishments for others. It would be hard to eliminate such behaviors. Second, limited resources often make it impossible to increase materials rewards. Third, much of our interpretation of our social standing lies in social comparison, and so increase in rewards across the board may not have the kind of impact we hoped.

6. There are several reasons why music might have such a strong effect on people. For example, people are attracted to highly structured patterns, and the tonal patterns and harmonies found in music conform to mathematical patterns that interest and stimulate us. Also, much like intonation and timing in language, music can convey emotional meaning and resolution very effectively. Still, the effects of music are still quite mysterious to us.

7. With an all-or-none response, you have a physical means for detecting things, rather than forcing some higher function to decide whether a neuron has fired with a great enough strength for something to be the case (e.g., there really was a noise, I really did have a memory). You also create a system that allows for the same information to be processed, while protecting the neuron from constantly having to be in some state of firing. As for neurotransmitters, the greater number allows for greater diversity of functioning in the brain and allows for one function to be active while other, less relevant or undesired ones remain inactive.

Unit 5. The Developing Child

1. Watson was devoted to behaviorism. He possessed a rather cold, objective view of the child, emphasized shaping and training, and discounted the importance of inherited traits and personality. Gesell emphasized that development depended on maturation. He contended that there was no point in training children or trying to speed up learning, because they couldn't learn until they were biologically ready.

2. Lack of knowledge or inappropriate expectations can cause unnecessary frustration and misunderstanding. Some child abuse may be related to unrealistic expectations, especially in toilet training and bed-wetting. In the past, parents were warned not to spoil their children by handling them too much. This was followed by a period of attentive indulgence. Currently, childrearing advice falls somewhere between these two extremes.

3. "Body language" of an adult primarily refers to facial expressions, movements, and gestures. The body language of an infant includes these, as well as physiological measures. A change in arousal level could be used in infants or adults to measure a response to a stimulus. These might include a change in temperature, heart rate, or brain activity. Adults also tend to look at what interests them. Tracking eye movements can reveal what a person notices, prefers, or recognizes.

4. Many very clever techniques for measuring topics, such as memory, perception, and preference, have been developed to study infants, who can have sophisticated abilities but who cannot respond to complex language or answer questions verbally. Some of these techniques can be adapted for use with other non-verbal animals, as long as their behavioral capabilities (such as grasping and looking) are well enough developed.

5. You can argue that anything that has general importance to rapidly learning about the world would have high interest for an infant. For example, language should be particularly interesting for the infant, and a predisposition to pay attention to language will allow the child to acquire a rich and powerful tool. As another example, infants should be predisposed to be interested in

events, actions that cause other actions to happen over time. Paying attention to causal relations will allow the child to learn principles governing physics and social order.

6. As people age, their interests and activities may need to be modified to fit their capabilities. Their interests may lead them to indoor, rather than outdoor activities, and their participation in physical activity may be redirected to watching children play outside. The good news is that, regardless of one's physical limitations, there are plenty of options for occupying one's time and occupying one's mind.

Unit 6. Language Development

1. Whether gorillas or chimps are truly capable of language is still debated. It really depends on your definition of language. Your textbook definition may include such characteristics as specialization, arbitrariness, displacement, productivity and novelty, and iteration and recursion. Although animals do use symbols, no animal other than humans consistently and naturally organizes symbols according to specific rules. Human language seems to be unique, and humans appear to be uniquely "programmed" to acquire it. Recent research has suggested that gorillas and chimps have higher-level communicative ability, and mothers trained in signs and symbols can transfer their learning to their offspring. The debate goes on.

2. Language helps structure thought, and people use words to think, solve problems, and define and use concepts. But thinking also involves visual and sensory images. Certain cognitive operations, but not all, are dependent on language.

3. Nonverbal communication includes body movements, postures, gestures, eye contact, and use of physical space. Other important elements of communication include such verbal features as voice intonation, hesitation, and volume. Nonlinguistic and other nonverbal elements account for a significant portion of the total message.

4. Having imaginary friends allows a child to practice several aspects of language. They can initiate conversation, hold long monologues, and practice turn-taking and other social skills related to language. They can also practice different kinds of language use that they otherwise wouldn't have opportunities for in the real world (e.g., when they "scold" their dolls). All of this helps them to master the phonological, working memory, and social skills related to language.

5. Parentese is characterized by a responsiveness to the child's level of language development. A parent whose speech does not adapt to the infant might not provide the optimal cues for discriminating sounds, recognizing important intonations of the language, or practicing social interaction patterns. Although parentese is not necessary, a child's language development might be somewhat delayed if there are no other sources of interaction.

6. By the age of six, most children have a skillful and functional command of their own language. However, people refine their use of language throughout their lives, including, but not limited to, expanding vocabulary and improving grammar.

7. Children seem to be equipped with the capability of determining whether, for example, "pewter" refers to the object itself, to what it's holding, or to what it's made of. If the child already has a word in her vocabulary for any particular aspect, they will assume that the new word refers to some other aspect of the object. So, for example, if a child's mother refers to "the pewter cup holding the juice," the child is likely to assume that "pewter" refers to what the object is made of. Such biases in language-learning are extremely helpful.

Unit 7. Sensation and Perception

1. The distinction between sensation and perception is an important one and will still be present fifty years from now. Whereas "sensation" refers to the registering of a physical stimulus on one of many different kinds of receptors, "perception" refers to one's experience of the stimulus. Sensations are translated through sophisticated neuronal structures into perceptions.

2. To improve the environment for individuals with visual deficits, one could print large labels on medicine bottles and other containers. For people with impaired balance, handrails in hallways and safety rails in bathrooms could be installed. To adjust for hearing loss, background noise could be reduced by better insulation, and blinking lights that indicate when the phone is ringing could be installed. For those with a loss of sensitivity to smells, smoke detectors or fire alarms could be installed. And, if loss of smell is affecting appetite, special effort should go into planning a diet to enhance flavors and ensure adequate nutrition.

3. Some people assert that those who practice and promote ESP are abusing science, particularly at a time when public decisions depend on the application of good science. Others criticize the spending of money on worthless books and gadgets. Admittedly, science cannot fully explain many phenomena, and people turn in frustration to mystics of various sorts, often accepting irrational explanations that do not hold up under rigorous and repeated scientific testing and that may put them at risk.

4. Items on the shelves have labels on them so that it's easy to group by perceptual similarity. Products belonging to the same category are typically stored within the same area of the store, allowing grouping by proximity. At the check-out stand, two different customers will typically leave a perceptible space between their clusters of purchases, allowing the clerk to group the clusters by the principle of proximity. Items moving together on a clerk's conveyer belt can be grouped by the principle of common fate.

5. By training yourself to pay close attention to visual and auditory elements, you can become increasingly aware of the purposeful choices directors make and how they use and combine various techniques to influence your perceptions. For example, children's toys are frequently photographed in ads so that they appear larger or sturdier than they really are. In films and television programs, dim lighting, a low camera angle, and shadows are used to create suspense or danger. Music is often used in television and film to evoke happiness, fear, or other emotions.

6. Perception of similarity, for example, in the quality of two people's voices, involves particular complexity, since it requires perception of two different things and the comparison between the

two. Because of this complexity, and because the comparison process depends on what one has experienced in the past, this might vary across people. Other perceptual experiences that might differ between people are those that involve evaluation of pleasantness. One person might perceive a shrill, unpleasant shriek, while another experiences a crisp, pleasant high tone. One person might experience pressure, while another might experience an unpleasant level of pain.

7. One possibility is that the tendency in primates to climb and to brachiate through trees required an extremely accurate three-dimensional perceptual system that would allow rapid navigation. Vision seems to serve this function best, although other animals who navigate at night seem to do well by using hearing, rather than vision.

Unit 8. Learning

1. Compulsive gambling could be considered a disease and a learned behavior. There is an organization called Gamblers Anonymous that is based on the same principles as Alcoholics Anonymous. However, analyzing compulsive gambling in terms of antecedents and consequences might suggest ways to eliminate cues that lead to gambling, thereby leading to extinction. The best policy might be to avoid all settings where gambling takes place. Because any winning would serve to reinforce gambling, the best goal for a behavior change program is no gambling at all. Because it is reinforced intermittently (on a variable ratio schedule), it may be very resistant to extinction.

2. You could provide positive reinforcement for keeping the school clean. For example, they could receive a sticker for every 50 pieces of litter they pick up. They could also be punished (e.g., with extra homework or reduced break periods) if they are caught littering. You might also try integrating other principles, like modelling, shaping, and ideal reinforcement schedules, into your program to increase the likelihood that students' behavior will conform to your goals.

3. Intention is not always a prerequisite for learning. We learn many behaviors without setting out to do so. However, if intention can help us focus attention, learning is enhanced. One exciting aspect of learning principles is that they do not require consent or knowledge of the learner in order for them to work. They can work on pigeons, mentally retarded people, and people who are resistant to change just as well as they can work on intelligent human adults. They are truly a universal phenomenon.

4. Parents generally don't reward or punish their children's grammar. Instead, they model good grammar for their children and do what they can to understand whatever utterances their children produce. So the learning of grammar does not depend on operant principles. Parents do, however, reward and punish other linguistic features, such as content (e.g., "That's right; that IS a doggy") and politeness (e.g., "Did you say 'thank you?' You're such a good girl").

Unit 9. Remembering and Forgetting

1. Helpful memory strategies include paying attention, minimizing distractions and interference, and encoding information in more than one way, such as reading out loud, outlining important points, or chunking information in some personally meaningful way. It is also helpful to add meaning by linking new facts and ideas to familiar information, to use visual imagery, to review material distributed in study sessions, to study before going to sleep, and to overlearn material.

2. The schema we used as children are very different from the ones we have developed as adults. And because young children are lacking in language, which normally helps us to label and organize memories, we may find that memories from our pre-verbal days are sparse or nonexistent. There is also evidence that early memories may be lost due to physiological maturation. Nevertheless, many memories, particularly from later childhood, are recoverable through good cues, and most people find that cues, such as family stories or photographs, can help in reconstructing memories.

3. The ABC song offers many devices to aid retention. The letters are chunked or grouped in units that conform to the capacity of short-term memory. The letters at the end of each phrase rhyme, which is a mnemonic device. The song encodes the information in sounds, as well as in movements. And the fun of it also motivates multiple rehearsals and performances.

4. Most of us are justifiably impressed with the capacity of our long-term memory. Society rewards people for good memories, starting in early childhood. Playing trivia games can set off a host of associations to events and ideas that we often don't even know we have in memory.

5. There is substantial controversy over what "leading" questions do to memories. The way a person perceives and recalls an event depends on perceptual and cognitive biases that even the eyewitness may not be aware of. Jury members are subject to their own biases when they hear and judge testimony. Jury members need to be especially alert to leading questions that might introduce details or prompt a witness to report an event in a particular way. The more informed a jury member is about how memory works, the better he or she may be able to weigh the value of testimony.

6. Not only does a good memory help in preparing for exams, but so do good metamemory skills. If you know how you learn and know what is most likely to work in your attempts to recall information, you can learn more effectively. Also, if you are good at gauging how well you have learned something so that you don't stop studying too early due to overconfidence, you vastly increase your odds of success on the exam.

Unit 10. Cognitive Processes

1. To interpret the poem you need to consider language rules and underlying structure—word order, forms, endings, and sounds and language patterns. Although there are many strange and made-up words, some clearly echo familiar words—so that there are some built-in associations that imply meaning.

2. Scripts might include types of activities and dress, level of education, achievement, income, social status, family patterns, interests, vacation ideas, restaurant preferences, and health status.

3. Children have scripts—expectations built on their knowledge of routine experiences. They are also able to learn procedural information and can store and manipulate visual information.

4. We draw meaning from events based on the implications we perceive, imagine, or anticipate that they will have. Events can have physical, intellectual, or emotional consequences, and these consequences can be direct or indirect. It is only because we are sentient beings who have goals and intelligence that anything has any "meaning."

5. Generally we use a variety of cues, such as context and intonation, to detect sarcasm in what our conversational partners say. Familiarity with the person, with cultural rules and conventions, and with the situation can help a lot. So you're at greatest risk for misunderstanding when you're speaking with someone you're unfamiliar with or who doesn't share these unwritten rules with you, such as someone from a different culture.

Unit 11. Judgment and Decision Making

1. Doctors might be basing their diagnoses on their experience with a biased sample of the population. They may also have a tendency to err on the side of caution, assuming a person has strep throat and treating it, rather than not treating a possibly seriously ill patient. In addition, doctors know that test results are not always 100 percent accurate, and they may have difficulty accepting a result that differs from their own opinion.

2. Pitfalls of problem solving include the inability to define the problem, to be illogical in situations in which emotions are involved, and reluctance to consider opposing points of view. People also depend on certain familiar approaches and strategies and often do not recognize when these are no longer useful. Cognitive bias and mental shortcuts also cause people to draw false conclusions or make bad decisions.

3. A child with these qualities might easily be considered precocious, disruptive, or difficult. Although most teachers respond positively to children with good verbal skills, schools typically put more emphasis on following the rules. This may be difficult for the creative, independent child.

4. Although you can certainly perceive more subtleties than your native language has words for, the way in which you think of complex situations, like campaign issues, can be influenced by the details of a situation that are made salient to you. Perhaps the best way to think about this seeming contradiction is to view the two phenomena as occurring at different cognitive levels. Concepts and percepts are more sophisticated than the language used to describe them. More complex cognitive processes involving elaborate knowledge structures can be vulnerable to framing.

5. According to the representativeness heuristic, we are prone to believe that an event is likely if it fits our stereotype of what usually happens. This makes us particularly likely to notice events that fit our stereotype, and it may lead us to overestimate how commonly stereotype-consistent instances are. Similarly, the availability heuristic can perpetuate stereotypes through the cues we provide ourselves with when conjuring up examples of or "typical profiles" of the groups with whom we hold the stereotypes.

Unit 12. Motivation and Emotion

1. An individual's sexual script is based on a unique combination of personal, social, and cultural beliefs and attitudes. Scripts are influenced by family role models, the media, and feedback from social experiences. Boys and girls are typically treated differently during development. Cultural stereotypes tend to reinforce some personal choices and not others. Sexual scripts are often not overtly expressed and may be a source of friction and disappointment in a relationship. If couples can talk about mismatched role expectations and values, they may be able to negotiate a shared script. The threat of AIDS and other sexually transmitted diseases may change the norms governing sexual activity and thereby rewrite the social scripts that guide sexual behavior. Expect to see changes in what characterizes an acceptable mate, dating patterns, and other relationship issues.

2. The optimist tends to emphasize global, external, and changeable or unstable reasons for failure, while claiming all the credit for success. The pessimist attributes success to luck or other random events out of his or her control and tends to take personal blame for failure.

3. Armed with this knowledge, you might couple a diet plan with stress management skills, such as meditation, time management courses, exercise, participation in a support group, and/or individual psychotherapy. You might also frame the diet plan so that the dieter doesn't feel deprived or self-restrained and is therefore less tempted by opportunities to binge.

4. People are typically motivated to approach activities or goals that increase pleasure and to avoid those that cause pain. Although food is generally thought of as something pleasurable, even as a reward or incentive, people with certain eating disorders see food as something to avoid. They modify or inhibit their eating behavior in an attempt to achieve an idealized body shape.

5. How you respond might be determined by your need for achievement. If you believed you could get an A, you probably would want a grade. Your motivation to study might be reduced by the less rewarding pass/fail option. If you thought you could only earn a C, a pass/fail option might be more appealing. You would eliminate the potentially handicapping stress of working for a grade. Working for a grade might also interfere with your intrinsic motivation to learn. If you were very interested in the course but didn't want the pressure of working hard, you would not need the incentive of being graded, and a pass/fail option would be more appealing.

6. According to theorists like Abraham Maslow, other, more abstract goals that might serve one's desire for self-fulfillment typically become secondary when more basic needs, like sleep and eating, are thwarted.

7. You may, for example, be perceived as overly familiar with people, expressing your affection for them in too forward a manner. Or you may be perceived as not expressive enough if, for example, you were raised to be relatively stoic and reserved but you find yourself in a demonstrative culture that expects more showy displays of love, surprise, or sadness.

Unit 13. The Mind Awake and Asleep

1. Filter theory states that there are limits on early stages of perception. Other sensory information is held briefly but not processed. Although attention reduces confusion and sensory overload, it is not an all-or-nothing phenomenon. There is generally some screening of the sensory input for meaningful information and some partial analysis below a level of conscious awareness.

2. Automatic processing, or "mindlessness," enables us to deal with far more information than we could handle if sensory inputs had to go through conscious processing item by item. But mindlessness can be maladaptive if a situation requires new discriminations and new adaptations.

3. In the sense that perception is influenced by norms and expectations, our selective attention can be determined by cultural context. We form concepts based on experience and language. Our perceptual habits are influenced by the environment and by the culture, which communicates what is important to notice and remember. Language helps to categorize elements of experience. But personal motivation and individual characteristics also create enormous variation within cultures.

4. REM sleep is critical, and when one is deprived of it, one generally experiences rebound effects. These can take the form of particularly vivid daydreaming, more rapid onset of the first REM phase when one falls asleep again, and a longer proportion of total sleep time spent in REM sleep.

Unit 14. The Mind Hidden and Divided

1. Illness, love, and grief can cause many changes in mental functioning typically associated with altered consciousness. Love and grief particularly can cause people to experience intense or extensive changes in consciousness and behavior.

2. Treatment should take into account social and psychological factors, as well as chemical effects and physiological factors. Drug education programs must prepare students to evaluate the social and psychological components of drug use that lead to dependence and addiction. Some drug education programs aimed at children attempt to establish a certain mind-set that counteracts peer and cultural pressures and promotes critical thinking about pro-drug messages.

3. Effects of extensive television viewing include heightened arousal and suggestibility, depression, and lowered motivation, as well as a distorted sense of time, disorientation, impulsivity, and hyperactivity, especially in children. Studies tend to be contradictory.

248

Prolonged inactivity can lead to a kind of stimulus deprivation. Young children do not have the intellectual ability or sufficient experience and information to distinguish fantasy from reality, so they may be confused by the distortions of reality they see on television.

4. People certainly differ in their ability to be hypnotized or the ease with which they can enter meditative states. It may take some practice, but you may well find that the benefits outweigh the investment you have to make up-front to learn to do it. In both cases, exposing oneself to quiet environments, practicing without imposing inappropriate demands on oneself, and following the instructions of an expert should help. You aren't guaranteed success, but it is certainly worth trying.

Unit 15. The Self

1. To the extent that standardized tests are used to categorize or place people, they pose some risk for inaccuracy and bias. What is normal or average in the larger population may differ from subculture to subculture. If members of a given subculture are compared to the larger population, they may be judged unfavorably, and this may lead to concrete consequences, such as a greater likelihood of being labeled as abnormal, or fewer job or social opportunities.

2. Shy people tend to be pessimistic. They have more social anxieties than those who are not shy. Shy people also tend to anticipate rejection and social failure and to interpret social encounters negatively, thus confirming their sense of inadequacy and helplessness.

3. The id is the driving energy of our passion, curiosity, and excitement. According to Freud, it is the life force that operates on the pleasure principle. On the positive side, it is the drive for self-preservation. It is also the place where sexual urges arise, thus ensuring the survival of the species. The fantasies of the id are the basis for imagination and creative endeavors. The id also contains aggressive and destructive drives that can be turned against the self or against society.

4. Your answer is probably yes, that different experiences of success or failure can change your sense of efficacy and your level of self-esteem. But success and failure are relative. If a task is too easy, it doesn't help a person with low self-esteem. Also, research has suggested that self-esteem is often affected by a social referent. An extremely attractive person sitting next to you before a job interview might make you feel dissatisfied with yourself, but a disheveled or unattractive person might make you feel better about yourself.

5. Although the Internet exposes us to lots of different kinds of people from all around the world, many of the social skills used with the Internet are specific to that particular medium. For people who substitute Internet-based interaction with face-to-face interaction, other critical social skills may be underdeveloped or lost over time. They may feel isolated, awkward in social situations, and shy. This is becoming particularly important as people find that identities are easy to slip into and out of in an Internet-based culture.

Unit 16. Testing and Intelligence

1. No. Environment still has an important influence on the expression of any trait or ability. This is obvious from studies of development in enriched and impoverished environments. Impoverished environments lower a person's test performance. Both heredity and environment play a role.

2. Some might say that people already tend to sort and segregate each other according to intelligence, even if judgments are based on informal, personal assessments. If IQs become public knowledge, this might have the largest effect on those at the top and bottom of the scale, leading to institutionalized forms of discrimination.

3. Both have tremendous value, and often in the same arenas of life (school, job, social success). Luckily, scoring high on one doesn't mean you're lacking in the other!

4. Intelligence tests and psychological assessments attempt to avoid personal bias and to obtain an objective measure of a person's abilities. However, the tests can be used as a short-cut in place of a more thorough and personalized evaluation. Tests are often misunderstood and misapplied. People have an inappropriate reverence for scores. Few people question the authority of a computer printout. Objections to the tests include claims that they are not objective and that they do not measure what they are intended to measure. People often use tests to focus on what is wrong with the individual instead of considering what is wrong with the system. Test scores have been used to argue for the heritability of intelligence, which has important public policy implications for immigration, education, employment, and affirmative action.

5. It is rare for someone to be universally more capable or more intelligent than the average person. A brilliant mathematician may be kinesthetically awkward, and a person with excellent spatial skills may be average or below average on verbal measures of intelligence. Looking around at our greatest models of mathematical intelligence, body skills, and social intelligence leads to outstanding models for those specific kinds of intelligence that may show no particular excellence on any of the other scales.

Unit 17. Sex and Gender

1. A person's sexual script includes knowing which behaviors are acceptable and unacceptable. It includes personal and social norms that prescribe what to do, when, where, how, and with whom. This may include rules that dictate who opens doors and who picks up the check. Gender roles are an important part of the scripts that influence interpersonal and sexual behavior. When people share complementary scripts, they may be more compatible than people whose expectations and preferences do not mesh.

2. Merely knowing if someone is male or female leads to interpretations based on stereotyped gender differences. From the beginning, infants are perceived to be female or male, although differences in appearance and behavior are negligible. Research shows how the same behavior may be judged differently, depending on whether it is done by a man or a woman. A man's

protest over a course grade, for example, may be perceived as assertive, but the same behavior by a woman may be judged as pushy. Judgments about the suitability of people for particular jobs and occupations sometimes ignore individual traits and are based solely on gender.

3. Children show different play and toy preferences. Research has shown that as early as toddlerhood, children choose to play with members of their own sex and in same-sex play groups.

4. Male traits are often perceived as more desirable by both men and women. Being assertive, achieving, and independent seems related to a better self-concept for both men and women. In general, the labels used to describe male traits are more positive. However, in judging the relative merits of masculine and feminine traits for adjustment, it is important to specify exactly what that means. For example, one study suggests that feminine traits contribute to happier marriages.

5. Some people insist that it doesn't make a difference, but many past studies have shown that both men and women make different judgments based on the sex of the author. In general, articles are viewed more favorably when readers believe they were written by a man. However, recent evidence suggests that this effect has diminished, and ratings of works by men and women are converging.

6. You would have a hard time! Other people who your child interacts with on a day-to-day basis, including young children and including strangers, will treat your child in a manner consistent with gender roles. If you try to disguise you child's gender in order to prevent this, by careful selection of clothing and a unisex style haircut, people may ask your child whether he or she is a boy or a girl in order to figure out what they believe to be the appropriate means of interacting, and other children might tease or reject your child for not following stereotypical dress and behavior patterns. Socialization and interaction based on gender is so strong in our culture that it is unlikely you'd be successful at your efforts.

Unit 18. Maturing and Aging

1. Until recently, the study of aging was dominated by pathology, studies of the sick elderly. Now that there are large numbers of healthy, active older people, the focus of research has changed. Statistics show that most older people do not fit the stereotype of the frail elderly. Some of the psychological problems and memory loss can be attributed to drug interactions, lack of stimulation, or the feeling of a loss of control. Studies can show the effects of lifestyle and environment on aging. Problems of depression, for example, might affect anyone who suffered the loss of loved ones, a job, intellectual stimulation, or control over his or her own life. Also, it shouldn't be considered an oddity that elderly people talk more about the past; they have more past than future. Comparing the status of the elderly in different cultures reveals the influence of cultural attitudes and social patterns.

2. The midlife crisis, an emotional upheaval or disorientation, is a process of self-assessment in which individuals confront such issues as the value of their lives, their social roles and

relationships, the gap between their dreams and accomplishments, and the realities of aging and death. Of course, not everyone goes through a crisis. In fact, some experts believe that "crisis" is too strong a word.

3. Any changes in intelligence depend on how one defines and measures intelligence. Not all cognitive abilities change at the same rate. Some decline, some improve, and some stay the same. There is also some evidence that shows that fluid intelligence, which is associated with speed of CNS functioning, tends to decline in adult years, while crystallized intelligence, primarily related to the application of knowledge, tends to increase.

4. Although the child would need some interaction with his or her parent in order to form an attachment relationship, there is no rule about how much time is necessary, nor how often there needs to be contact. Still, having only occasional contact with a child (such as when a parent doesn't have primary custody) may pose a particular challenge in developing a relationship with the child. In order to test the effects of divorce on attachment, a well-controlled study would need to rule out alternative explanations. For example, it might be interesting to include other groups in the study, such as families that are intact but that have a lot of aggression or animosity, or families in which one parent is frequently out of the house because he or she is traveling for business reasons. Data from these other groups would help to isolate the specific effects of divorce from other factors (hostility, frequency of contact) that might affect the attachment relationship.

5. Social attitudes and economic conditions determine which changes and responsibilities are considered appropriate for adult roles. For example, the age at which marriage is acceptable or at which children are expected to become self-supporting is often set by economic and social conditions in the larger society.

6. Being a parent was once the norm. Taking on the responsibilities of parenthood was one of the major milestones in adult development and was considered the step that moved a person from a stage of selfishness to a stage in which nurturing and intimacy become a priority. However, not everyone accepts the idea that having children is the only way to be productive, creative, and nurturing.

Unit 19. The Power of the Situation

1. The participants in Milgram's research could avoid blaming themselves if they reasoned that the situation was influencing their behavior. They could rationalize that they were only following orders and did not have to accept responsibility for their behavior. Therefore, they could avoid guilt, much as the Nazis did when they claimed they were only following orders.

2. People who have only known oppressive conditions like this may be susceptible to other psychological phenomena, such as pressures toward conformity or toward following new charismatic leaders. They may also lack the sophistication in thinking about controversial issues that have been developed by others who have spent a lifetime debating all sides of them.

3. Roles involve expectations about behavior. Roles and social obligations are sometimes perceived as social traps, especially when behavior is dictated by social expectations and norms rather than by personal feelings and individual tastes. You may conform only to win approval or to avoid social rejection. For example, being respected in the community might require church attendance, even if you are not a believer. When social expectations conflict with feelings, alienation or resentment may result. When behavior coincides with role expectations, it reinforces a sense of true identity.

4. Everyone has had good and bad teachers and bosses. Choose specific situations and analyze the style of authority or leadership. Analyze your participation and performance. In which situation did you learn or accomplish the most? In which situation did people support and help each other the most? Which situations were most relaxed?

5. Although extreme examples of blind obedience, such as Nazi Germany or even Milgram's experiment, are easy to identify, there are many ambiguous situations in which the difference is not so clear. In schools, churches, and the workplace, cooperation is highly esteemed and compliance is usually rewarded. Efforts to undermine authority are typically considered to be a threat by the leader of the group. Parents and teachers tend to reinforce obedient behavior in children. It may be useful to cite examples of people who buck authority and to help illustrate possibilities for legitimate dissent. However, most research on social influence shows that unquestioning obedience is the norm in the presence of perceived authority figures.

6. You should artificially create a situation in which people do not feel as though they are part of a large group of people who could act. You should individually identify someone and ask them to help you. In such a situation, it would be unlikely that he or she would fall prey to diffusion of responsibility.

Unit 20. Constructing Social Reality

1. Individuals do not respond to situations identically. Some individuals have such strong personal values and self confidence that they do not seek social approval as much as others. Also, people usually choose what they hear and watch. They can turn off the television, ignore a program, or walk out of the movie theater. They can read selectively, actively looking for articles that support their ideas or challenge them. They can associate with people who share their beliefs and opinions or purposely expose themselves to new ideas and experiences.

2. Nationalism can be a source of pride and cohesiveness for a population. However, this is all too often gained at the expense of making certain classes of people into internal or external enemies. These out-groups are used to divert attention from national problems and often become a target for anger. Nationalism can encourage "us versus them" thinking and escalate conflicts. An "us versus them" mentality is simple to create. It depends only on drawing some distinction—relevant or arbitrary—between groups of people. Such opportunities for perceiving differences and exaggerating them are bigger in times of war or cold war, and since people at war tend not to socialize with each other, negative stereotypes and negative

interactions aren't easily overridden by positive exchanges. As borders between cultures and economies become blurred, globalization might counteract some of these forces.

3. Dissonance reduction, the self-serving bias, and defense mechanisms are very similar. They are all efforts to reduce anxiety or resolve an apparent conflict between desirable self-perceptions and unacceptable attitudes and actions.

4. Children who watch television tend to think that there is more violence in the streets than there really is. At the same time, they rarely experience the true impact of violence. They tend to see men and women in stereotyped roles and relationships; in most situation comedies, problems get resolved in thirty minutes. Since "reality tv" focuses on unusual situations but presents itself as an honest view into the lives of typical people, children may come away with a particularly distorted model of how other people live.

5. People who are made aware of their identities and responsibilities are more likely to follow cultural norms. The de-individuation and anonymity of big cities foster irresponsible and aggressive behavior. In addition, in accordance with the principle of diffusion of responsibility, the large number of people who can intervene to help or to correct a situation tends to lower the likelihood that anyone will intervene.

Unit 21. Psychopathology

1. Courts differ on how they deal with the insanity defense. In order for a person to be excused from legal responsibility for criminal actions, the defense must demonstrate severely impaired judgment and lack of self-control. A person is not considered legally responsible if he or she is unable to distinguish right from wrong. The definition may vary from country to country, from state to state, even from court to court. It is a highly controversial issue.

2. The *Diagnostic and Statistical Manual* has been criticized for inflating disorders, basing some criteria on myth, instead of empirical evidence, and for stigmatizing people. It is also, clearly, a relative assessment guide subject to cultural forces. For example, homosexuality was once characterized as a disorder. Today, the self-defeating personality has been proposed as a disorder to be included. Women's groups and others are very concerned that such a label will lead to a blaming of the victim.

3. Statistically, homosexuality is relatively less common. However, cultural standards are relative. Psychological assessments show no differences in personality or adjustment between heterosexuals and homosexuals. Today, the DSM-IV does not list homosexuality as a disorder. It is considered a problem only if it causes guilt or self-hate.

4. Women may be more willing to talk about distress and emotional problems. They are more often denied opportunities for independence and achievement and may feel angry, hopeless, or helpless, justifiably. There is a male bias toward traditional concepts of mental health.

5. Many psychological problems are just extreme instances of behavior that most of us exhibit at one time or another. If you are extremely worried about a certain behavior, if the behavior is disruptive to relationships, or if it has become a persistent problem, you might consider getting a professional evaluation.

Unit 22. Psychotherapy

1. It is difficult to determine the success of a particular therapy because faith in the effectiveness of any treatment may be enough to bring about changes in a patient's feelings or behavior. Also, some problems resolve themselves over time without professional intervention.

2. A given psychological problem is often associated with clear abnormalities in the functioning of the brain. We know, for example, that depression is associated with the functioning of the neurotransmitter serotonin. We also know that serotonin can be affected in multiple ways, including through either direct manipulation of serotonin re-uptake in the brain, as is accomplished through some anti-depressants, or indirectly, through one's psychological experience. Psychotherapy is intended to provide people with the skills and experience that will allow changes in one's behavior, environment, experience, and relationships. Although it is not intended as the ultimate goal, a change in brain functioning co-occurs with these other changes. One's movement toward greater happiness and self-efficacy is reflected in one's brain.

3. Finding the right match between a problem and an approach to therapy starts with how you define the problem and your attitude or beliefs about the kind of help you need. A person might seek assistance in making the decision from a physician or person in the community who is familiar with available resources and services.

4. Unit 22 describes therapies that focus on illness and problem solving, as well as on those designed to address life management issues, self-esteem, relationships, and potential. Most people, at some time, could benefit from professional intervention.

5. In American culture, there is typically a stigma associated with seeking help of any kind. Our culture emphasizes individuality, self-sufficiency, and strength, especially for men. That makes it harder to admit weakness or the need for support.

6. Although drug therapies can be enormously helpful in correcting abnormal neurochemistry, it cannot fix a marriage or magically raise someone's self-esteem. People who expect too much from drug therapies may fail to do the additional work necessary to make headway on their problems. In addition, people may come to be dependent on or addicted to their prescription drugs, creating an additional problem that they'll need to address.

7. Although it is confrontational and can be aversive, exposure therapy is also quite an effective treatment strategy. If you are committed to facing and overcoming a phobia and you trust your therapist, you might consider this very efficient therapeutic strategy.

Unit 23. Health, Mind, and Behavior

1. Friends can help reduce stress in several ways. They can offer practical help. For example, when there is illness or a crisis in a family, friends can relieve temporary concerns about money, child care, food, or transportation needs. They can also offer emotional support, being there to listen and empathize with you about what you are going through and reassuring you that you are not going crazy even when you feel most vulnerable and confused. Friends may also offer advice in an unfamiliar situation, helping you to think through decisions. Social support makes people less vulnerable to stress-related problems. Social networks counteract a sense of isolation by providing a sense of belonging. In support groups, individuals help each other by providing a social reference group. They share advice, feelings, and information specific to the situation.

2. Victims of a curse may feel such intense or prolonged fear that it wears down the body's ability to cope. One theory suggests that the body's attempt to counteract an extreme emotional reaction may go too far, slowing down important systems and processes to the point of death.

3. Most people use defense mechanisms at times. Some defenses help us gain time to adjust to a trauma or other type of problem. Rationalization may be a stress-reducing strategy in the face of frustration or failure. Any defense mechanism can be part of a coping approach, but it may prevent us from confronting and solving our real problems if it becomes habitual.

4. Self-defeating thoughts undermine a person's sense of self-esteem, optimism, efficacy, and control—all necessary for adequate coping.

5. Perfectionists unnecessarily stress themselves by setting impossible goals and standards. They may compare themselves with inappropriate models of achievement, never being satisfied with their own accomplishments. They may feel they have inadequate resources to measure up to their unreasonably high standards. These attitudes can create stress and can undermine their ability to perform.

6. Although the traditional gender roles for running a household have changed over the past several years, men still typically find themselves in more stressful, powerful job situations. Such work conditions are associated with poor lifestyle habits, such as caffeine, nicotine, and alcohol abuse, and with insufficient sleep and lack of exercise. Add to that a cultural tendency to foster aggression in men, and we see that such a combination puts men at risk for cardiovascular disease. Women are also at risk. In the workplace, they may find themselves in situations where they have less control than men do, making them also prone to stress-related health problems, including cardiovascular disease. And as gender roles continue to shift, women become more and more vulnerable to the traditional "male" stress-related risks.

7. Meditation and yoga allow the body to physically relax, making stress responses like rapid heart rate and muscle tensing less likely. Because these practices lower stress and because stress is associated with health outcomes, meditation and yoga improve health and create the experience of greater peace.

Unit 24. Applying Psychology to Life

1. Basic or pure research is done for the sake of knowledge, while applied research is designed to solve concrete problems. For example, investigators doing basic research that focuses on the genetic influences on brain chemistry may simply be interested in defining, understanding, and predicting the effects of chemical reactions in the brain. Eventually the information may be applied. It may be used to plan treatment to correct abnormal brain conditions or to alter brain chemistry in an attempt to cure certain diseases. Although they have different goals, neither is more important than the other, and their border isn't always clear.

2. When we call a machine "user friendly," we mean that it is easy to use. Its controls and displays are designed with human comfort and sensory and motor abilities in mind. The design of the machine minimizes mistakes and may even anticipate and correct mistakes. Organizational psychologists also address practical concerns and quality-of-life issues in the workplace. They influence organization effectiveness by applying their skills and insights to solving problems of human relations, communication, mediation, employee selection and training, leadership, job satisfaction, and stress.

3. Yes. People can use principles of persuasion and coercion to influence the behavior of others. For example, cults use carefully structured methods to recruit and convert new members. Advertisers might design campaigns to persuade people to buy things they don't need. Con artists use techniques to sell products and enlist cooperation from people.

4. It might be best to play the odds. If a candidate is going after a particular demographic, then it may work to use a roughly homogenous set of campaign ads, knowing that people will react quite differently to it but aiming to have one's targeted audience respond favorably to it. Another possibility would be to create different kinds of ads, aimed at different demographic groups, that have been tailored to elicit the desired reaction from them. What we now know is that historical references can indeed be risky to use in a campaign, and such references should be chosen carefully.

CUMULATIVE GLOSSARY OF PROGRAM TERMS

agonist—a chemical or drug that mimics the action of a neurotransmitter.

amnesia—partial or complete memory loss of information or past events.

androgynous—having both masculine and feminine traits.

antagonist—a chemical or drug that blocks the action of a neurotransmitter.

applied psychology—the practical application of psychological knowledge and principles to concrete problems.

arousal—a heightened level of excitation or activation.

autocratic—governed by one person with unlimited power.

autokinetic effect—a phenomenon whereby a stationary object in a darkened room appears to move.

behavioral confirmation—a form of social feedback in which our self-beliefs determine how we are perceived and evaluated by others.

beta-endorphin—a type of opioid which, under conditions of maternal deprivation, can block the action of the early regulators of insulin and growth hormone.

biological biasing—a genetic predisposition that increases the likelihood of getting a disorder if exposed to prolonged or intense stress.

biological senescing—growing older physically, or biological aging.

cognitive control—the power of beliefs to give meaning to a situation.

cognitive developmental theory—the theory stating that children use male and female as fundamental categories and actively sex-type themselves to achieve cognitive consistency.

democratic—practicing social equality.

developmental strategies—behaviors that have evolved to conform to the sex roles typical of the adult members of a species.

disposition—a person's internal or personal characteristics.

double-blind procedure—an experimental procedure in which neither the researcher nor the subject knows which subjects are receiving the real treatment and which are getting the placebo.

dread factor—the fear of unfamiliar or potentially catastrophic events that makes us judge these to be riskier than familiar events.

enzymes—protein molecules that act as catalysts in body chemistry by facilitating chemical reactions.

ERP (event-related potentials) —variations in brain waves, as recorded by the electroencephalogram (EEG), which are triggered by specific internal or external events.

field study—research carried on outside the laboratory where naturally occurring, ongoing behavior can be observed.

framing—the way information is presented that tends to bias how it is interpreted.

genetic counseling—counseling that advises a person about the probability of passing on defective genes to offspring.

glucocorticoids—substances produced by the adrenal cortex that act on the hippocampus to alter the stress response.

Heisenberg indeterminacy principle—a principle stating that our impressions of other people are distorted by how we observe and assess them.

human factors—the field of psychology interested in the characteristics of humans that relate to the optimal design of systems and devices.

hypnagogic state—a period of reveries at the onset of the sleeping state.

hypnotic analgesia—lack of pain perception while under hypnosis.

IAT (Implicit Attitudes Test)—uses response time as a means of detecting unconscious prejudice.

independent way of being—associated with the individual as the focus and locus of action.

interdependent way of being—focuses on social relationships and views action as distributed across and caused by a network of people.

invariance—the principle stating that preferences between options should be independent of different representations.

jet lag—a sense of disorientation caused by disruption of internal circadian rhythms.

laissez-faire—allowing complete freedom, with little or no interference or guidance.

language acquisition device—the innate ability to acquire language; a hypothesis put forth by Noam Chomsky.

legitimate authority—a form of power exercised by someone in a superior role, such as a teacher or president.

life-span development—developmental changes continuing throughout the life cycle.

LSD—lysergic acid diethylamide, a hallucinogen.

lucid dreaming—the awareness of dreaming without awakening, and sometimes the ability to control the content of a dream.

maternal deprivation—the lack of adequate affection and stimulation from the mother or mother substitute.

micro level—the smallest unit of analysis in psychology; for example, studying P-300 brain waves or other neural or biochemical changes.

molar level—the analysis of larger units of behavior of the whole person in complex situations, taking into account cultural background and social experiences.

molecular level—the analysis of discrete, observable behaviors, such as body language, crying, or laughing.

morpheme—the smallest unit of language that has meaning.

mutual constitution—the process of culture and individual shaping and being shaped by each other.

narcolepsy—a sleep disorder, brought on by strong emotion, in which REM sleep occurs suddenly during the day.

optimism—the tendency to attribute failure to external, unstable, or changeable factors and to attribute success to stable factors.

parentese—modified speech that parallels children's level of language development.

parietal lobe—the part of the brain responsible for math skills.

pessimism—the tendency to attribute failure to stable or internal factors and to attribute success to global variables.

phoneme—the smallest unit of sound that affects the meaning of speech.

plasticity—the ability of the brain to restructure itself as a result, for example, of learning.

posthypnotic amnesia—forgetting selected events by suggestion.

prejudice—a bias for or against someone formed without sufficient information.

priming—a speeding up in response time as a function of recent exposure.

psychic numbing—being emotionally unaffected by an upsetting or alarming event.

psychogenic—organic malfunction or tissue damage caused by anxiety, tension, or depression.

psycholinguists—scientists who study how the structure of language is related to speaking and listening.

psychological adolescing—developing psychologically to full potential.

Pygmalion effect—the effect of positive and negative expectations on behavior.

random sample—an unbiased population selected at random.

receptor—a specialized nerve cell sensitive to particular kinds of stimulus energy.

reference standard—a norm or model of behavior that is used to decide how to behave in a particular situation.

selective optimization—making the most of what you have.

self-handicapping—a process by which we try to explain away potential failures by blaming them on something other than our lack of ability.

senile dementia—biochemical and neuronal changes in the brain that lead to a gradual reduction in mental efficiency.

sex typing—the psychological process by which boys and girls become masculine or feminine.

similarity heuristic—an error based on the tendency to see a connection between belonging to a certain category and having the characteristics considered typical of members of that category.

sleep apnea—a sleep disorder characterized by heavy snoring with repetitive pauses in breathing.

social learning theory—the theory stating that children are socialized by observing role models and are rewarded or punished for behaving appropriately.

stage theory—a theory that describes development as a fixed sequence of distinct periods of life.

status transaction—a form of interpersonal communication in which we establish relative degrees of social status and power.

stereotype—the belief that all members of a group share common traits.

subjective reality—the perceptions and beliefs that we accept without question.

syntax—a set of rules for combining words into phrases and sentences.

time-limited dynamic psychotherapy—a form of short-term therapy.

NOTES

NOTES

NOTES

NOTES

NOTES